UNDERSTANDING LIBYA SINCE GADDAFI

ULF LAESSING

Understanding Libya
Since Gaddafi

HURST & COMPANY, LONDON

First published in the United Kingdom in 2020 by
C. Hurst & Co. (Publishers) Ltd.,
41 Great Russell Street, London, WC1B 3PL
© Ulf Laessing, 2020
All rights reserved.
Printed in Great Britain by Bell and Bain Ltd, Glasgow

Distributed in the United States, Canada and Latin America by
Oxford University Press, 198 Madison Avenue, New York, NY 10016,
United States of America.

The right of Ulf Laessing to be identified as the author of
this publication is asserted by him in accordance with the
Copyright, Designs and Patents Act, 1988.

A Cataloguing-in-Publication data record for this book
is available from the British Library.

ISBN: 9781849048880

This book is printed using paper from registered sustainable
and managed sources.

www.hurstpublishers.com

For Tahani, with love

CONTENTS

ACKNOWLEDGEMENTS

I always wanted to write a book about Libya, as Tripoli was the most interesting and also the most intense posting I've had as a foreign correspondent for Reuters.

I'd like to thank Mary Fitzgerald and Umar Khan, two friends I made during my time in Libya, for urging me to go ahead with my plan. I would have given up without their constant encouragement. Mattio Toalda, Hend el-Amry and Ehab Abdulgader were also a great source of inspiration.

Jalel Harchaoui and Tarek Megerisi, two other distinguished Libya experts, and my former Reuters colleague, Ghaith Shennib, and the current Reuters team on the ground, Ahmed Elumami and Ayman al-Warfalli, gave me invaluable advice and shared their immense knowledge of Libya with me. Mary was kind to introduce me to Michael Dwyer at Hurst, who helped me finetune my original idea.

I would also thank my employer, Thomson Reuters, for allowing me to write the book. Of course, the views expressed here (along with any errors) are my own, and should not be attributed to my employer.

I'd also like to thank my editor, Colin Cooper from Grand Apostrophe.

Finally, I can't thank enough my dear wife Tahani, and my parents, who have supported me throughout the project.

LIST OF ACRONYMS AND ABBREVIATIONS

EUBAM	EU Integrated Border Management Assistance Mission
GECOL	General Electricity Company of Libya
GNA	Government of National Accord
GNC	General National Congress
HoR	House of Representatives
HRW	Human Rights Watch
ICRC	International Committee of the Red Cross
IS	Islamic State
LAAF	Libyan Arab Armed Forces
LIFG	Libyan Islamist Fighting Group
LNA	Libyan National Army
NOC	National Oil Corporation
NTC	National Transitional Council
PSF	Price Stability Fund
RCC	Revolutionary Command Council
SSC	Supreme Security Committee
WHO	World Health Organization

INTRODUCTION

Libya combines within the borders of one country virtually all the obstacles to development that can be found anywhere: geographic, economic, political, sociological, technological.

Benjamin Higgins, UN-appointed economist, 1951

At first glance, one might think Libya's descent into chaos after the toppling of Muammar Gaddafi need not have happened. The North African country sits on Africa's largest proven oil reserves and contains within its borders significant natural gas reservoirs. Its central bank had, by the time of the first anti-Gaddafi protests in February 2011, more than $120 billion in its coffers. The Libyan sovereign wealth fund owned assets around the globe in the form of Chinese bonds, stakes in Italian and Bahraini financial institutions and investments in tourism and agricultural projects around Africa worth a total of $65 billion.[1] A wealthy country with a per capita income of $12,065 in 2010, Libya looked like the perfect investment opportunity.[2]

The country needed to overhaul everything: roads, banks, hospitals, hotels, schools and universities had all suffered under Gaddafi's socialist-style state mismanagement. The desert nation also boasts unique tourist attractions such as the Roman ruins of Leptis Magna—an entire ancient city with a port, theatre, public

1

sauna, market square and wide plastered avenues—as well as spectacular natural environments. Wave-like Saharan sand dunes and prehistoric rock carvings stand, largely ignored, outside the ancient oasis caravan town of Ghat.

Libya's assets extended beyond Fezzanian charm, and indeed beyond national borders: many educated Libyans—having graduated in Europe and North America—were willing to return in the absence of Gaddafi, ready to tap into new opportunities and help rebuild their country.[3] Of course, Libya faced a bumpy transition: weak state institutions and weapons looted by former rebels posed a significant threat to stability, but surely—went the thinking of many of the Libyans I met during the 2011 uprising and two years later when I returned to Tripoli—anything was better than the old regime.

In 2014 I sat on a plush couch in Tripoli's foreign ministry, overlooking the Mediterranean. I was trying to think of questions for a press conference with the foreign minister and other officials of an unrecognised administration that had seized the capital by force and expelled the official government, whose members had fled to eastern Libya. It was the latest of several administrations trying to impose its authority on a country slipping into anarchy. They had invited me and the handful of other foreign reporters left in Tripoli to press us to report that they were now the legitimate rulers.

Suddenly, a security guard drew a gun on a reporter sitting next to me. My colleague had complained that the conference had been delayed for almost two hours, and during this time the guards had moved us between a series of holding rooms. Aided by two plain-clothes guards failing to conceal their gun holsters, the official dragged the screaming Libyan reporter outside and began beating him. I should have come to the aid my colleague, but I was frozen in shock.

Coming to, I whispered to the cameraman sitting on my other side:

INTRODUCTION

'What shall we do? Shall we leave?'

'Maybe we should.'

The cameraman and I fled quickly and quietly. The guard was now kicking the journalist down a staircase that for decades prior had been used by top foreign officials and diplomatic delegations sent to visit the Libyan foreign minister. His head hit a set of red-carpeted stairs on the way down. I had never been so scared—not even when dodging bullets during the revolution, when I was embedded with the rebels marching on Tripoli. That was three years ago, in August 2011, at the end of Gaddafi's dreaded 42-year rule, when the promises of the Arab Spring still gripped the Middle East.

Officials were quick to downplay the incident and vowed to punish the guard, but no action was taken. Libya had descended into a state of quasi-anarchy, with hundreds, maybe thousands, of former rebel factions now the only power brokers, refusing to disarm after toppling Gaddafi and carving out precarious fiefdoms like the one to which the offending guard belonged. In the new Libya, Tripoli had only limited control over the west of the country, and its current overlords would lose the capital within two years, when another UN-backed administration took over—with the help of militias.

But in 2014, retired Gaddafi-era general, Khalifa Haftar, declared a coup, starting his own war in the east and setting his sights on Tripoli, triggering a counter-offensive and effectively breaking the country into two halves—a division from which Libya has never recovered. This was the turning point for Libya, and signalled the death of any illusion of a peaceful transition and the dreams of Libyans who craved democracy and stability. Indeed, many ordinary Libyans have long given up hope of their lives changing for the better. They avoid political discussions (at least in public) and are careful about venturing out late at night for fear of kidnappings and shootings. They live in stark contrast to the final days of the uprising, when many Libyans were euphoric, as the rebels—with the help of NATO and sympathetic Arab states such as Qatar—swept away the strongman who had suppressed all forms of dissent.[4]

'Now we build a free and democratic Libya. We want freedom!' Rebel fighters had shouted as they tore along the coastal road to Tripoli in the final push towards the capital,[5] repurposing slogans heard in Cairo's Tahrir Square when the uprising there had unseated Hosni Mubarak earlier the same year.

I heard such vows every day while embedded with rebels in the western mountains, which served as a launchpad for the eventual taking of Tripoli. For weeks after the seizure of the capital, rebel fighters were firing guns into the air on Green Square—the erstwhile venue for Gaddafi's speeches and rallies. Now renamed Martyrs' Square, the site of the uprising's climactic moments is located a short drive along the seafront, near the foreign ministry, where three years later a guard would point a gun at a journalist beside me. Who could forget the celebrations?

* * *

In 2015 I moved to Nigeria as Reuters' bureau chief in Africa's most populous country. I was fascinated by the country's turbulent history, politics and corruption, and how that sat alongside its rich cultural life. I also needed a break: having spent eight years covering a Middle East gripped by crises, I needed a break from the region's autocratic regimes. I had been expelled by Saudi Arabia in 2011[6] during pro-democracy protests that erupted at the start of the Arab Spring and headed straight to Khartoum to cover the breakup of Sudan as its southern region became the world's youngest nation. I also reported in Iraq, Yemen and Egypt—where in 2013 the military deposed the elected Islamist President Mohamed Mursi following mass protests against his rule. I had hardly had a day off when I moved to Tripoli later that year.

INTRODUCTION

I lived with my wife, who also worked as a journalist, in Tripoli from September 2013 until July 2014, before the fighting made a permanent residence too dangerous.[7] Even then we didn't have much of a private life, having to be at home by 8pm for security reasons. There was no such thing as a cinema or theatre visit in Tripoli: the highlight of our social life would be a waterpipe at 6pm at a popular café on Algiers Square, next to a former Italian cathedral. But we met and befriended many Libyans, whose thinking often contrasted with statements from top officials.

Thinking my journey as a reporter had turned a corner, away from the Arab world to sub-Saharan Africa, I found I couldn't shake my connections to Libya so easily. Boko Haram, the jihadist group haunting northern Nigeria had links to Islamic State (IS),[8] which had seized territory in Libya, establishing a stronghold in Gaddafi's hometown, Sirte, in 2015 and regrouping to the southern desert after Libyan forces, backed up by US airstrikes, expelled it in December 2016. Many Nigerians I met tried to escape poverty by attempting the perilous journey from Libya to Italy: at a Tripoli naval base I met a group of crying women whose dreams of reaching Europe had been shattered when the Libyan coastguard intercepted their inflatable boat.

I returned to Libya as Reuters' North Africa bureau chief in November 2017 for a three-week reporting trip in the west of the country. The capital was highly dysfunctional and hostile towards reporters despite a UN-backed government which, on paper, was meant to restore order and build up a functioning state. I had hoped the dark days of the unrecognised and Islamist-leaning Libya Dawn administration—the one whose officials had put a gun to my colleague's head—would be at a close. Unfortunately, conditions for journalists on the ground had worsened. Reacting to a barrage of negative coverage about its powerless Prime Minister, Fayez al-Serraj, officials made it very difficult for foreign reporters to gain press accreditation and visas. It took me six weeks to cajole an approval letter from the foreign media office, which (like the rest of the country) had split into competing factions, complicating the process beyond the familiar Kafkaism of the Libyan state. The abusive head of the office had refused to leave his post, even after ministers had packed up after the arrival of Serraj by boat from Tunisia. He slept in his office until he was forcibly removed by the new administration, which reinstalled the rather more cooperative senior official I had known from my earlier stint in Tripoli, even if some of the new staff held back paperwork in a bid to obstruct their new boss, who was also undermined by intelligence agents and other officials from the old Gaddafi apparatus. Suspicious of foreign media, this group's gradual re-emergence saw them penetrating the foreign and interior ministries and pressuring the new head of the foreign media office to issue fewer visas. I and a colleague were the last to receive his approval, just before the new administration took away his stamps.[9]

Even after I had the necessary approvals from Tripoli, this didn't mean I had a visa. The chaos of rival governments, who themselves faced internal divisions, meant you had to find an embassy official who would accept a visa from the capital. The Libyan embassy in Tunis, where the consul is affiliated to a prominent militia leader,[10] refused to issue me the visa, with staff claiming they couldn't find the email from the Tripoli administration—a claim they would make with some regularity.[11] I had to collect my visa in London, home to one of the few Libyan missions still somehow functioning normally.

But you couldn't simply board a plane to Libya like before: now you needed separate approval from Tripoli, or the airline would refuse to check you in. Gone too were the days when a bored airport official would stamp your passport without looking. Now, intelligence officers questioned foreigners arriving at Tripoli's Mitiga airport (the principal gateway to western Libya, since the main airport in the capital was closed after being shelled, along with 90 per cent of all planes parked there, three years earlier).[12] Unless someone could vouch for you—like a colleague or a member of the foreign media office—you faced likely deportation on the same plane you arrived on whether you held a valid visa or not. Since the country split, airport security in Tripoli and the east had become very suspicious—not just of foreigners, but also of Libyans suspected of belonging to rival camps.

Upon leaving the country, plain-clothes police would ask what you had been doing in Libya. In my case, the focus would be on who I had interviewed and where. I would reveal the names of high-profile commanders but was careful not to reveal details of anyone who might get in trouble for cooperating with me, and these clandestine interlocutors would stamp my boarding pass with the word *mabahith* (security). The stamp was an indication that Gaddafi-era intelligence officials had returned and were working with the Salafist Islamist Rada militia that now controlled the airport, running a prison patrolled by bearded militiamen on the same premises. There had been rumours about a return of former security officers who had fled abroad or gone into hiding after the revolution, but this was, as with so many things in Libya, almost impossible to prove. It made sense for Rada to work with former Gaddafi officers, as the militia had fighters with experience in street battles but not necessarily in basic intelligence work, nor in how to screen or interrogate travellers.

Luggage checks remained as lax as ever, with young men in uniforms only cursorily glancing at x-ray screens. Almost no foreign carriers returned to Libya, not even Tunisair, which used to operate more than ten daily flights. The company was concerned about insufficient luggage checks and the risk of staff kidnappings: whenever Tunisian authorities would arrest a militia commander, his men would respond "in kind"—by abducting

Tunisians.[13] Since the Tunisian consulate in Tripoli had closed for a lack of security, the comparatively vulnerable Tunisair staff would surely become a target.[14]

Perhaps the worst was that some of the most restrictive rules from the Gaddafi era had been reinstated for journalists. It was no longer possible to walk into ministries and ask to speak to an official—a relaxed set-up I had always liked about Libya. Now a letter from the foreign media office was required for every interview, detailing who would conduct it and the subjects that would be covered. I spent half of my time just trying to get the papers to allow me to do some reporting. As in the old days, some freelance journalists had been forced to hire a minder, whose fee would then be shared between officials in the foreign media office. One of them told me over coffee that accreditation was only afforded to minders or fixers who gave such kickbacks. Another official even asked my team for a laptop in exchange for a visa extension, although he was fired days later, before we'd ascertained if he was serious. The ever-changing and complex rules prompted some journalists to travel on business visas, risking detention. They got usually away with it, but the practice just made things even more difficult for those of us playing by the rules, as officials became ever more suspicious of the media. On the other hand, I could understand freelancers taking these risks: without an office in Libya you stood almost no chance of receiving accreditation through official channels.

The obstacles didn't end there. When you went to another city, like Misrata, you needed to request permission to report from the local council, even if (as we did en route to the central city of Sirte in November 2017) you were just passing through. A plain-clothes agent approached our multimedia team at the hotel asking to authenticate our stay, which unfortunately cut short our day trip to see the heavily damaged city after it was liberated from the clutches of IS. It was also necessary to sign a form titled 'Misrata Municipality Journalism Controls', which outlined the council's ground rules. This included a directive 'not to do any media work without the media facilitators' and another 'not to do any journalistic work ... before getting specific written permission.' Such rules (which necessarily disallowed talking to ordinary people) were routinely ignored, but were nonetheless discomfiting.

In the east, the situation was even worse. Our reporters had been unable to get a visa for the east for several years (although I managed to obtain one in February 2019), with officials linked to General Haftar refusing to cooperate. Although Libya is still one country, its division into a Tripoli-based government and a rival administration in the east means you need a separate eastern visa, or at least a letter stating you are allowed to board a plane bound for an airport there. Even now, very few foreign journalists travel east, where independent reporting is all but impossible, with minders linked to Haftar's fighters acting as uninvited escorts on all visits to Benghazi. During a 2018 visit I found out that the Tripoli government had set up similar rules.

In Tripoli, little had changed with the arrival of a new government, meaning mediators would struggle to find someone in charge who could enforce either peace deals or basic rules. Diplomats could now return, but the new government struggled make an impact, as the power of its ministers rarely extended beyond the confines of their offices. The new rulers were without a real army or police force and so were instead, like previous administrations, dependent on militias—among them some of the major factions that had carved out fiefdoms district by district since 2011. Security remained poor, with Mitiga airport regularly forced to close during shootouts between rival groups. The only Western embassies operating were those of Italy and Turkey. The UN mission and some other European embassies had reopened their compounds, but diplomats rarely spent time there, preferring the safety of Tunis. Power cuts and interruptions in water supply were frequent, which made life difficult for residents worn down by years of chaos. A few more foreigners could be seen in the capital, but very little had changed since the 2014 attack on Tripoli, which had sent Western expatriates (and indeed many Libyans) packing.

The main business of the Government of National Accord (the official name of the new administration) seemed to be to update the letterheads of official documents that had played host to the monikers of other short-lived administrations (for instance, the National Transitional Council set up after the revolution; the Interim Government headed by Ali Zeidan; the unrecognised National Salvation Government based in Tripoli from 2014 to 2016) in lieu of power or influence, which remained in the hands of militias—some of which had also backed previous administrations. There was also the eastern-based House of Representatives and the Tripoli-based state council, a body advising Serraj's government to broaden power by including as many figures as possible. All had their own stationery.

During the revolution you would hear from rebels, defected officials and the general public of the wish to end Gaddafi's police state. Unfortunately, Libya's post-revolution rulers have since established a similarly repressive environment in which nobody dares to talk freely, and those criticising the new rulers are likely to end up in jails run by armed groups and without any formal charges or access to legal representation, in the same way that inmates were locked up by Gaddafi's revolutionary committees. Beatings and torture remain commonplace.

* * *

In Chapter 1 we will look at Libya's modern history to try to understand the difficulties faced by those who might try to build state institutions after four decades of Gaddafi. Libya was a state created rather by accident: stitched together by world powers after World War II and led initially by a reluctant regent whose modest achievements in institution-building were quickly wiped out by Gaddafi when he took power in 1969.

Chapter 2 shows how the former rebels who, with the help of NATO, toppled the autocrat and attempted to fill the subsequent security void. These groups became the new state by force and by de facto, blackmailing weak ministers to hire and empower their fighters in the absence of a national army and police.

In Chapter 3 we take a closer look at one militia commander, Ibrahim Jathran, who in 2013 seized Libya's oil export ports, resulting in losses to the national economy that ran to tens of billions of dollars. Jathran's story illustrates why civilian rulers never had a chance in post-Gaddafi Libya. Indeed, there would be plenty of others like him, but Jathran is a case study for what went wrong, and I dealt extensively with him and his fighters during my tenure in Libya.

Chapter 4 sheds light on another commander, General Khalifa Haftar, whose trajectory is crucial to understanding why Libya's democratic transition failed. Haftar helped Gaddafi in his 1969 coup before the pair fell out and Haftar took up residence in Virginia. Haftar joined the uprising in 2011 and has since used his considerable military influence to shift proceedings in and about Libya, with foreign diplomats and international organisations including him in their visions for the future of the country.

In Chapter 5 we will see why Libya has struggled to build national institutions and a consensus over the post-Gaddafi transition due to deep-rooted divisions driven by Libya's fractious society and complex identity politics. The power struggle since 2011 has opened new wounds, making it even more difficult to reconcile and build a cohesive state.

Part of the challenge of state-building are Libya's vast oil and gas revenues, which are spent almost exclusively on an unproductive civil service and subsidies, as discussed in Chapter 6. Libya's public sector stifles work, discourages private sector enterprise and benefits militias who have been milking the state ever since the uprising, putting fighters on the payroll indefinitely, mirroring the way the system was abused by Gaddafi.

Soon after the uprising, Western powers largely left Libya to its own devices, allowing them to hijack the state and dominate its weak institutions. But there was one part of the Libyan state that did receive assistance—the coastguard. The European Union's vested interest in stemming the flow of migrants and refugees arriving on its shores from Libya led to a range of interventions, as we will see in Chapter 7.

Libya is dominated by militias, but with most only controlling limited territory, IS militants have entered the fray after having made inroads in Iraq and Syria. The group lost its stronghold in Sirte, but has regrouped in the southern desert and has staged several attacks inside the capital, shattering the illusion of relative stability. Building on this, Chapter 8 discusses the inability of yet another government in Tripoli to address the incursion, and indeed to provide basic services.

The Epilogue discusses General Haftar's campaign to conquer Tripoli by force, which dramatically escalated tensions again, after eight years of conflict and chaos. Militias in western Libya overcame their differences almost overnight in a bid to stop Haftar in the biggest military mobilisation since 2011. The offensive killed UN plans for peaceful power sharing, displaced more than 120,000 people and the hopes of those who thought their county might soon meet the aspirations of the revolution.

So where did it all go wrong? This book is my attempt to explain why this North African country, with its embarrassment of riches and wealth of natural resources, has descended from a popular uprising against a dictator into a failed state and major security headache for its neighbours in Europe, the Middle East and West Africa. Mine is by no means an academic take: I base my analysis of this complex country solely on personal experience of covering the civil war in 2011, and then again from 2013 to 2015, for the Reuters news agency. I came back to Libya in 2017 when I took up a new role as regional bureau chief, and I have been one of the few foreign correspondents on the ground in Libya since Gaddafi's overthrow. In my current role as bureau chief for Egypt and Sudan I am based in Cairo. As a result, I monitor developments in Libya less closely, although it is impossible for me to look away entirely.

But before I talk about my work and daily life in a land now run by militias, we need look at Libya's modern history to understand what prompted the revolution in the first place, and why the hopes of ordinary people have gone unfulfilled.

1

AN ACCIDENTAL STATE

To understand why Libyans have struggled to build an efficient state in the wake of Gaddafi's 2011 overthrow, we need to look at how what is known as Libya today was created. It was not, like in the case of its neighbour Algeria, the result of an eight-year independence struggle against an imperial overlord in which up to 300,000 people[1] were killed, creating a national identity and narrative which helped the rebel party retain power until the present day. Neither does Libya share Tunisia's experience of its first president, Habib Bourguiba, whose autocracy built an education system that stands out in the region and developed a culture of compromise which allowed Tunisians to negotiate peaceful democratic transitions, such as the one that followed the fall of Zine El-Abidine Ben Ali in 2011 and helped to avoid a civil war.[2] Libya doesn't share Egypt's long tradition of a strong military as a power centre. Gaddafi, an officer, was inspired by Gamal Abdel Nasser, who removed the Egyptian King Farouk, but Libya never had much of an army.

Instead, Libya was stitched together by Allied powers after World War II, merging three autonomous regions: the eastern

Cyrenaica, Tripolitania in the west, and the sparsely inhabited Fezzan, south in the endless Sahara.[3] All three regions had, until then, limited contact with one another. Though the fourth-largest country in Africa after Algeria, the Democratic Republic of Congo and Sudan (with an area of around 1.76 million km),[2] Libya has always been sparsely inhabited. Apart from a mountain range in the west and east, it consists mostly of desert, with most inhabitants settling on a fertile coastal strip. The desert stretches from the centre to the Mediterranean coast, creating a natural border between Tripolitania and Cyrenaica. Upon unification, there were only isolated cities to be found inland, aside from in the mountainous hinterland of Tripoli and the eastern Green Mountain region. Fezzan's main town of Sebha was located about 1,000 km south of the coast. Before the discovery of oil and gas, Libya—sandwiched today between Egypt, Sudan, Chad, Niger, Algeria and Tunisia—was, at its formation in 1951, a desolate place subjected to summer temperatures of up to 50°C in the desert.

The country's chaos since 2011 has once again cut contact between the different regions as the domestic airline network—once one of the region's largest—has largely collapsed. There is no railway, but decent (if potholed) roads can be found along the country's Mediterranean coast. The coastal road between Tripoli and Benghazi has become dangerous due to checkpoints run by militias with changeable loyalties. The three main roads leading south from the coast are often blocked due to fighting between tribes and other armed groups. With the few flights operating between the south and Tripoli or Benghazi booked weeks in advance, residents regularly find themselves stranded.

A foreign creation: 1911–1951

The sparsely populated region now known as Libya was ruled by the Ottomans from the 16th century, but their control was limited. 'Although Ottoman influence did reach Fezzan and beyond, most of the empire's attention concentrated on the littoral, relying on shallow and indirect measures to manage the hinterland,' said Libya researcher Jalel Harchaoui.[4] The Italians took over and occupied Tripoli in 1911 and built roads, elegant villas and palaces there and in Benghazi, the second-largest city in the east. But they did little to create an efficient state, and failed to launch any major infrastructure projects or develop the hinterland. Libya is the only North African country that has not inherited a railway system from its French (Algeria, Morocco and Tunisia) or British (Egypt, Sudan) colonial rulers. In contrast to other Arab countries, no coloniser has seriously attempted to build a national army.[5] For Rome, the land grab was a means to exploit the region's vast agricultural resources and to establish the 'fourth shore'—advancing the expansionist ambitions of Benito Mussolini's fascist regime. Their colonial masters had excluded Libyans from political life, brutally suppressing an insurgency that started right after their arrival and lasted, in the east, until the 1930s. More than 100,000 Libyans were imprisoned in camps and as many as 50,000 may have died.[6] The Italians also made a lasting impression with their building activity in Tripoli and Benghazi: Tripoli's old city is made up of Italian-made residential and administrative buildings as well as schools notably grander than those constructed by Gaddafi (who erected Soviet-style shopping malls and the luxury El Kabir Hotel). Even the palace of King Idris, the country's first ruler, was commissioned by Italian governor Giuseppe Volpi and executed by Milanese architect Meraviglia Montegazza.

Italian rule failed to diminish the role of Libya's tribes, whose influence even the Ottomans had failed to curtail. After Italy's defeat by the Allies, both Britain and France fostered tribal links via indirect rule when they administered what would become the modern state of Libya. The world powers tasked King Idris al-

Sanoussi, a member of a prominent Muslim movement which had led the resistance against Italian rule, with running the underdeveloped desert nation when it became independent in 1951. The new country depended on foreign aid from day one. Some 90 per cent of its citizens were illiterate in 1952, living on a per capita income of just $35 annually. Only 1.2 per cent of land was suitable for agriculture and just 5 per cent was being irrigated. The Italians had built large-scale farms, but many projects (including vast tobacco farms and vineyards, established in violation of Islamic law) had been abandoned since their departure as they did not necessarily benefit the local population.[7]

For the United States, Britain and France, Libya had mainly strategic value due to its position on the Mediterranean, hosting several military bases linking air and sea routes to India and the Far East. The biggest testimony to that was the Wheelus air base outside Tripoli, now the Mitiga civil and military airport, which between 1943 and 1969 operated as the US's largest military base abroad. The discovery of oil in commercial quantities in the 1960s made Libya even more valuable: oil could be safely exported to Europe without the use of tankers, unlike shipments from the Gulf which had been made impossible by Egypt's closure of the Suez Canal after Israel's Six-Day War in 1967.[8] Amid the Cold War and the Algerian War of Independence, the Allies sought to bolster their position by granting aid to the new Libya, but the prolonged presence of foreign troops and technical experts became a source of contention among ordinary Libyans—something Gaddafi would eventually tap into during his 1969 coup.[9]

The Idris era: 1951–1969

Lacking a unified sense of national identity, King Idris was (despite his frail health) a natural choice for Libya's monarch. His order found credibility among ordinary Libyans, especially

18

those from his region, Cyrenaica. The order had been founded by Idris's grandfather, Sayyid Mohammed ibn Ali al-Sanoussi, who sought to revitalise and purify the practice of Islam in the country and founded the most important socio-religious movement in the region.[10] Sanoussi led the resistance against the Italians and later became an ally of the British, providing support during World War II against Nazi Germany's North Africa campaign. For 40 years Idris had lived in exile in Egypt, where he acted as a leader in opposition to the Italians, and later supported the British, who seized Tripolitania and Cyrenaica in 1943 (the southern Fezzan came under French control).[11] Idris later negotiated with Britain towards independence for Cyrenaica and Libya.[12] King Idris was also seen as a compromising figure in Tripolitania, where residents expected him to establish an independent state, while he won support in the Fezzan, where people hoped not to be 'dominated by Tripolitania'.[13]

Libya,[14] despite being home to only 1.5 million people, ended up with two capitals: Tripoli, the most developed city in the west; and Benghazi, a major port in the eastern Cyrenaica. Ever since then Libya has struggled to stay together: despite Benghazi losing its co-capital status in 1969, 2014 saw the de facto re-establishment of the dual-capital system and, for now at least, Libya functions with capitals in the west and the east. The country's 1951 constitution established a federal power-sharing system headed by King Idris to balance power among the regions. The three provinces were represented in the two chambers of parliament, which had to approve all laws in a highly inefficient and costly political system. The provincial governorates of Tripolitania and Cyrenaica employed more public servants than the federal government, which remained weak. The provinces managed local affairs and often exercised their powers to obstruct federal initiatives. The federal government was even restricted by the provinces in budget planning, as taxation needed provincial approval.[15]

This loose federal union reflected Libya's lack of identity and was 'designed to balance the rivalries and jealousies of the three historically disparate provinces'.[16] Libyans, while benefiting (from the 1960s onwards) from a welfare state financed by oil exports, developed a distrust of state institutions. As a result, decision making was dominated by tribal and familial links that operated outside of the formal system, which was all too often weighed down by maximal bureaucracy with little sign of an efficient state.[17]

Idris, a pious Muslim, did little to foster a sense of national identity. He was a reluctant ruler who spent much of his time at home in the east, keeping the country together with patronage and tribal alliances. Idris was hesitant to impose his will, and spent the summers in Bayda, a small city in the Green Mountain region known for its mild climate. His presence made Bayda the summer capital in a country with a tiny population and strained public finances. Adding to his detachment from political life, Idris would also often stay with his family in a palace in Tobruk, another small city in the east, close to the Egyptian border— closer, in fact, to Cairo than to Tripoli.

When first negotiating with the British, Idris aimed to achieve autonomy for Cyrenaica, hoping that the wider region's independence would follow later. 'He always seemed to care more for the affairs of Cyrenaica alone rather than Libya as a whole,' wrote John Wright, a Libya specialist. 'He put political matters second to religion and regretted to have to spend much time on running the country.'[18] So unassuming was Idris that he even asked that official buildings not be named after him, with the exception of Tripoli's airport.[19]

The resistance against the Italians had also helped foster a special identity in the east which would undermine the formation of a national identity (and has ultimately played a big role following the overthrow of Gaddafi). There were violent protests against the Italians in Tripoli in the 1910s and 1920s, but much less than in the Cyrenaica, as residents in coastal cities lacked united leadership and showed little interest in combat.[20] In Cyrenaica, the fight lasted much longer, as insurgents used the Green Mountain region as a hideout until their leader, Umar Mukhtar, was caught and hanged in 1931. Even today, pictures of him can be found in homes and public buildings in the east, but much less commonly in western Libya. 'Umar Mukhtar was the greatest Libyan,' Mohamed, a young student who was helping to build a museum in the eastern city of Tobruk, once told me.[21]

Idris had fostered personal and tribal links, with a focus on Cyrenaica, and was against political parties because they cut across families and tribes. He had little interest in developing a national spirit, leaving Libya fractured in regions where citizens, when asked where they were from, would offer their town, tribe or region before saying they were Libyans. This reluctance was not shared by the citizens of Libya's neighbours, whose rulers and citizens were also struggling to turn former colonies into viable and cohesive nation states. Where they differed, perhaps, was in ancient heritage, in the case of Egypt; or a liberation war against French colonial rulers, in the case of Algeria; from which to carve out a national identity. In Libya, independence was the result of neither ancient heritage nor armed struggle—it was a country created by world powers who looked to someone like Idris to lead it.

The kingdom saw only modest development (thanks to foreign grants) until the discovery of oil in the late 1950s, which transformed the economy and allowed for the development of a welfare state. Oil majors had begun conducting seismic surveys in the 1950s, and Esso had concluded there was oil in commercial quantities to be explored under Libyan soil.[22] Government expenditure rose from just 7 million Libyan pounds in 1952/3 to an estimated 345 million in 1968/9. GDP per capita income surged from $35 in 1951 to $514 in 1963, and $2,028 in 1969.[23]

Idris launched the country's first Five-Year Plan in 1963, aimed at improving the infrastructure and living standards of Libyans and achieving food security based around self-sufficiency. In 1958, the government decided that 70 per cent of oil revenues would go into development, with the remainder to be used by provincial and federal governments.[24]

On paper this spending looked impressive, but the reality was somewhat different. Libya, like other countries enjoying a sudden uptick of massive oil revenues, could not spend the oil money quickly enough for it to make a substantive difference to its people. The crude wealth helped to build a welfare state, employing Libyans in the civil service and allowing young people to enrol in schools and universities. But more time was needed to overhaul the infrastructure that could create institutions and attract experts to execute development plans. The welfare state also discouraged private entrepreneurship, as it created decent (though non-productive) administrative jobs. Libyans are haunted to this day by the problems associated with having the public sector function as the country's biggest employer, as we will see in Chapter 6. Idris tried building a national army, but the new oil wealth made the army less attractive as an employer, even for notable families.[25]

Part of Idris's first Five-Year Plan was to promote industries to diversify the economy beyond oil extraction and agriculture, but the results were disappointing.[26] The scheme envisaged that 17 per cent of the plan's budget would go into agriculture, but Libya, which had previously produced its own food, soon became a net importer of agricultural products—a classic curse of oil exporters, where the inflow of oil revenues keeps the local currency's foreign exchange rate high, making imports cheaper than local production. As a result, ordinary people suffered high inflation, which could only be contended by the 1 per cent of the population who found (skilled) work in the oil industry.[27]

Libya remained an undeveloped country: with farming remaining the mainstay of Libyans: 'Oil had raised expectations that no regime at no time could have satisfied, for the new wealth could not be distributed fast and fairly enough,' wrote Wright.[28] The country needed long-term planning and some 100,000 skilled workers to execute the ambitious plans. Some projects were started, such as new housing in Tripoli, though Gaddafi would eventually take the credit for this. When driving around today's Tripoli, our photographer, who has a keen interest in history, always points out white residential blocks that were inaugurated by Gaddafi but planned and commissioned before his coup. A similar problem arose after the 2011 revolution, when Libyans eagerly demanded an overhaul of the country's dilapidated infrastructure, which was impossible to achieve in the short term.

To address the shortcomings of the political system and manage the arrival of oil revenues, Idris agreed a constitutional amendment which gave the federal government more power. 'It constituted the single most critical political act during the monarch's tenure', wrote Vandewalle, calling it a 'watershed'.[29] Under the old constitution, even budget planning had been difficult to execute. However, while this amendment gave more power to central government, the main factors in decision making were still the familial interests fostered by the king. For example, tribes in Cyrenaica had initially worried about Tripoli's dominance, but that fear faded with the discovery of oil reserves in the east. To win the support of the east many leaders from Cyrenaica were also given jobs under a power-sharing deal and the country's name changed from the 'United Kingdom of Libya' to the 'Kingdom of Libya'.

Despite the new constitution and name, there was widespread political lethargy and a sense of permanent crisis, exacerbated by oil revenues fuelling corruption which had disconnected the elite from the public, mere bystanders in their own politics—something of a recurring theme in modern Libyan history. The continued presence of troops from Britain and the United States—two backers of Israel—on Libyan soil was an additional source of dissent at a time when pan-Arabic rhetoric against the Jewish state was growing, with some campaigning for a single Arab state to nullify the borders created by colonial powers. Oil revenues benefited an elite patronage network, giving critics room to describe the kingdom as backward. As Idris approached 80, the prospect of Crown Prince Hasan's ascent was even less appealing. Appointed at the age of 28 in 1966, Hasan had little personal following and no political influence, and many questioned whether he could provide the leadership and stabilising influence of his uncle.[30]

The kingdom's crisis deepened in 1967, with the Arab defeat in Israel's Six-Day War, when the Jewish state seized East Jerusalem and the West Bank from Jordan, the Gaza Strip and the Sinai Peninsula from Egypt and the Golan Heights from Syria. Some Libyan aircraft took part in the fighting, but more notably, angry youths attacked Jewish shops in Tripoli and hunted for Jews in the streets.[31] Groups also attacked British and US properties, such as the US information office in Benghazi, while some port workers also refused to serve Western tankers. Government offices were also targeted over the kingdom's pro-Western stance.[32] Some ministers fled abroad, and tensions continued to run high for weeks, until Idris dismissed what had become a defunct government. This did not bring the kingdom's state of crisis to an end.[33] Pan-Arab demands were fuelled by a hatred of the Western powers accused of aiding Israel and Libya's inability to help Palestinians. Idris was, as Pargeter puts it, 'no match for the powers of the Arab nationalist ideology',[34] unable to match the expectations of a generation and build a modern state. Libya needed a new start.

AN ACCIDENTAL STATE

The Green Revolution: 1969–1978

Having tapped into these frustrations, Muammar Gaddafi seized power with his fellow army officers on 1 September 1969, declaring a Libyan Arab republic and promising development and an end to repression and dependency on foreign powers. Said to have been born in a tent in the village of Qasr Abu Hadi near Sirte in 1942, he developed (even during his time as a schoolboy in Sebha and later in Misrata) a plan to overthrow the king, who he accused of corruption and working against the Arab cause, framing his critique in the wider pan-Arab rhetoric of the time. He began recruiting fellow students, enrolling with some of them in the army in 1963 to pursue his long-planned coup. In Libya, as elsewhere, the army is the natural place to go to pursue regime change, thanks to its key domestic role and international roles. Military officers had toppled rulers in several Arab countries: Gamal Abdel Nasser seized power from King Farouk (whose dynasty the British had installed) in Egypt in 1952; in Iraq, putschists toppled King Faisal II. Gaddafi founded the Free Unionist Officers Movement, seeking to repeat the success of Nasser by forming a Revolutionary Command Council (RCC) which met in secret and recruited officer cadets from across the country. It took years for the coup to happen, and some of his fellow revolutionaries had begun to doubt it ever would. When the hour of the coup finally arrived, there was no bloodshed—neither the British nor any other foreign power rushed to defend the old regime.

While Gaddafi and his fellow officers were charismatic, they lacked a clear strategy beyond their plan to oust the monarch. A new constitution empowered the RCC, allowing a gradual purge of figures of the old regime, as well as elite tribal elders who had backed Idris. Western banks were nationalised, the British and Americans were ~~forced~~ asked to abandon their bases and the last of the Italians were expelled and their property seized.[35]

In 1971, Gaddafi, who had systematically sidelined his fellow plotters to emerge as the dominant force of the new era, created so-called 'popular congresses' to move the revolution to the next level. But faced with a lack of enthusiasm from ordinary Libyans (who were once again treated as something of an afterthought) the new rulers moved towards a more controlled system, creating an Arab Socialist Union based on Nasser's model and intended to mobilise the masses. After its failure, Gaddafi, frustrated by the lack of revolutionary fervour among the general public, launched what he called a 'popular revolution' in a speech in Zuwara, a small town near the Tunisian border in 1973. He stunned even his closest allies by declaring all laws nullified, calling on citizens to take up arms and dissolve the state. From 1975 onwards, authority was handed over to so-called people's committees in line with the slogan of his Green Book: *lijan fi kuli makan* (committees are everywhere).[36]

And so began 'Gaddafism', an obscure mix of socialism, Islam and pan-Arab ideology penetrating every aspect of life in its rejection of foreign influence and ban on private entrepreneurship, among many other restrictions.[37] Some 2,000 committees oversaw the implementation of the new revolution, which seemed to consist of arresting opponents, settling old scores and creating bureaucratic chaos as the number of official state bodies surged.[38]

Gaddafi's idol had always been Egypt's President Nasser, but his hopes of a union between Egypt, Libya and Sudan failed to materialise when the Egyptian leader died in 1970. Gaddafi's subsequent plans to unite Libya with other Arab states also failed when he was dismissed by many as an obscurantist. Shunned, he turned his attention to Africa, hosting its leaders at lavish summits in his home city of Sirte and funding development projects as well as rebel movements across the continent. With his revolutionary rhetoric, he helped inspire South Africans to revolt against apartheid and, unlike in the West, he was and still is respected in much of Africa. Nelson Mandela named a grandson after him, while during my time as Reuters bureau chief in Nigeria I met ordinary people in several West African countries who spoke fondly about the roads and other development projects he funded in their countries. In 2019, eight years after his death, his Green Book was still being sold by online and retail bookshops in Nigeria.[39]

After the coup, Gaddafi's regime forced foreign oil companies to agree on tougher production terms, increasing the government's profit share from barrels pumped from deep beneath the Libyan soil. This allowed Gaddafi to fund his 'state of the masses' (called *Jamahiriya*, from the Arabic word *jumhur*, or masses) and foreign 'revolutionary' activities backing rebels or friendly regimes in various countries, especially Africa. Libya's oil revenues rose from $2 billion in 1971 to $6 billion in 1974.[40]

The creation of the Socialist People's Libyan Arab Jamahiriya in 1977[41] entrenched a parallel authority with power bundled in so-called revolutionary committees and courts. The crushing of dissidents at home and abroad would intensify in the 1980s, with committees acting as police, state prosecutors and judges— arresting, torturing and sentencing people at will.[42]

Gaddafi kept the army weak to minimise the danger of a coup d'état and set up competing security agencies to keep watch on one another. Special brigades were recruited from his own tribe, the Gadhadfa; the Warfalla, a tribe from the city of Bani Walid, south of Tripoli; and the Magarha, another tribe from deep in the south, and from which his spy chief Abdullah el-Senoussi hailed. Like rulers before him, Gaddafi used the tribes to secure his power: he first sidelined tribal notables to break the dominance of elites allied to the monarchy; then, after dissolving state institutions, he restored their powers selectively, offering jobs, patronage and cementing ties through marriage.[43]

GDP continued to rise until 1983, which helped Gaddafi expand the welfare state to buy loyalty. This included free education, health care, jobs in an overstaffed civil service as well as subsidies for anything from petrol to bread to domestic airline tickets. However, the implications of the Green Book for ordinary Libyans were grave, making life difficult and unpredictable despite the country's oil revenues. Under the pretence of wealth being shared equally and empowering the masses, private businesses were confiscated and landowners were stripped of property, with rules often changing overnight. The Libyan currency was taken out of circulation with a week's notice in 1980, triggering a run on banks, with personal savings wiped clean or moved to accounts which could not be accessed.

These bizarre economic policies stifled private production, which remains a problem to date: there is hardly any non-oil production in Libya, with even basic foods such as milk and cheese being imported from Europe. Moreover, the expansion of the welfare state to foster political loyalty meant Libyans had no incentive to develop an entrepreneurial mentality, as public service jobs were readily available. Other promising business sectors (such as tourism) went unexploited. Authorities would nominally open the country in the final years of the regime, but with Gaddafi's distrust of foreigners (who he regularly branded as spies) and the influence of media, politicians and most governments' travel advice against non-essential travel to Libya, its full potential was never realised.

While the welfare state ensured survival, it created frustration among young Libyans who were underemployed in the public sector. Up to 75 per cent of Libyans were on the public payroll by 1987,[44] often doings job that were not really necessary. They would be the driving force behind the anti-Gaddafi uprising. 'The majority of the population lived on a combination of badly paid public sector jobs and subsidies, with young people being particularly affected by widespread unemployment,' wrote the German Libya researcher, Wolfram Lacher.[45] With the old education system destroyed and manipulated by the regime to teach the ideology of the Green Book, and with English banned, Libya never developed the educated middle class, labour unions and professional organisations that would later drive the uprisings in Tunisia and Egypt.

Life under Gaddafi: 1978–2011

In an attempt to understand why Libya swapped a police state under Gaddafi for instability and militia rule, I have tried to learn from ordinary Libyans about life under the dictator. One of my best guides was one of our photographers in Tripoli. Having navigated three political systems—the kingdom, Gaddafi's regime and the current chaos—he is the kind of local reporter without whose help no foreign reporter could survive. He would often discreetly advise me against filing a story or would suggest omitting certain details from an interview if my questions had breached one of the many unofficial red lines you face in a country run by gunmen who only want to have it their way. At times it seemed as though he knew someone in every government office or remote village whose trust he'd won during his decades of work. Whenever I'm unsure what to make of a comment in an interview or some new policy restricting the movement of journalists, I ask him for advice. He will then have a quiet word with someone or offer me his interpretation which is usually spot on. When my wife first came to Tripoli in November 2013, a month after my arrival, and was worried about arriving alone at the airport, he went to the airport to pick her up when I couldn't make it due to a press conference.

'Not only would we not dare express any criticism, we wouldn't even dare thinking anything critical in our heads,' he told me once while driving his battered white car. (He didn't want to buy a new vehicle, fearing a militia might snatch it at one of the many checkpoints that sprung up in Tripoli after the 2011 uprising.) 'People put up with his rule out of fear. It was terrible.'

As part of Gaddafi's obsession with crushing the private sector he deemed so dangerous to his rule, Libyans needed to supply (and staff, and shop at) 180 state-run department stores, which were supposed to provide every product needed for daily life at extraordinarily low prices.[46] Touring Tripoli with me, my friend would explain the history of the buildings we passed by—remnants from the rules of King Idris or Gaddafi: 'You waited in queues for five hours, not daring to complain and not knowing what you could buy.' He pointed out a grey tower made of concrete and steel not far from the National Oil Corporation headquarters, with *Suq al-mujama* (shopping complex) on its placard, like something from Soviet Moscow. Gaddafi banned private firms, calling entrepreneurs "parasites" in a speech in 1980.[47] 'Once your turn came in the queue, you just took what was thrown at you by an employee,' my photographer friend would say. 'You got trousers, socks or shoes, but couldn't check whether they were the right size. You later tried to trade your shoes with someone with the right size. But nobody would complain. You were too afraid, and too busy trying to survive.'

The stress of survival was part of Gaddafi's strategy to stay in power—keeping his citizens in uncertainty and destroying any trust they had in state institutions. One day the dictator would declare private firms evil, the next it was forbidden to withdraw more than a meagre stipend from state banks. On top of this, living standards had—despite the country's oil wealth—steadily deteriorated in the three decades the country spent under US sanctions for its role in supporting armed groups abroad. The situation worsened in 1992 when the United Nations imposed an embargo for Gaddafi's refusal to hand over suspects involved in the downing of Pan Am Flight 103 over the Scottish town of Lockerbie four years earlier, which had killed 270 people.[48]

The oil kept flowing, but Libya was largely cut off from the world, as Western firms pulled out while the country was put under air embargo. When Gaddafi finally handed over the prime suspect, Abdelbaset al-Megrahi, in 1999, the embargo was lifted and ties with Western countries were restored, triggering an influx of foreign firms signing multibillion-dollar business deals. The bonanza mainly enriched Gaddafi's family and henchmen, leaving out the citizens who had felt the force of the sanctions: Tripoli residents in need of hospital treatment, for example, had to travel for five hours by car to Tunisia, as clinics at home were running out of drug stocks and equipment.

Gaddafi's most prominent son, Saif al-Islam,[49] pushed for limited reforms, helped by the reformist Prime Minister Shukri Ghanem, an economist and friend (in office from 2003 to 2006). While studying in Vienna in the late 1990s after receiving his degree in architecture from the University of Tripoli, Saif made headlines by bringing his pet tigers, Fredo and Barney, to Vienna before receiving his Master's degree and doctorate at the prestigious London School of Economics. He also launched a foundation which became the platform for political and economic ambitions, appearing in Western media, where many mistook him as reformist who desired genuine change. Understanding that Jamahiriya was in need of reform after years of isolation, he presented his country as an investment destination in speeches at the World Economic Forum. His slick business talk was a world away from the ideology of the Green Book and his father's public spats with fellow Arab leaders at gold-gilded summit conference halls. He played a role in the compassionate release of Meghrahi from the UK and solved a hostage crisis in the Philippines, among other headline-grabbing activities.[50]

Domestically, he sensed Libyans' frustrations with the political system. Saif started talking about human rights abuses (without pointing the finger at senior regime figures, of course) in a public campaign against torture. In 2007 he launched a dialogue he called 'Reform and Repent' with imprisoned Islamists, the Muslim Brotherhood and jihadists, which eventually led to the release of hundreds of dissidents from the notorious Abu Salim prison. Saif also launched TV stations, websites and two newspapers, which were permitted to cover sensitive issues like poverty. But this was still much less than other Arab rulers allowed their local media to cover, and Saif al-Islam's outlets never challenged his father's grip on the country.

Libya did see some economic reforms in the 2000s, including steps to integrate with the global economy by consulting with the International Monetary Fund on structural reforms and passing stock market, real estate, tax and other regulations to attract foreign investment.[51] The opening up of the economy saw international restaurants and fashion retailers setting up shop.[52] The Ben Ashour district, where I lived with my wife from 2013 to 2014, also saw luxury fashion shops open. Walking along the main shopping avenue, with its displays of designer shoes and handbags, you might think you were in Europe—as long as you didn't look at the potholed roads or crumbling residential buildings. Indeed, given that Libya was an oil producer, Tripoli was far less glitzy than Dubai, Kuwait City or even Cairo.

In the end, the limited economic reforms mainly benefited Gaddafi's family and their cronies but offered little to the underemployed and frustrated youth. The idea of economic or political reform was in contradiction to the theory and implementation of the Green Book, or what Vandewalle calls 'too much state, too little state'.[53] That is, a state that seeks to control every part of life, but which has failed to create efficient structures. Saif ended his reform campaign in 2008 when he met with fierce opposition from his father for a constitutional draft, which called for the formation of a special council to broaden popular participation without easing Gaddafi's grip on power.[54]

When the uprising against the regime first broke out in the east in February 2011, Saif al-Islam brought foreign reporters to Tripoli in a bid to demonstrate that rumours of a protest movement were wildly exaggerated. The government even appointed a spokesperson, British-educated Moussa Ibrahim, who gave daily news conferences from the five-star Rixos Hotel, right next to Gaddafi's own Bab Aziziya compound. Hard-hitting reporting was difficult to do as, after a brief period of (relative) freedom of movement, no one could leave the hotel without an escort, turning the Rixos into a bubble. Reporters took selfies in front of green flags and giant Gaddafi pictures, but risked expulsion if they tried sneaking out through the garden or dared challenge the official line. An army of minders would routinely bus the foreign press corps to the central Green Square or other locations where diehard Gaddafi supporters would be lined up shouting anti-NATO slogans. Even among the acolytes, words of dissent could sometimes be heard if the minders were absent for a moment. At the time I was covering Sudan, a colleague of mine, Peter Graff, wrote a story about a baby allegedly wounded in a NATO airstrike on Libya. A member of the hospital staff attending to the child gave a reporter a handwritten note that contradicted the official line: 'This is a case of a road traffic accident. This is the truth.'[55]

* * *

Many African and Arab countries have struggled to build nations from different ethnic groups and communities thrown together by colonial rulers. Citizens' first loyalties are often to an ethnic group, tribe or family, rather than to the state, which provides them with comparatively little. British, French and Italian colonial rulers have much to answer for: forcing completely different (and often hostile) tribes and ethnicities to live together while dividing others across international borders. This process left behind a fragile public, often held together by military or police enforcement, an Islamist regime or—as in the case of Idris and Gaddafi's Libyas—an oil welfare state in which rulers traded loyalty for political rights, generous salaries and benefits for jobs the state didn't need. As state budgets are used to fund an overstaffed public sector or spent on security, fuel and other subsidies, education, health and technical innovations are neglected. The more state services and infrastructure deteriorate, the angrier people become, prompting further spending on secret police and patronage for allies. The brightest and most skilled people seek better lives abroad, leaving behind an unproductive, corrupt and impoverished country where people with no faith in the state turn to tribes, and therefore tribalism, to survive. I could see this when I was based in Sudan as Reuters correspondent from 2011 to 2013. The health ministry, like other state bodies, spent much of its budget on salaries or patronage in accounts not included in the regular budget, known as *tagneeb* (setting aside). Hospitals in Sudan often lack the basic medication and equipment, especially in rural areas. If services are provided at all, they often come from private hospitals unaffordable to most, or from INGOs.

Libya fits this bill, with stronger divisions than other Arab countries, as the state is in most areas far less present. In Jordan, for example, the royal Hashemite family relies on largely unproductive tribesmen staffing security agencies and the army, while the economy depends on urban Jordanians of Palestinian origin. But despite this split the country has carved out some sort of national identity and has a rather more efficient bureaucracy than can be found in the rest of the region. While there have been large protests against the government against corruption and unemployment, most agree on a political system headed by the king. Whenever I visit, friends there tell me that their country, despite its divisions and human rights abuses, is one they are proud of.

AN ACCIDENTAL STATE

When Gaddafi was toppled in 2011, there wasn't much Libyans could hark back to that could help them reinstitute a sense of statehood: 42 years of revolutionary talk and chaos inflicted by a figurehead bent on instilling fear and division in institutions he had systematically weakened had taken its toll. During the eight-month uprising, residents and rebel groups quickly brought back the old tricolour—red, black and green horizontal strips with a white crescent and star in the middle. Idris's flag flew while his national anthem played on radio stations under rebel control. Most Libyans acknowledge the shortcomings of the state under Idris, but he is seen as much less repressive than Gaddafi, which partly explains the rose-tinted wistfulness for a monarchy that precedes living memory for much of Libya's relatively young population. The nostalgia was, for me, reminiscent of my native Germany where many in the east, worn down from the hardships caused by the collapse of the Communist regime, developed positive memories of the police state they had despised for decades.

WELCOME TO MILITIALAND

The luxury Rixos, with its pillared lobby and opulent decor, had always seemed like a gilded cage set amid the eucalyptus trees. Even before the rebel assault, correspondents were prohibited from venturing out of the hotel on their own. [Since the uprising], government minders hovered nearby during interviews and coached residents on their answers. They carted [reporters] to and from pro-Gaddafi rallies and showed ... gory sites where they said NATO air strikes had killed civilians... the government saw [foreign journalists] as an extension of the Western effort to bring down 'the brother leader'.

Extracts from a report for Reuters by Missy Ryan[1]

Very few foreign journalists lived in Libya during the Gaddafi years. Indeed, this North African country remained an enigma, not just to the world but also to the Libyan diaspora, whose access to information was stifled by fears that domestic phone lines might be tapped by security services. Journalists who were present, like BBC correspondent Rana Jawad[2]—who arrived there as the first resident foreign reporter in 2004—were forced to walk a tightrope between their journalistic duties and the expectations of the authorities that they glorify the leader.

Western news agencies relied mainly on local freelance staff who filed routine reports from business conferences and filmed Gaddafi's rallies. Most interviews had to be conducted in the presence of a minder, or required written permission to film and take pictures, but even when reporters manged to slip away to do street interviews people were mostly too afraid to talk or be quoted. One major obstacle to opening a news bureau was that the government preferred that a Libyan national be appointed as bureau chief, who would then be under pressure from officials to toe the line—an unacceptable condition for some news outlets.

Come the 2011 uprising, a different kind of conflict of interest presented itself to reporters. Covering the rebels meant teams of reporters embedding with them for access. At first, we were welcomed—brought to the front line by fighters hoping for positive coverage to boost their cause. While Gaddafi and his aides framed the civil war as a struggle against Islamists and 'rats',[3] the rebels spoke of freedom, but with little thought for the details, save for the high-minded expectation that the country would take a turn for the better. We embedded reporters could talk to ordinary people more freely than our counterparts in Tripoli, but it was hard, being so close to the rebels, to find anyone willing to criticise them. Out-and-out Gaddafi enthusiasts were quieter still.

There was genuine support for the various rebel groups—though political and regional fault lines were already emerging. The media's focus was on the chances of the uprising's military success rather than the divisions that would prove fatal in the years to come. It was difficult not to get carried away: reporters and rebels—travelling and sometimes living together during the fighting—often became friends, which led to problems when it became necessary to report critically about the rebels, which it did, as these self-styled freedom fighters neared the capital, with its Gaddafi loyalists and, later, its power vacuum.

During the anti-Gaddafi revolt, several hundred rebel groups emerged across the country. There were army units who defected in the east (where the regime fell quickly) and the western Zintan region, allowing rebels to build upon existing infrastructure and giving them an advantage when the regime fell. Such groups were in competition with the Islamists they had worked with to topple Gaddafi, many of whom had absconded from the notorious Abu Salim prison. The Islamists joined the uprising in the east, where the regime collapsed quickly, or worked in underground cells in the west until the revolution there gained momentum.

Often, rebel groups were borne of a spontaneous effort by apolitical, religiously moderate civilians—many with no discernible military background—to rise up. Most units were just ragtag groupings of fighters acting with only loose coordination with other rebels in the area. Coordination was difficult, and much depended on local initiative: in Misrata, which saw some of the fiercest fighting during the revolution, 236 rebel groups with a total of almost 40,000 members existed by October 2011.[4]

From rebels to militias

The switch came immediately after the fall of the Gaddafi regime. Rebel factions consolidated their positions and rushed to loot arms depots and government offices to equip themselves for the post-war struggle for Libya. The Zintani forces, for example, occupied Tripoli International Airport and the surrounding southern area of the capital they had seized as part of the rebel advance on Tripoli in August 2011. In Misrata, the rebels began working with businessmen who had funded them during the revolution and now hired them as guards for the local steel factory, free trade zone, air and seaports. Some militias ran protection rackets or were hired to guard buildings and resources coveted by rival militias.

Former rebel groups saw themselves as saviours of a nascent state. 'We are keeping our weapons, not because we want to end the state, but [because] we are waiting for a real organisation to appear,' said Khalid Imohamed, a former militia commander in Zintan.[5] But that was only part of the truth. The post-war period presented huge business opportunities, as militias would force weak authorities to hire their men. That pattern would repeat itself across Libya where the local *thuwar* (revolutionaries) set up local military councils which then self-declared their authority over an area. That made it very difficult for the National Transitional Council (NTC), which managed the country until the first free elections in 2012, and subsequent weak governments in Tripoli, to build up a regular army or police force—both of which were doomed to rivalry with the *thuwar*. It also meant there would be no centralised command of the former rebel groups, which worsened existing regional, tribal and political schisms. 'Libya is a very localised country; no group can dominate the others,' said Frederic Wehrey, a journalist and researcher who covered the revolution and its aftermath.[6]

Officials would claim the former rebel groups had united to form an 'army', but in reality the power of the Tripoli-based chief of staff didn't stretch beyond the capital, or even cover all of it: every district of Tripoli, including some major thoroughfares, were overseen by groups who were technically working for the state, but did so with flexible loyalty. That became clear when, a month before I interviewed Prime Minister Zeidan, I travelled to the eastern city of Tobruk to see whether the 'army' would end by force a blockade of the oil ports by the rebel Ibrahim Jathran's forces. Zeidan had threatened several times to clear the terminal blockage, but the army commander in Tobruk refused to move his troops, which were based in a barracks some 5 km from Hariga. 'We cannot prevent people from blockading tankers. We cannot confront our own people. Political conflicts need to be sorted out peacefully,' said Colonel Abdelnasser Shalsha, sitting in his base in the city centre. Even if he wanted to clear the port, he added, his forces would stand little chance against the militias. In reality, the weapons and equipment of the port rebels weren't that powerful: they only had anti-aircraft cannons mounted on a few Toyota four-wheel cars—practically standard issue for militias—but the armed forces had even less, lacking any tanks or artillery cannons. 'We don't have any heavy weapons,' said Shalsha.[7]

While the rebels united over ousting Gaddafi, their loose alliance fell apart as the various groups pursued different agendas and distrusted each other for political, regional or religious reasons. Other groups were not political, but used their firepower to bully their way into the cross-border smuggling of drugs, subsidised products such as gasoline or flour, and illegal migrants from African countries headed for Europe—a lucrative trade booming in the absence of a state.

Right after the seizure of the capital, while the rebels were continuing to fight on several fronts in Gaddafi's strongholds of Sirte and Bani Walid, working conditions for foreign reporters remained good; the rebels still had a positive opinion of the media. But one could sense that problems lay ahead: after the reopening of the Corinthia, the most prominent hotel on the corniche in Tripoli's centre, two days after the liberation of Tripoli, a rebel brigade set up a checkpoint at the door with a scanning machine, not to search for weapons but 'to make sure there is no alcohol in the hotel,' a guard said. They also put a carpet emblazoned with Gaddafi's visage by the front door, for anyone entering to trample on. Patrons who failed to do so would be admonished and told to go back and try again 'to support the revolution'.[8]

From militias to an army

Politicians, who formed a series of weak central governments and the first transitional parliament, the General National Congress (GNC), tried to co-opt the former rebels by putting them on the state payroll as a supposed regular security force or army. Any militia, even Islamist militants like Ansar al-Sharia, who was fighting for a state based on Sharia law, gained access to government money, for example to protect a hospital in Benghazi.[9] Once on the list, operators were rarely removed, even when members of Islamist groups recruited into government service joined Islamic State (IS) in 2015. They, along with anyone else approved by the state, would go to the state Jamahiriya Bank on the last working day of each month to collect their paycheque, even with ID and past payment records pending—no questions asked.

The transitional government, running Libya from the toppling of Gaddafi until the 2012 national elections, paid out more than $1.4 billion to former rebels and those who claimed to have fought Gaddafi. Authorities stopped the initiative after a few months due to massive fraud, but these and other payments for those claiming to have fought in 2011 later resumed.[10] 'The corruption is too much,' said Mohammed al-Harizy, a spokesman for the NTC. 'Some of the people on the lists aren't even alive.'[11] Others claimed entitlements—4,000 Libyan dinars[12] for married former rebels and 2,200 dinars for singles—several times. Local councils, themselves made up of former rebels, had been put in charge of drawing up lists of recipients to be submitted to the central bank. Unsurprisingly, council members made their fighters state servants, and whoever was on the initial lists would be able to claim salary payments. Investigations into the corruption were repeatedly promised, but the weak state had no means to act on findings, and for the most part there were no probes.

Having put their members on the public payroll, the militias now cemented their position by setting their eyes on Libya's 2012 elections—the first free vote in half a century. The main parties elected to the first GNC were somehow linked to or backed by militias. The National Front Alliance of civil war Prime Minister Mahmoud Jibril, a rather secular-minded group that opposed Islamists, had the support of the Zintani former rebel groups and defected army units in the east. This bloc later hooked up with General Khalifa Haftar, a strongman leader who emerged in the east with a mission to crush Islamists.

Islamists would be allied to former members of the Libyan Islamist Fighting Group (LIFG), which had tried toppling Gaddafi in the 1990s, or other groups, such as the Muslim Brotherhood. Many had spent years in prison before being released prior to the revolution under a reconciliation initiative by Saif al-Islam.

The 1996 massacre in the Abu Salim prison, in which Gaddafi's security forces killed around 1,200 mostly Islamist inmates after a protest, was a major catalyst for Islamists to unite, whatever differences they might have had before. The shared experience of torture, lack of adequate food and cramped cells created the unintended consequence of strong bonds in a police state where people did not trust easily. Such ties were reactivated when the revolution broke out. 'Many imprisoned there speak of it as a formative experience, during which ideologies, strategies and tactics were debated,' wrote Irish journalist Mary Fitzgerald, who has written much on Libya's Islamist scene.[13]

The brutality of the Gaddafi era was also a driver in the post-revolution era, as many Islamists took on former regime security agents or officers, especially in Benghazi—former prisoners fighting their long-time captors. Many former soldiers or secret service agents running away from Islamists ended up as fighters under General Haftar.[14]

Government institutions were formed to integrate competing rebel units into the new state. Islamist former rebel groups fell under the purview of the defence ministry, while the Zintanis and units close to them were organised under a Supreme Security Committee (SSC) belonging to the interior ministry. From then on, both groups would only support allied militias, providing them with contracts and routinely undermining the state. The so-called Petroleum Facilities Guards Force was formed as an employment scheme for former rebels tasked with guarding vital oil facilities—in reality they would quickly realise they could make more money occupying the oilfields and terminals they were meant to protect, forcing the government to hire more of their friends and relatives or increase their salaries. Another massive employment scheme for rebel groups was the Libya Shield militia, set up with several regional branches in 2012 in an attempt to buy loyalty and bestow upon them a sense of official authority. Libya Shield was the new 'army', while the SSC was the 'police'—but only on paper; neither group was ever folded into a coherent structure with national reach. Several more, similar groups would be created in different parts of the country. The militias were a continuation of Gaddafi's revolutionary committees—a one-stop secret police, court and state prosecutor able to suppress dissent by locking up and killing anyone who opposed the regime.

Perhaps unsurprisingly, then, a militia working for the interior ministry in Tripoli kidnapped the daughter of Gaddafi's former spy chief, Abdullah al-Senoussi, in September 2013. She was snatched following a visit to her father, who was in prison for entering the country illegally. Members of her Magarha tribe in southern Libya stopped pumps in the Great Man-Made River, one of Gaddafi's main industrial projects, piping water from aquifers deep under the Sahara to cities in the north, cutting off supplies to the capital until Anoud Senoussi was released.[15]

The group responsible for the abduction was led by Haitham al-Tajouri, a role model for militia leaders with flexible political views. Since the toppling of Gaddafi he changed his loyalties several times, always aligning himself with whoever was in control of Tripoli and its state money, allowing him keep control of army barracks and other assets. His men worked for the government of Prime Minister Zeidan, then the unrecognised National Salvation Government, which expelled the legitimate cabinet (of Zeidan's successor al-Thinni) in July 2014.

A few months earlier, then US Ambassador Deborah Jones praised him—to the shock of many Libyans. 'Like Captain Haitham Tajouri, all Libyans should join together to build their country's future,' she wrote in a tweet in December 2013[16]—it was a time when Western governments still hoped the militias would work together for the sake of a stable nation. With the arrival of the UN-brokered government in 2016, Commander Tajouri was quick to voice support, all the while his men were involved in endless shootouts with rival groups and there were claims of kidnappings and assassination attempts, although most of these went unconfirmed.

When Tajouri released the daughter of Gaddafi's spy master in 2013, he justified the abduction by saying his group only wanted to protect her amid an overall security vacuum[17]—the standard line from militias, which served at once to excuse their existence and make it impossible to form regular army and police forces. Later, Tajouri became a major player, running a kind of 'super-militia', which in 2019 began to take control of Tripoli along with three other major groups, carving out districts they would squeeze for funds by sophisticating their businesses. Public salaries for his men would become only one source of income, while he forced the government bodies and banks whose perimeters he controlled to give him contracts and other benefits, like preferential access to cash in the liquidity crisis which ensued in 2016. In 2019 he was heading a business empire with real estate investments in the UAE and travelling in a private jet, while formally allied to the Tripoli-based Government of National Accord (GNA), the internationally recognised administration.[18]

Libyan-British researcher Tarek Megerisi said the country after the revolution resembled a schoolyard in which naughty children—in this case the militias—were constantly testing how far they could push their teachers. Each time authorities bowed to a request, more demands were made.[19] The water blackmail scheme would be repeated over and again: in October 2017 parts of Tripoli were cut off for weeks after a southern tribe attacked a power station belonging to the Great Man-Made River system to stop flows and press for the release of a relative in Tripoli.

The general-purpose force

There was an attempt by Western and some Arab countries, mainly the US, Britain, France and Turkey, to build up a Libyan army, a so-called general-purpose force, but the plan never really got off the ground. The hands-off approach was due to NATO's reluctance to send troops into Libya following the fall of Gaddafi (which it helped to precipitate). Most Libyan players, especially the Islamist forces, would have rejected intervention anyway, while US President Barack Obama was trying to avoid another costly Middle East adventure after the wars in Iraq and Afghanistan. The Iraq war alone cost at least $2 trillion and killed at least 134,000 Iraqi civilians, while 4,488 US soldiers had been killed by the end of 2012.[20]

After much hand-wringing, it was agreed that the general-purpose force would be trained outside Libya, since training providers were reluctant to come, and Western embassies had few staff on the ground for security reasons.[21] Bulgaria was chosen as the principal location, with additional training to take place in France, the UK, Italy and Turkey. Several Arab and Asian countries also trained Libyan soldiers, some using existing army academy exchange programmes from the Gaddafi era, such as Sudan, Egypt and Jordan. Some of these locations had conflicting interests that mirrored Libya's own: the Islamist-led Sudanese regime, for example, reportedly backed Islamist forces, while Egypt supported former army officers such as Khalifa Haftar, hoping he would contain Islamists groups like the Muslim Brotherhood.

There were delays in working out detailed training regimes, but one of the biggest problems was that Tripoli struggled to identify candidates or even to estimate how large its existing army was. I kept asking top officials but never got an answer: how many soldiers from Gaddafi's regular army remained after the revolution? There was no functioning administrative structure resembling a military or state bureaucracy. Some officials put the number of soldiers (who were, incidentally, still collecting pay cheques) at more than 100,000, but less than 10,000 showed up.[22] Lacking any qualifications for the private sector, many former soldiers would have struggled to find a better paid profession. It was a similar economic transition to the one experienced in Eastern Europe after the fall of communism in 1990, when employees of bankrupt state enterprises were pushed into unemployment; only with the difference that former state employees under Gaddafi kept on getting paid.

The defence ministry, like other state bodies, was now dominated by former rebel groups. People working in the ministry dressed in a mix of military, police and civilian uniforms, occupying huge desks and issuing orders. But like the rest of the country, there was no central command or someone thinking of national strategy. On one visit to the police headquarters, fighting illegal immigration in Tripoli, I found no fewer than four 'directors' (and their secretaries), each occupying a large office with a Libyan flag behind a desk, each seemingly free to process my request to visit a detention centre.[23]

Former revolutionary forces could be forgiven for thinking, then, that it was easy to control the state (and therefore its funds) if only their fighting groups or militias managed to stay in power. Most rebel fighters were not really interested in the training programmes for the new army. Some would commit to training sessions inside or outside Libya, but militias offered a better life, along with the freewheeling and laid-back attitude of locals enjoying a generous welfare state. 'Sometimes people would not show up for training, though they first said yes,' said a Turkish diplomat in Tripoli. 'Sometimes out of 15 people, only ten or seven would show up on the day training started.'[24] It was simply more attractive to work for a militia that—thanks to their various protection rackets—could afford to pay higher salaries than the ones received by government-paid soldiers. Commanders put forward members for foreign training, selling it as quasi-holiday.[25]

Perhaps worse, political infighting blocked payments for the training for almost two years. Western countries insisted that Libya paid for the training of its new army. Prime Minister Zeidan kept complaining that Islamists in his own government and the GNC were holding up budget transfers to derail efforts to build up an army. Zeidan referred especially to Khalid al-Sharif, his deputy defence minister, a veteran Islamist leader and one of the founders of the LIFG which tried to topple Gaddafi in the 1990s. Sharif denied the charge[26] but the Islamist movement had, like the rest of the players, their own militias. They in turn were worried that a new army would be limited to former officers from Gaddafi's army, excluding the revolutionaries—one of the motives for Libya Dawn's Tripoli attack in July 2014 was the fear of a counter-revolution by the old establishment. Likewise, defected army units were often reluctant to form alliances with Islamists.

For Western countries, another concern was that they did not know where cadets went after completing their training. I met several soldiers who, after training had returned to their old units, which were in many cases former rebel groups. There was no national army or military structure to absorb them or put their training to use. Others, like a soldier guarding the western border with Algeria, had been trained in Turkey to operate a radar technology not present at his unit. He had only a Kalashnikov, like his comrades. 'It was good, but I didn't really benefit from the training, as we don't have radar,' he said.[27] But NATO members couldn't afford to be picky about candidates, as so few were committed to join.

Then there was the problem of reaching agreement with Libyan officials. Zeidan, like his predecessor Abdulrahim el-Keib (prime minister from November 2011 to November 2012), ordered the formation of a new army unit to be trained abroad, announcing this in a televised news conference, but there was little follow-up from the defence or interior ministry, where different militias were in charge. Diplomats struggled to find government officials they were sure represented a particular ministry or the government as a whole. With the exception of the National Oil Corporation (NOC) and the central bank, the most organised entities in an otherwise lawless country, few Libyan officials used their government email accounts, relying instead on Yahoo or Gmail. I dealt with senior central bank officials who also had no corporate email address, leaving open the question of whether they were speaking to me in a private or official capacity.[28] For legal reasons, the US and its European counterparts were often unable to approve training requests made using unofficial email addresses.

The plan initially conceived by the US, the UK, Italy and Turkey was to train around 20,000 troops.[29] In the end, a few hundred Libyans were trained. France never started its programme, as Libya did not make the necessary payments. All training came to an effective end when Libya Dawn militias attacked the Zintani militia controlling Tripoli International Airport in July 2014, as Western embassies—already running on a skeleton staff in the previous months—moved out, cutting ties with the unofficial government which ran Tripoli from 2014 to 2016.

The last regular Western training ended when the UK sent home some 300 Libyan cadets based in Cambridge in September 2014 after a series of alleged sexual crimes against the local community were blamed on members of their cohort.[30] A more fundamental problem was that pay and life in the militias was better than in the armed forces, where a disciplined, rigid system forced recruits to get up early in the morning to report for duty. Those who were sent on programmes abroad were often selected by militia commanders who ordered them to go to gain more experience, regardless of how interested or committed the cadets really were. Some, abroad for the first time, struggled to adjust to life in a country like the UK, where you could not run around robbing motorists at checkpoints or refusing to pay for restaurant meals, calling your commander if you ran into trouble.

Some European countries offered broad training courses in 2016 (when Libya once again had a recognised government, this time led by Fayez al-Serraj) for the fledgling Libyan coastguard, to stem the flow of refugees and migrants trying to reach Italy by boat. But there was little talk among Western circles of building an army anymore. Some countries discreetly helped Khalifa Haftar, who also enjoyed support from Arab countries, with France putting special forces on the ground to help him, but there was no training effort like before.[31] The US and Britain have also had commandos in western and eastern Libya, but again this was not part of a broader effort to build a national army.

Several Muslim countries stopped accepting Libyan cadets,[32] but Egypt, the UAE and Jordan continued training soldiers after the country split into two administrations in 2014, investing heavily in Haftar. They saw him as a bulwark against what they saw as an Islamist threat in western Libya, where the Libya Dawn government (with its Islamist ties) sat from 2014 to 2016. Even after Libya Dawn had been replaced by the internationally recognised GNA in Tripoli in 2016, they maintained their backing of Haftar and kept working with the eastern-based government—even though Thinni had lost his status as an internationally recognised premier—sending aircraft, vessels and ammunition and even building an air base.[33] Thinni accused Sudan of having shipped weapons to Tripoli's Mitiga airport. Sudan said the delivery had been meant for a joint border force in Kufra, an oasis near the Sudanese-Libyan border. But suspicions that arms were being supplied by Islamist president Omar al-Bashir to the unrecognised Tripoli government were fuelled by a UN report showing a Sudanese C-130 military transport plane parked at Mitiga in October 2014.[34] At least one militia commander fighter trained in Sudan ended up with the Libya Dawn fighters, which confirmed to critics that Khartoum was playing its own game. Thinni also accused Turkey of shipping arms to Tripoli. Turkey, one of the only states to receive official visits from Libya Dawn ministers, denied the claim, but another UN report confirmed at least one arms shipment from a Turkish port.

While Western efforts to build up a Libyan army were going nowhere and militias were enjoying easy state money, many groups began to racketeer and form street gangs. When I met them for interviews they sermonised about democracy and the rule of law, but would take that law into their own hands as soon as one of their number was detained, even for legitimate, low-level crimes such as driving without number plates. Militias kidnapped diplomats from Egypt, Tunisia and Jordan, and even the latter's ambassador[35] to press for the release of fellow commanders and fighters detained in those countries. These countries then pulled out of Tripoli, adding to the hardship of ordinary Libyans trying to obtain visas for hospital treatments unavailable at home for a lack of staff and equipment. In November 2013, residents, tired of fighting and of the presence of militias in Tripoli, marched on the headquarters of a Misrata militia which then opened fire with anti-aircraft guns, killing more than 40 people. Victims were rushed to the Salam Hospital, where I was counting the wounded to compare numbers with those provided by medics and officials—some of whom are known to inflate such numbers to build up the case for their own particular worldview. For the relatives of those who did pass away, there was no time to mourn—space needed to be made for the arrival of more wounded civilians. Those who could not be saved were wrapped in white blankets and moved elsewhere. There was so much shouting that the overworked doctors and nurses were hardly able to understand each other while working on patients on operating tables. 'This is the new Libya,' said a tired-looking hospital guard (dressed in army uniform) who took me around the hospital.[36]

Prime Minister Zeidan went on television the next day, sitting among visibly angry lawmakers and officials who blamed him and his cabinet for failing to send reinforcements. 'We called the army but there was no response,' said a stoned-faced official in the eastern Tajoura suburb, the scene of heavy clashes, in a press conference televised while the shooting was ongoing. 'We are building up a state; an army,' said Zeidan, pleading for patience. 'This takes time.'

Tellingly, when fighting started I, along with my Libyan colleagues Ghaith Shennib and Feras Bosalum, reporters in the Tripoli bureau, struggled to ascertain what was going on: officials at the interior and defence ministries switched off their phones for several hours. Whenever militias started to fight, officials would either disappear or refuse to comment—tacit acknowledgement of their powerlessness. Then the government would issue a statement: that Libya's temporary government urges all sides to respect the law, or similar. Then again: silence. There was nothing else officials could do to stop the carnage.

* * *

What helped cement the dominant role of the militias was an approach by politicians to first pursue the interests of their local communities before thinking of what Libya needed, if at all. While Prime Minister Zeidan talked of building an army, members of his government were busy securing contracts for their local armed groups. The first defence minister to hold the post after the toppling of Gaddafi, Osama al-Juwaili, spent much of his time organising work for his community in Zintan, giving his former comrades lucrative security jobs at the El Feel and El Sharara oilfields deep in the Sahara, or at crossing stations on the Tunisian border. Tripoli International Airport became a major employment and money-making scheme for the Zintanis. Passport officers, guards and administrative staff (as well as the transport minister himself) were mostly from Zintan, as well as owners of small, private businesses such as cafés.[37] In Misrata and other cities militias were put on the state payroll.

The militias who would eventually cost Zeidan his job in March 2014 were not the Misrata militias attacking Tripoli, but those led by Ibrahim Jathran, the defected commander of the state oil guard force. Jathran's story helps explain why Libya has failed as a state: weak rulers never managed to tame him, instead they hoped they could buy his loyalty. He cost the Libyan state tens of billions of dollars in lost oil revenues after he orchestrated a blockade of eastern oil ports in 2013 and 2014, trying to break up the NOC by attempting to sell oil on his own. Certainly, there are hundreds of other militias commanders just like him in Libya, but I use him as an example because I dealt regularly with him and his fighters.

3

THE OIL PORT REBEL

Ibrahim Jathran was a controversial character from the start. Under Gaddafi, he and four of his brothers sat in Tripoli's Abu Salim jail, home to hundreds of Islamists, for their opposition to the regime—or so his aides would have you believe.[1] With no access to reporting basics like court documents—if indeed they ever existed—it was often impossible to get to the bottom of what was happening in Gaddafi's Libya. The only solution was to ask as many people as possible, and judge veracity on the weight of corroboration.

The son of a civil defence officer, Jathran (who has 22 siblings—11 brothers, 11 sisters) was raised in Ajdabiya, an oil town west of Benghazi.[2] While in fact a member of the Maghraba tribe, his dark skin meant opponents often falsely claimed he was from Chad or undeveloped southern Libya—smears in a country where people from sub-Saharan Africa are often treated with disdain, and where black Libyans are unlikely to forge successful careers in politics.[3]

Indeed, there was no shortage of people willing to denounce him as a thug who bullied his way into post-revolution politics, and it is certainly true that he used the seizing of oil facilities as a means to press powerless politicians into financial and political demands. Whatever the veracity of the claims made by supporters and detractors, Jathran was in many ways the archetype of a post-Gaddafi Libyan militia commander, and his blockade of oil export ports in eastern Libya during 2013 and 2014 cost the state more than $30 billion in lost oil revenues.[4]

The sometime Director of the Politburo of the Federalist Cyrenaica Movement

After the 2011 uprising, during which Jathran could be seen fighting in military fatigues and sporting a long beard, the weak new government put him and his estimated 2,500 rebel fighters in charge of protecting oilfields and ports in Libya. He was then in his early 30s—very young in a conservative society where tribal elders are the dominant figures. But the parameters of society had shifted, empowering anyone with weapons and troops, regardless of their leadership qualities or standing in society. A special headquarters was created for Jathran in the port city of Brega, close to Ajdabiya. But in August 2013, he decided to rebel once more, this time against Tripoli's central government, demanding an end to what he called corruption in the oil sector and pushing for eastern autonomy according to the federalist system introduced by King Idris in the early years of his reign. His goals would change over time, always setting the bar higher than officials could possibly agree to, but just getting this far was a rare success for a government which many Libyans thought existed only on paper.

Jathran actually had a point when it came to oil corruption, which is widespread in Libya and harks back to the earliest days of Gaddafi's kleptocracy. There are, as ever, no reliable figures, but a report commissioned by the toothless Ministry for

Inspection and Popular Control in 2010 revealed that almost 5 million barrels of oil—then worth half a billion dollars—had gone missing from just one Libyan oilfield two years earlier.[5] Libyan oil ports were supposed to have meters monitoring oil export flows down to the barrel once a tanker had docked and begun loading. Indeed, I had been shown such a device at Hariga port in Tobruk by an oil worker who printed out a ticket, like at a petrol station. He insisted cheating was impossible: 'This is all legal here,' he said.[6] But there were ways to circumvent the metering, for example, when port engineers deliberately filled tanks and then diverted the supply to an emergency line through which the crude would be loaded onto tankers unmonitored. At Es Sider[7], the biggest oil terminal held by Jathran's men, the metering system had been destroyed altogether.

In July 2013 Jathran seized Es Sider and three other eastern oil ports he had been charged to protect. A fifth terminal in Tobruk was added after a student-led protest demanding state jobs ended its blockade and armed men moved in. One protest group was followed by another. The port seizures stopped the export of 600,000 barrels a day, halving the country's output and sparking a budget crisis as Libya began losing $3 billion each month.[8] The Zeidan government first sought to buy Jathran off—a move typical of powerless officials dealing with heavily armed militias. A lawmaker was dispatched from Tripoli, offering Jathran cheques which his aides showed to me and other journalists before posting pictures of them online as examples of the political corruption common in Libya. When the money failed to lure him, Zeidan's government asked Interpol to issue an arrest warrant for Jathran's brother, who had travelled to Dubai to scout for potential buyers of the stolen oil.

Meanwhile, Jathran used Zeidan's buyout offer to start a broad discussion about corruption, appearing clean-shaven and in a suit to talk about the need for rule of law and what he called 'real democracy' in Libya. It was not the first time he had changed his views: according to his aides, when the revolt against Gaddafi broke out, Jathran had pretended to government officials that he was on the side of the dictator, only to walk away with the weapons he had been supplied with. In 2013, as during the revolution, Jathran used the legitimacy extended to him by the state to weaken it, retaining the Brega headquarters, offices, phones, vehicles and guns.

He was eager to talk to the media then, inviting me and my Tripoli-based colleague Ghaith Shennib to his lair, a two-hour drive from Benghazi. We had to cross a checkpoint manned by the Islamist militant group Ansar al-Sharia on the city's western side, where bearded men patrolled the junction of coastal road leading all the way along to Tripoli and on to the Tunisian border 1,500 km to the west. When we arrived at Jathran's office it was packed with aides and military men dressed in the usual mix of army, police and civilian clothes. Two Toyota pickup trucks mounted with machine guns were parked outside.

We waited for six hours while aides and officers fed us anecdotes and lectures about Libya's transition into a democratic state of law. 'We want freedom and dignity,' Jathran explained when we were finally given an hour-long audience reminiscent of university seminars in political science. 'We want to build a state based on the rule of law,' he said, before apologising for the long wait; he had a different time scheduled for our interview in his smartphone. Ghaith, a media officer and the master himself then began arguing over who was to blame for the delay. We managed to squeeze all of eight questions into our allotted hour, as Jathran pontificated about the new democratic state he wanted to build. He rejected all suggestion that his own revolt against the central government was undermining efforts to establish a state, alleging that Tripoli was controlled by Islamists: 'How can we allow the export of oil which is used to fund the Muslim Brotherhood and other extremists?'

He also demanded that Libya reinstate King Idris's 1951 constitution, which guaranteed the sharing of power and oil revenues between the three historic regions. 'How do you want to do that? Do you want to reinstate the king?' Ghaith asked. Unruffled, Jathran clarified his position: Libya could adopt the previous constitution 'minus the king'. While Jathran was talking, aides in the adjacent room were watching a televised news conference from Tripoli, in which a member from the Libyan Revolutionary Operations Room boasted of kidnapping Prime Minister Zeidan, dragging him out of bed at dawn and interrogating him until he was eventually freed by a sympathetic militia.

During the interview, Jathran claimed to be speaking for the whole of the east, using the historic Arabic name 'Barqa' for Cyrenaica, as it had been called by the Italians. The east holds at least 60 per cent of Libya's oil wealth, but had long been neglected by Gaddafi as punishment for its groundswell of opposition to his rule. Buildings in the city of Benghazi were still damaged from World War II, when it changed hands between British and German troops. It was an obvious choice for Jathran to tap into the eastern sentiment for autonomy (or even secession) but many didn't see him—a man deploying force to have his way—as an ideal champion of federalist reform.

While we were waiting for the interview, we kept pressing his aides to grant us access to one of the occupied oil ports. After all, we reasoned, Brega was just a short stroll from his headquarters. It was clear why his aides were not keen on such an excursion, but after hours of pleading we were allowed a brief visit. Contrary to his claims, Jathran's men didn't control the entire harbour. While crude exports from the state-run Sirte Oil Company (a unit of the National Oil Corporation [NOC] based in the port) had indeed been stopped, the Yara fertiliser firm located next to the Sirte oil facilities remained open. 'The residents here have decided to reject the blockage,' explained Awad

Elsaber, an angry chief technical officer from Yara. Elsaber refused to be intimidated by Jathran's men, referring to them derisively as 'these people'.

'We don't agree that they close the port,' he said, sitting stone-faced at his desk. It also became clear from the visit that Jathran did not command as many men as he claimed. In fact, it was a small force that an army in most other countries could have dealt with. Tragically, Libya's military existed only on paper, which only empowered militia commanders like Jathran.[9]

An engineer in the port's control room in Brega also ignored Jathran's aides, but criticised their leader more cautiously: 'I sympathise with their goals but also think dialogue is important,' he said, giving his view diplomatic cover while watching a huge electronic display showing gas flows. But there were also workers who supported Jathran, like an engineer for the oil company who later drove us to a storage tank blocked by Jathran's men to showcase the effectiveness of their protest. 'I don't want to work for a state where oil is stolen,' he said, by way of justification.

While Zeidan's government asked repeatedly for tribal elders to persuade Jathran to end the oil blockade, giving several deadlines not followed up by any military action, Jathran took matters into his own hands. His politburo set up its own oil firm to offer the oil in port tanks under his control to international buyers.[10] In a bid to drum up business, he even hired a Canada-based Israeli lobbyist, but later denied the relationship when details of the deal were posted on the internet, sparking outrage about the Israeli connection.

Jathran's actions lacked the transparency he had complained was missing from Zeidan's leadership. Ghaith, who like many in the east had initially expressed modest sympathies for Jathran, were soon disillusioned. Jathran had appointed a head for his new 'state' oil firm, but he hung up the phone when we called, and was never heard from again.

Perhaps most audaciously, Jathran defied the leaders of his own tribe, the Magharba, who were trying to convince him to reopen the ports, demonstrating how the traditional tribal power balance had shifted with the rise of militiamen in 2011. 'We met on 10 December and stressed the need to open the ports and ... Ibrahim Jathran confirmed to those assembled and to all Libyans that he would open the ports on 15 December,' said Saleh Atawich, the tribe's top leader, in an interview in January 2014. On the same day, Jathran made a defiant statement on television, vowing to continue his protest until the east was granted autonomy. Reuters and other news outlets sent reporters to Ajdabiya to cover the event, but he refused to take questions. The reporters were only allowed to listen to a brief statement before Jathran disappeared. 'Shutting down ports is not acceptable. Oil is Libya's only income and [it] belongs to all Libyans,' said Atawich, sitting in the reception room of his farm on the outskirts of Benghazi.

Some in Benghazi supported the idea of a federal state allocating more oil revenues to the east, but were against a port blockade as it might affect their own salaries. Residents denounced Jathran, who did not receive a secondary school education, as the wrong person to promote the cause. Youssef al-Gharyani, a federalist activist who works for NOC told me, 'He asked me to work for him. He said "you know English". He wanted me to join to help sell oil [bypassing Tripoli], but I declined.' From his small office, not far from the former US diplomatic compound that was ransacked in 2011, he lashed out at Jathran: 'Ninety per cent in Benghazi are not with Jathran because of who Ibrahim Jathran is,' he said. 'What is his education? How can he lead?'

Jathran himself decided to go silent after welcoming us and other foreign reporters to Brega in the first weeks of his port seizures. He invited journalists to events billed 'press conferences', usually at short notice, but when our Benghazi reporter Ayman al-Warfalli rushed to one, driving 180 km on the potholed coastal road to the venue in Ajdabiya, his aides merely transferred a statement filmed by his team onto a USB stick. The man himself was nowhere to be seen.

Jathran badly damaged the reputation of the federalist movement with his oil port blockages, which almost brought Libya to its knees. But his influence was undeniable, and he found an imitator, who some in the east call the 'little Jathran'. In Tobruk, a different group of tribesmen joined in Jathran's October 2013 port blockade, though they also travelled under the federalist banner. The group's leader, Mansour Salhin, became Jathran's deputy in the politburo, but he lacked the charisma with which Jathran had rallied supporters. He was at least 15 years older than his boss, an unusual constellation in a conservative tribal society respecting age—power in Libya was now defined by the number of Toyota trucks with mounted anti-aircraft guns you could muster.

When I met Salhin in Tobruk in February 2014 over tea in the Salam Hotel, he had policy papers in front of him, matching the points Jathran would make in his televised speeches. Salhin mainly read from his papers while declining to discuss how the port blockade conflict with Tripoli could be ended. 'We want our rights and share in the east from oil revenues,' he said, keeping it vague. When pressed, he got agitated and raised his voice, saying firmly, 'We want our rights, we want our rights,' without specifying what they were. His joining Jathran's politburo showed the flexible and often temporary nature of alliances that were formed in post-revolution Libya, where players often teamed up for short-term gains. Mohammed Younis, a lawmaker member for Tobruk, said Salhin was representing just a few families who had for a while been eyeing a share of oil revenues and local power. 'They all have different opinions and agendas,' he said, describing the divisions in his hometown. He was visibly tired when I met him in his house, having tried for months to end the port blockade.

THE OIL PORT REBEL

As the blockade dragged on, we asked for another interview, but Jathran's aides were evasive. 'Mr Jathran is in meetings. Call us back tomorrow,' was the standard response. His deputy, Abd Rabbo al-Barassi, signalled that he might be willing to meet us in Ajdabiya, though it was also hard to arrange an appointment. Jathran had appointed him as a representative from the Barassi tribe based in Bayda, east of Benghazi, to broaden his powerbase, and he was (technically) the prime minister of Jathran's Cyrenaica government. He seemed to have very little to say to reporters, but meeting him might still have provided an opportunity to gain an insight into the thinking inside the Cyrenaica movement. Despite having no confirmed appointment with Jathran or Barassi, I took my chances and booked a flight to Benghazi.

Setting out early in the morning with Ayman, our Benghazi reporter, a photographer and a security adviser hired by Reuters, we crossed the Ansar al-Sharia Islamist checkpoint. Driving on the empty highway to western Libya, we stopped only at makeshift checkpoints where bored militiamen sat on plastic chairs, enjoying cups of tea instead of searching cars. When Ayman called Jathran's office, we were told to go to the town's biggest hotel, a landmark spot in the centre. Advertisements from the Gaddafi era showed it was once a busy place that welcomed tourists, but now we were the only visitors. We had just ordered cappuccinos in the lobby café when we learned from Jathran's politburo that he would not be available (he was, as usual, in meetings all day), but that Barassi would see us. When we asked where we could meet him, we were told to wait in the hotel. An hour later someone else called and asked us to come outside. Ten minutes later, a white pickup truck stopped in the parking lot in front of the hotel. We had no clue where he was going to lead us, but in Libya you often need to trust your life to strangers.

We set off, following him on the main road that crisscrossed the city until he suddenly made a sharp turn into a dirt track populated only by a stray dog. 'So maybe now we get kidnapped,' said Ayman, who was driving. I thought he was joking, but his stern look told me otherwise, and in any case there wasn't time to ponder our options. Our guide made another turn, leading us into a walled compound. There we spotted a small building, a typical place that Libyans call an *istraha*, a kind of rest house. Many Libyan families, mostly former farmers, use such buildings to enjoy a barbecue on the weekend. Young people sometimes have a drink there, away from the prying eyes of disapproving family. I immediately relaxed when I saw Barassi emerging from the small house, greeting us on the veranda in a pyjama-like gown of the type commonly worn when at home on the weekend. This was how the region's self-declared prime minister governed, sharing mattresses on the floor with four family members and, of course, his aides.

There had been much hype from global banks and oil dealers about the Cyrenaica government's plans to sell oil and rule the east, but evidence of this on the ground was hard to come by, proving once more that covering Libya from afar was impossible. According to Jathran, he had appointed ministers with portfolios in education and finance and met with them regularly to discuss the rebuilding of Benghazi and other ambitious development projects. When I asked Barassi what he was actually doing as prime minister, whether he was chairing cabinet sessions to discuss budgets or policy plans, he simply said: 'We haven't anything to do yet because we still need a budget. We need to sell oil first.'

He was optimistic about reaching a deal with Tripoli to reopen the ports: 'We have agreed on two of three points with the government,' he said. 'I think we can reach an agreement within three weeks.' That was hot news for oil traders hoping for a return of Libyan crude, but it became clear that, at least until then, he had little to do in his modest guesthouse. We parted after an hour, having drunk sweet green tea and eaten imported cookies. He had no other appointments that day.

While Barassi was negotiating an oil deal, Jathran, who also appointed his own oil minister and central bank governor, was pursuing another lead: he had found a buyer for the oil in his port tanks, invalidating talks with Tripoli. One night in March 2014, workers at Es Sider reported the arrival of an oil tanker, the *Morning Glory*, flagged first to North Korea, but whose ownership changed several times as the deal became public, with shippers getting cold feet. We never established who the buyer was, as there were several middlemen and a Dubai-based shipping company involved. A supporter of Jathran eventually bought the ship while it was being loaded with crude at the port. Barassi gave a televised speech at Es Sider announcing the first eastern oil export while, in the background, a camel was ceremonially slaughtered. Then, Prime Minister Zeidan's office suddenly claimed that navy boats had intercepted the tanker after it set off from Es Sider, and were escorting it to western Libya the next morning.

Zeidan had been in Rome when the tanker arrived, and had struggled to explain to Western partners what was going on in his lawless country. When I arrived at his office with a cameraman and a photographer, the mood was strangely subdued. Zeidan's aide kept telling me I would not be able to ask questions during the interview. In a country run by militias, you sometimes have to make concessions for your own wellbeing, but conducting an interview in which the interviewee reads out a statement, like on state television, was too much. After two hours, I was still arguing in German with Zeidan's aide—a lady who had studied at the German University of Mainz—until I stopped at his office door. 'I cannot do an interview where I won't be able to ask any questions,' I told her. More wrangling followed with the help of our photographer, a veteran when it came to dealing with uncooperative Libyan officials. The aide finally agreed to let me ask three questions.

While we were setting up, I asked Zeidan whether the situation with the tanker was really under control. 'Kind of,' he responded, smiling nervously. When the camera was on, he gave his statement: navy boats loyal to Tripoli had stopped the tanker, which would be brought to a port under the control of his government the next day. But once the camera was off, he acknowledged this was wishful thinking. 'The situation is not entirely under control,' he said. 'But, God willing, it will be in the morning,' he said, before his aide led us out.

By morning, the tanker was gone, crossing into Egyptian waters after a brief firefight with navy boats loyal to Tripoli. It was up to US Navy Seals to end the drama when they stormed the tanker off the Cyprian coast after the Pakistani captain had sent several SOS alerts. Barassi kept calling us to complain about this perceived injustice, which he framed as an attack on Libya's sovereignty. Parliament ousted Zeidan the day after my interview. He boarded a plane to Malta, but was only allowed to take off after being hassled by militias, who kept his plane waiting on the runway for several hours after the state prosecutor—also pressured by militias—launched corruption charges against him.[11]

The episode showcases the dilemma powerless officials faced as former rebel groups led by the likes of Jathran called the shots in the new Libya. Zeidan's opponents from the Muslim Brotherhood and other parties, backed by their own militias, just had to wait for his failure to stop the tanker. Libya's main problem was not the infighting in the General National Congress (GNC) or the Islamist parties' opposition to a secular-minded prime minister like Zeidan, but the former rebel groups operating a state within the state, filling a void after the revolution.

Meanwhile, the US navy handed the tanker back to the Libyan 'navy', which in reality just meant civilian boats loyal to

Tripoli. But so weak were the authorities that they diverted the tanker bound for the western Zawiya oil port, where the crude was supposed to be discharged to feed the local refinery, to Tripoli, mooring it just out of sight from land. 'We are worried that something might happen to the crew,' said a Zawiya port official. Militiamen had been gathering at the port all day, waiting for the *Morning Glory* to dock. The men had entered through the main gate, where security guards were supposed to make sure no unauthorised visitor gained access. But the guards were from the same militia, who were now parading a machine-gun on a speed boat in the bay while bored cameramen, standing on the roof of the administrative building, waited in vain for the tanker to appear. The Pakistani captain later told me that Jathran's gunmen had boarded his tanker and forced him at gunpoint to load the crude—claims that were confirmed by his crew and other port workers.

With the tanker deal off and the UN Security Council outlawing any oil sales that bypassed the NOC, it was game over for Jathran, who was by now struggling to pay his men occupying the oil ports. Donations from businessmen in Ajdabiya, who had initially sympathised with his cause but later worried that the blockade would lead to state collapse, were drying up.

The oil port rebel swiftly made a deal with Tripoli to open two ports immediately and the rest a month later, though the 'agreement' read like a capitulation.[12] None of his federalist demands were included, and the document was published by Tripoli to prevent him claiming otherwise. Jathran still told his local TV station that the government wanted to look into the Cyrenaica matter, but that was just talk. Now he faced mutiny: seven members of his leadership team had quit in protest to both the deal and his autocratic style.

In a classic post-Gaddafi deal designed to keep Libya glued together with oil money, Jathran's men were put back on the state payroll, while the man himself was reinstated as head of the petroleum protection force, working out of the same Brega headquarters as before, charged with protecting the very ports he had seized with his troops. Jathran played the statesman, giving dramatic speeches on his federalist TV station, claiming the blockade had been necessary to democratise Libya and establish the rule of law.

It would take several months for Libya to ramp up oil production after nearly a year of closures at the major ports. Even worse, at the eastern Zueitina port, protesters decided to continue the blockade, breaking away from Jathran, once a symbolic figure for their protest and now someone whose cash payments had given them ideas. In the Hariga port, guards now regularly staged port seizures—they too wanted to see whether they could get payouts like Jathran's, wagering that toothless authorities would always meet their demands.

My colleagues and I had been busy for months with Jathran and his oil blockade, but in the weeks after the deal he stopped giving interviews to the foreign media and his aides stopped getting in touch. It was a welcome break: they often complained that we described Jathran as a militia leader willing to use violence, and insisted we include his 'official' title and refer more to his federalist ambitions. Then one day our Benghazi reporter Ayman got a call from one of them Reuters had won an award for having covered the 'federalist cause' objectively, and we were duly invited to collect it at a ceremony. Of course, we didn't want the award or any other public recognition (let alone attend an event organised by a militia), but we also had to be careful not to offend a group with the means and motivation to exact revenge. We told them we couldn't accept the award, but the ceremony went ahead without us.

THE OIL PORT REBEL

Operation Sunrise

When Libya split into two governments in 2014 with the expulsion of the recognised administration in the east, Ibrahim Jathran made headlines again. He became useful for the eastern government, which needed his men to fill the vacuum caused by the departure of state military guarding the oil ports he had seized in 2013. The few troops who could have been deployed were busy fighting in Benghazi, where Khalifa Haftar had begun a campaign to seize the city from Islamists and other groups.[13] Once again, we are confronted with the symbiosis between a weak state and the militias operating within it: a militiaman seizes key oil ports, causing tens of billions of dollars in lost oil revenues, but then becomes key to the state and its overstretched military in resecuring those very same ports.

While the oil tanker debacle had cost premier Zeidan his job, Jathran helped his successor, Thinni, by defending the Ras Lanuf and Es Sider ports, Libya's two biggest oil ports located in a region known as the 'Oil Crescent', against a military offensive launched by the Libya Dawn administration in Tripoli. It was a power grab, but the rump GNC in Tripoli provided some legal cover for the operation, citing a decree signed by Parliamentary Speaker Nouri Abu Sahmain, an Amazigh politician with somewhat flexible political views. He had actually issued that decree in February 2014 to threaten Jathran, but it had never been implemented, as Islamist forces sought to weaken the moderate Zeidan. Now the rump parliament, again dominated by Islamists, dusted off the old decree for a cause it deemed just—another example of a militia using parliament to justify its actions.

The military offensive launched on the two oil ports from Misrata nevertheless ended in farce. Jathran swapped his suit for military fatigues once more, and a video on social media showed him directing artillery fire towards the invaders from Operation

Sunrise, the official name of the attackers who were camped out some 20 km from Es Sider. The attackers never made it any further, failing to reach either port. The three-month battle laid bare the madness engulfing a Libya in which two governments claimed to command armies but in reality allowed militia leaders to fight it out for them.

That was not the only madness. An Operation Sunrise unit I embedded with wore the same uniforms as Jathran's men: standard army kits with boots, trousers and shirts delivered straight from the Tripoli defence ministry's storage facilities. 'We are the Libyan army,' said a commander called Mussab Bala. 'We fight for legitimacy, for the revolution, and report to the chief of staff at the defence ministry.' Over tea in a farmhouse-turned-barracks, his comrades showed us the official militia identity cards issued by the defence ministry in Tripoli. 'This is a just war,' another fighter said. They were all in their early twenties and poorly trained, but they were highly motivated, repeating verbatim the propaganda of their leaders. Their enemies, holed up in trenches a few kilometres to the east, were citing General Haftar and Jathran, using language strikingly similar to that of Gaddafi, who justified his actions by deploying obscure slogans from his Green Revolution diatribe.

The most difficult interview I conducted during my visit to the front was with a fighter who lost a leg in 2011 during the anti-Gaddafi revolt. He had spent months in a hospital in northern Germany waiting for a transplant. Now he was back on the front, close to where he had been fighting four years ago. Struggling with these brainwashed young people—who should have been at university or working in business instead of fighting their fellow countrymen—I abandoned my role as a reporter, urging him to come to his senses. But he insisted that their fight was justified and in line with the rule of law: 'Haftar keeps attacking us so the UN dialogue won't succeed. He attacks us every day with his aircraft,' he said, sitting on a wooden bench in the reception room of an administrative building now being used as a front line operations room. Downstairs, civil servants deployed from Misrata served lunch for soldiers coming from companies in the western city. I suspected they had been forced to man the field kitchen, as they did not want to give their names or have their pictures taken.

At the same time, in an adjacent room, officers were plotting the next day's attack. Up to 30 Operation Sunrise men were killed when the commanders ordered their young fighters, dressed in new army uniforms, to advance towards Jathran's tank and artillery lines, around 5 km away and close to the Es Sider port, whose tower-shaped terminals you could barely see from the last Misratan positions.

The day before, I had visited an Operation Sunrise forward position at a front line in the sand next to a Soviet tank and cluster bomb remains, where soldiers were dozing beneath a damaged solar panel. I hurried my interviews while our photographer took some shots—I was nervous about being in the firing line on the desert plane. Later—in our comfortable Tripoli villa—I thought about their advance the next day, when Jathran's artillery guns literally shot the young fighters to pieces. 'Our boys are advancing,' texted a senior government official in Tripoli. But one hour later the advance was called off, ending in bloodshed. It was the last major advance before Operation Sunrise commanders finally saw reason, agreeing to pull out a month later.

The night before the front line trip I had another telling encounter with a militia commander who was supposed to arrange transport to visit his troops at the front. I had agreed to pay his men a fee of 500 Libyan dinars (almost $400)[14] against an official receipt from the Tripoli-based foreign media office which had arranged the trip. He showed up with an entourage of a dozen men at the hotel where we were staying for the night before our trip the next morning. We ordered cappuccinos and the commander got straight down to business. 'How much money can you pay me?' he asked. I struggled to follow his colloquial Libyan Arabic, made rougher because he appeared to be drunk. Since I was not really in the business of paying militiamen-turned-soldiers, I wasn't willing to spend more than I had already paid. I pretended not to understand his question while searching in my bag for the receipt. When he looked at the paper he erupted: 'What is this? Do you think Libyan soldiers are so cheap? You cannot buy a bottle of vodka from that,' he said, drawing support from his enraged men, who also began shouting. He demanded the phone number of the Tripoli official who had signed the receipt, and he put his phone on speaker so his men could hear the call.

'What is this you think that we are so cheap. Why did you agree on 500 dinars?' he barked down the line.

'But Mr M...' the timid official pleaded.

'Can you believe this guy is selling us so cheap?' the commander asked his audience. Then he went on, 'Look, you know what I will do. Tomorrow I will bring these journalists for free to the front and then I will visit you in Tripoli, rape your sister and kill you.'

The commander hung up, and he and his men rose, confirming they would pick us up the next day. I shook the commander's hand, trying maintain the fragile goodwill. My cameraman and I were frightened. In parting, one of Mr M's aides said politicians were 'nobodies'. 'They are nothing without us. We are in charge of Libya,' he said, translating his commander's words to make sure I got the message. They left us to pay for the coffee.

After that meeting I took a walk to try to calm down when I noticed right behind our hotel a crowd gathering around several white billboards upon which typed lists had been pasted. Curious, I approached, and realised the lists were roll calls for at least 500 militiamen, organised by *katiba* (brigade). Their members were asked to report to their barracks with guns, ammunition, food, clothes and 100 dinars. People from all ages and professions gathered to find out if it was their turn to join the oil port battle.

While both sides—Jathran's men and Operation Sunrise—claimed to represent the Libyan state and its 'legitimate army', the Oil Crescent battle reinstated the historic border between Tripolitania and Cyrenaica. Residents on both sides disagree over exactly where the line drawn during the Italian colonial period lay, but suffice to say it would have been near to the 2015 front line, outside the small town of Ben Jawad. Sandbags blocked the road at the last Misratan position, cutting of the vital road linking Tripoli to Benghazi. The numbers of passenger cars and trucks shipping goods from Misrata to an embattled Benghazi (where Haftar's forces fought the Islamists) went down drastically. Taking a detour to the south was no longer an option, as Islamic State (IS) militants had made that route too dangerous. When the soldiers of Operation Sunrise eventually pulled back, the coastal road was reopened.

* * *

Self-declared Tripoli-based Prime Minister Omar al-Hassi[15] warned me of what had been on the minds of most Libyan politicians: the fear that they could no longer control their own militias. 'There are many angry youth [who are] impossible to tame unless their demands are met,' he said. The ultimate absurdity of the militias' quest for the Oil Crescent was exposed when Jathran and the east's top military man, Haftar, fell out in 2016, fighting over control of the two ports they had defended against the Operation Sunrise assault two years earlier. For around 18 months, Haftar had cooperated with Jathran to confront the joint enemy from Misrata until autumn 2015, by which time he had expanded his own forces and political clout and no longer needed Jathran's help.[16]

While Jathran still controlled the terminals and his headquarters in Ajdabiya, he tapped into the booming business of human trafficking. The oil town turned into a transit hub for illegal migrants brought to the western coast—the launchpad for boat departures to Italy. A UN report found that Jathran's men provided shelter in houses where migrants were held (and abused) until their relatives sent funds for onward travel. Eritreans and nationals of other sub-Saharan countries told me in 2015 that they had been tortured while being held in Ajdabiya with their jailers forcing them to call relatives while they were beaten. I didn't make the connection to Jathran until I read the UN Security Council panel report from June 2017, which contained an even more shocking revelation about the militia leader: he had forced migrants to clear minefields without any protective equipment.[17] I was reminded of Jathran's high-minded vision for a new Libya with a constitution that enshrined the rule of law.

Jathran's career as militia commander appeared to be over when he lost control over the oil terminals and fled the country while some of his family members were held in Tripoli. The defeat also showed that his forces were much smaller than the 15,000 or so he had claimed to command. In the end, he met the fate of other militia commanders who lost their men when a series of failures led to insolvency and a subsequent inability to pay wages. But he made another comeback in 2018, assembling fighters from his old force, the Tebu ethnic group, Chadian, Sudanese and others[18] to attack the Ras Lanuf and Es Sider ports, forcing an evacuation of staff and halting exports of up to 400,000 barrels a day before Haftar's forces expelled them.[19] Several storage tanks were hit by rockets, reducing capacity at the Ras Lanuf port alone by 400,000 barrels a day.[20] Jathran announced the attack in a video claiming his forces were only there to restore order and security.[21] The six-minute clip lacked any mention of a federalist agenda, with rhetoric now honed to accuse Haftar's forces of being oppressive to the people of Barqa (Cyrenaica) and Libya in general. During the video, Jathran visibly struggled to express himself coherently, resulting in the repetition of platitudes about the ending of suppression— another trope used flexibly by Libyan militiamen to justify their actions (and existence).

I had first described Jathran in my Reuters dispatches as an 'oil port rebel'—a term which was at that time used by diplomats and colleagues alike. But I wasn't entirely comfortable with this designation: nothing in Libya was ever so clear cut. Back then, Jathran seemed to have genuine political objectives, like the establishment of federalism. But by 2018 he could no longer fool anyone: he was a militia leader with no discernible political agenda. As the British Ambassador Peter Millet put it, Jathran's 'offensive in [the] Oil Crescent serves no one but his selfish greed.'[22]

At the time of writing, Jathran was rumoured to be in hiding somewhere in Bani Walid, a town in the hilly hinterland south of Tripoli, assembling a new force. Some experts also suspect he is involved in trafficking migrants from Libya's southern neighbours.[23]

There are many other examples of militia leaders operating in post-Gaddafi Libya, but I decided to focus on Jathran as the scale of destruction and economic damage inflicted by his forces stood out and kept me busy for much of my time covering Libya. His political career was finished, while his last opponent during the 2018 Oil Crescent battle, General Haftar, rose to prominence, using his forces to control much of eastern Libya and embodying the new archetype of a post-Gaddafi Libyan militia commander.

4

LIBYA DIVIDED

The security situation deteriorated dramatically in 2014, with fighting between militias escalating, splitting Libya into two halves with their own governments and accelerating the country's fragmentation. Most embassies in Tripoli closed in summer 2014 when the capital turned into a battlefield between rival groups. Foreign firms moved out their business or evacuated staff. Foreign airlines stopped flying to Libya.[1] Almost 300,000 people[2] were internally displaced as a result of worsening fighting and a political conflict that would surely tear the country apart. Hundreds of thousands more ended up in neighbouring countries, mostly Tunisia, where Libyans don't need a visa, and for those with the means to obtain a visa, to Egypt or Europe. Libya has simply never recovered from that division. For my part, while it was never easy to cover Libya as journalist, 2014 was when things got really dangerous.

Ever since 2011, Libya's militias had fought each other in intra-city confrontations that lasted anything from a few hours to a few days, until some sort of ceasefire would be found and residents could move on with their lives. But a new level of conflict was reached when in May 2014 a Gaddafi-era general, Khalifa Haftar, launched an attack on radical Islamists using helicopters and aircraft from Ansar al-Sharia and other groups which had carved out fiefdoms in Libya's second city. This kicked off a battle that would turn parts of Benghazi into ruins, kill thousands and close its air and seaports for three years. Haftar would turn into one of the most divisive figures in Libya, but in 2015 he was beacon of hope for many Libyans tired of chaos, and not just in Benghazi.

We have to go back a bit to understand the factors that led to Haftar's rise. An elite army unit[3] called Sa'iqa (*Lightning*) was trying to impose some sort of order in Benghazi from 2013 to 2015, clashing with Ansar al-Sharia and other Islamist groups they blamed for a wave of assassinations of lawyers, intellectuals, army and police officers. It wasn't always clear whether Ansar members, most of whom had also fought during the revolution, were behind the murders, but Islamists acknowledged that they were responsible for at least some of the killings, especially of police and intelligence officers from the Gaddafi era, who were suspected of having tortured Islamists in prison.[4] Ansar al-Sharia had steadily expanded its territory in Libya's second-largest city, manning checkpoints and guarding a state hospital for a hefty payment under the militia payments system set up in 2012. As mentioned in the previous chapter, many claiming to have fought Gaddafi in 2011 were put on the payroll—regardless of political views and with very little oversight. The security situation in Benghazi, the cradle of the 2011 uprising, steadily worsened as shootings and car bombs became part of daily life. In autumn 2013, Al Qaeda flags could be seen at some checkpoints and official buildings.[5]

Special army forces commander Wanis Bukhamda kept asking for reinforcements and material support from officials in Tripoli, but no substantial help arrived. Instead, the government made unrealistic demands, such as arresting a prime suspect in the storming of the US diplomatic compound and nearby CIA annex by militias in September 2012, during which visiting US Ambassador Christopher Stevens and three other Americans were killed.[6] Washington blamed Islamist militiamen from Ansar al-Sharia for the attack, which sparked a heated domestic debate in the US that lasted years and even became a prominent debating issue during the 2016 presidential campaign. Republicans and their candidate Donald Trump accused the Democrats' nominee Hillary Clinton of having failed to provide adequate security for the Benghazi compound when she was Secretary of State.

So Bukhamada and other commanders turned to a retired general called Khalifa Haftar, who assembled some 200 men and helicopters in May 2014 to start his Benghazi war.[7] He was yet another rebel commander and surely one of the most divisive figures in Libya—he tends to pop up whenever the country is in upheaval. Similar to Jathran, Haftar is another example of a former rebel who became a top official, but always acted like a militia commander. He is now one of the most powerful figures in the country and commands the largest armed group.

Khalifa Belqasim Haftar was not on many people's radar. Few books on modern Libyan history published before 2011 mention him. Born in 1943 in the eastern city of Ajdabiya, Haftar grew up in eastern Libya. He is a member of the Ferjan tribe and a career soldier who received his training in the Soviet Union. He had once been close to Gaddafi, helping him to power in the 1969 coup before the two fell out in the 80s after a disastrous Libyan military invasion of the country's southern neighbour. Libya had first invaded northern Chad in 1973, claiming a strip of land called Aouzou, just south of its border. Gaddafi moved more troops there in 1980, backing various rebel groups in Chad and entangling his country in a war that lasted almost a decade over just 60 miles of land. The war took a decisive turn in 1987 when French-backed Chadian forces, driving Toyota pickups, seized Libya's main air base in northern Chad—despite up to 5,000 Libyans stationed there with the latest Soviet weapons. The fleeing Libyans left behind nearly 200 tanks and several fighter jets.[8]

Haftar was taken prisoner along with between 300 and 400 others, after which Gaddafi disowned him. The former general then formed an exile opposition group, the National Salvation Front of Libya, plotting to invade Libya and topple Gaddafi and backed—allegedly—by the CIA. Gaddafi got wind of his plans, and the CIA airlifted him and some 350 men to Zaire, from where he moved to Virginia and lived for 20 years.[9] He stayed in contact with opposition groups, but he did not return to Libya until March 2011, gathering together former members of the army units he had once commanded. But he fell out again with his comrades as he competed with Abdel Fattah Younis, the former Gaddafi interior minister who was later killed over the rebel leadership. Haftar disappeared from public view, staying mostly in eastern Libya[10] until he published a video in February 2014, posing in front of a Libyan flag and announcing a coup of parliament, due to its failure to tackle the Islamists. Nothing happened, and few Libyans initially took grey-haired man wearing an immaculate army uniform seriously, but this didn't stop Haftar's determination. He saw himself as a saviour, there to drag Benghazi out of chaos. 'There was no justice and no protection,' he said. 'People no longer left their houses at night. All of this upset me greatly ... Everybody told me the same thing: "We are looking for a saviour."'[11]

Bukhamada and other army and air force units pledged support for his 'Dignity' (*Karama*) campaign after Haftar declared war by launching airstrikes on suspected camps of the Majlis al-Shoura, an umbrella of Islamist brigades in Benghazi to which Ansar al-Sharia belonged. He allied himself with Zintani militias from western Libya who, two days after the start of Haftar's Benghazi campaign, stormed the General National Congress (GNC), the parliament in Tripoli, to demand its suspension and to appoint a caretaker government.[12] Haftar named his forces the Libyan National Army (LNA),[13] which proved to be a PR coup: many analysts, foreign observers or even governments mistook it for a real army, which helped Haftar with his ambitions to present himself as Libya's new strongman, capable of saving the country by commanding a real army. In fact, the LNA is an umbrella for former army units, militias and street fighters with loose ties. He even had some Salafist Islamist brigades fighting with him, which have become a key element of his forces, as well as foreign mercenaries from Chad and Sudan.[14]

General Haftar starts his own war

Haftar's war kicked off Libya's final descent into anarchy and instigated a rift between eastern and western entities, taking a full-scale military campaign into the cities. Two months after Haftar started his war, fighting reached Tripoli when Libya Dawn, fearing a coup of Haftar and other old regime figures and militias from Misrata, moved on the capital and expelled the recognised government of premier Abdullah al-Thinni to the east.

In a showcase of quickly shifting alliances in post-revolution Libya, Thinni and the elected House of Representatives (HoR) allied themselves with Haftar, who offered protection. Haftar was promoted to top army commander, though the move was legally questionable as he had long passed the age for active service. Sensing that the appointment of a divisive figure like Haftar might split the east, it was never made official. We spent weeks trying to get a copy of the decree, and when we did we found that the signature, supposedly from the parliamentary speaker (in his other role as de facto commander) was illegible. No name accompanied the scribble, and Deputy Speaker Ihmed Shoaib—a more moderate politician who was sceptical of Haftar—long denied the appointment, saying he had never heard of such a signing. I believe he wasn't consulted when the decree was signed by speaker Aguila Saleh, a Haftar supporter, but later had to swallow the decision. Lawmakers knew there was a risk of Haftar going rogue, but he was the principle force in the east, commanding several small air force bases—the only real weapons on the ground apart from the standard militia equipment: the ubiquitous Toyota pickup mounted with a heavy gun.

It wasn't long before new trouble erupted. Those who have worked with Haftar describe him as someone who wants to dominate and control everything—the opposite of a team player.[15] Haftar tried in February 2015 to stop Prime Minister Thinni from visiting Benghazi, which he considered his own. Officers manning the Benghazi control tower first tried stopping his plane and then stopped his convoy when going back to Bayda, Thinni's government seat, triggering a shootout at a checkpoint in al-Marj, an eastern town then home to Haftar's headquarters and main base.[16] Few dared criticise the general. When I visited the east in February 2015, ministers would stop talking when the word Haftar came up, as if just the very mention of him would invite reprisal.

The words 'general' and 'army' were not appropriate labels for Haftar and his men. He kept calling his troops a 'national army'. 'He calls anyone who joins him "army", even Majlis al-Shoura would be called army if they decided to join him,' said Khalid al-Sherif, an Islamist figure.[17] From the very beginning, Haftar enjoyed enthusiastic support from Egypt, which was keen to prop up an eastern anti-Islamist bulwark against Tripoli. Egyptian officials used to a country controlled by generals for decades had been waiting for someone in Libya's chaos to claim to have built an army. A UN panel report showed pictures of

Egyptian helicopters delivered to the eastern government with their Egyptian banners painted over.[18] But the general's popularity among those hoping for a saviour faded in 2015, when even supporters realised his use of Soviet warplanes and helicopters was turning parts of Benghazi into rubble without achieving much on the ground. 'He was a bluff,' said a prominent businessman, who had first believed in him, hoping, like others—including many of the Western diplomats I met—that the general would restore stability. Many supporters, even once close aides, have broken ranks with him since 2014, citing various personal fallouts and his crackdown on dissent.

When I interviewed Haftar by phone in May 2014, two weeks into his Benghazi campaign, he was optimistic that he would expel the Islamists within a few months. But he was vague on what was going on at the battlefront, and about the weapons he had at his disposal.[19] 'There is for sure progress ... [but] it is not appropriate to tell you this,' said Haftar, speaking from an undisclosed location in eastern Libya. He also claimed that he had arrested foreign fighters from Sudan, Egypt and other Arab countries, but again declined to give any figures. He rejected the Islamist-backed businessman Ahmed Maiteeq, who was for a few months in 2014 in Tripoli prime minister-elect in a disputed parliamentary vote, not just because of the vote, but for another reason: 'We are open to talk to anyone who can defend the nation,' but 'he is a businessman, not a man of war.' Like autocratic Arab rulers, he spoke in first person plural when talking about plans which were almost certainly his alone.

Haftar has surrounded himself with former army officers as well security and judiciary officials from the Gaddafi regime. The eastern Interior Minister, Ibrahim Bouchnaf, served as state prosecutor under the autocrat. Other indicators of his attentions abound: he described himself as a 'saviour', claiming that Libyans saw him this way in a thread which also endorsed postponement of the then forthcoming elections. The roadsides of the cities under his control were plastered with pictures showing him in military fatigues. He also gave control of the best-equipped units of his 'army' to two of his five sons. A UN report in September 2018 accused one of them having stolen €159,700,000, $1,900,000, as well as 639,975,000 Libyan dinars (worth $457 million based on the official rate at the time) and 5,869 silver coins from a central bank building in Benghazi.[20] The money was moved to an unknown destination, and explanations by an official that most of the banknotes had been damaged by sewage water flooding were 'contradictory and incomplete'.[21] When I went to Benghazi in February 2019, several people who worked near the branch discreetly talked about a bank heist, but it was impossible to prove and too dangerous to write about.

With the help of Egypt and the UAE (and to a lesser extent Jordan), Haftar expanded his military power in the following years, acquiring new supplies of arms and having his old Soviet planes fixed. The UAE even built an air base in Al-Kadhim, through which to bring in supplies, as various UN reports have since established.[22] His hard-won air superiority helped him finish the Benghazi battle, seize Derna (another eastern city) from Islamists, and allowed him to launch an offensive to 'secure' southern Libya in January 2019. His force based two MiG aircraft near the biggest southern city of Sebha. There was also some tactical French aid.

There are no reliable figures for how strong his 'Libyan Arab Armed Forces' (in English the force still carries the title of Libyan National Army)[23] are. Officially, the force is made up of 85,000 men, but when I pressed LNA spokesman Ahmed Mismari during a visit to Benghazi in 2019, he admitted this figure in fact represents the overall number of soldiers in Libya from the Gaddafi days, which the LNA hopes will prove loyal to Haftar, and so includes an untold number who are not active and whose allegiances are unconfirmed. Before April 2019, when Haftar moved on Tripoli, the LNA was for the most part only present in eastern and parts of southern Libya, so it makes no sense to count loyalists in western Libya. The most professional contingent, the Saiqa, are just 3,500 strong, as Commander Wanis Bukhamada told me in February 2019. Analysts and diplomats put the total number at between 10,000 and 25,000 including non-regular forces, but these are just rough estimates.

Rough LNA elements also shatter the illusion of an organised army, as the case of Mahmoud al-Werfalli, an LNA commander with Salafist ties, shows. The International Criminal Court, based in The Hague, issued an arrest warrant for his involvement in the execution of some 33 people in areas retaken in Benghazi from Islamists. Authorities later said they were investigating him, but in November 2017, Human Rights Watch (HRW) blamed LNA forces for having executed dozens more opponents, which undermines the idea of the properly trained army Haftar claims to command. The man himself remains at large, and could be seen working out in a gym when I last visited Benghazi, declining to be interviewed.

While Haftar's forces remained popular in the east, many were afraid of him. The only person willing to say much in 2015 was then Interior Minister Omar Zanki, who had just been fired after making public Haftar's attempt to ban Thinni from Benghazi. Haftar's guards opened fire before the convoy was eventually allowed to pass. We ran that story based on what Zanki and Thinni's enraged aides had told us, though the prime minister categorically denied the charge when I asked him, in the typical Libyan post-revolution style.[24] Despite having lost his job over the story, Zanki agreed to meet us in Bayda, though he was careful not to criticise Haftar while the camera was running. When arrived at his villa he had been sleeping but invited us in, still in his pyjamas. A luxury sportscar was parked outside, but when I pointed at it Zanki was quick to say: 'It's not mine. I don't drive such a large car.' He was very friendly, making us stay for a traditional couscous lamb dinner during which he confided that people were afraid of Haftar. The next day he headed to a court to challenge his dismissal, showing us the letter he had written and stamped in his reception room, where we sat on pillows with the TV playing in the background.

Before we left, Zanki warned that Islamic State (IS) would become much more active in Libya, demanding that both governments overcome their split to work together. Later, there was even an arrest warrant issued for Zanki, but he continued to work out of his Bayda villa, insisting he was still in office, showing us the official letterhead he was using. That was how contradictory statements would pop up in the media: ministers and officials had access to stamps and official paperwork and used them to express what they thought was the state's opinion. However, for all his pragmatism, Zanki was arrested in 2017, and was still in jail at the time of going to press for staging an alleged plot against Haftar.[25]

Libya elected a new parliament in June 2014 as part of the post-Gaddafi transition agreed by the main players in the previous assembly. The new assembly was given a new name, the HoR, and an initial mandate of just 15 months,[26] replacing the ineffective GNC. Voting took place without major incident (polling stations didn't open in Derna and some southern towns due to fighting), though interest was minimal, as many Libyans had given up any faith they might have had in the country's nascent democracy. Only 41 per cent of 1.5 million registered voters took part, much lower than in the 2012 vote, when 60 per cent of 2.8 million registered voters went to the ballot box.[27] The new parliament was meant to be based in Benghazi as part of efforts to decentralise the country's institutions and quell demands for greater autonomy and even independence.

Relocation would have proven extremely difficult, though, with the growing conflict in the city likely to dissuade lawmakers from making the move there.

One morning in Tripoli we woke to the sound of distant artillery booms, struggling for hours to understand who was fighting whom—something that wasn't always clear amid Libya's shifting alliances. Officials didn't pick up or return calls, and residents reported that fighting had closed the airport. I and my colleagues were sitting, dumbfounded, when one station suddenly showed footage of planes engulfed in smoke. On pickup trucks mounted with guns you could read banners suggesting the attackers belonged to an Islamist-leaning militia from Misrata, a city some 200 km east of Tripoli. The militia was trying to wrestle away the main airport from a rival group from Zintan, a mountainous region southwest of Tripoli.

In the next days the motives of the attackers became clearer: they cited fear of a military coup by Haftar and other figures from the old regime who were backing him. There had been talk among some that Libya might take a similar course to its neighbour, Egypt, where General Abdel-Fattah al-Sisi removed the elected Islamist President Mohamed Morsi in 2013, following popular mass protests against his rule. The conflict between supporters of Haftar and militias in Misrata touched on a division between former rebels—on one side, the ex-general and his former soldiers from the old regime and on the other, the Misrata militias, many of whose fighters were Islamist-leaning and had spent years in Gaddafi's jails. This latter group feared the newly-elected parliament, the House of Representative, would be controlled by Haftar because it was now set to be based in Tobruk.[28] With Haftar in charge of parts of the east, there were concerns about his motives. His Zintani allies had, as mentioned above, stormed the Tripoli assembly in May. Having first favoured a postponement of the election, Haftar now backed the HoR after anti-Islamist and federalist lawmakers had made a strong show-ing. One of Haftar's supporters, Tareq al-Joroushi, won a seat, and was thus able to lobby for both Haftar and his own father, Saqer, to be appointed air force commander.

There was another motive for the July attack: the Misrata militias leading it had first backed the 2014 elections, but rejected the outcome as Islamists had a much weaker presence in the HoR than in the previous assembly.[29] Once they had seized Tripoli they reinstated remnants of the old parliament, the GNC, claiming that this assembly alone could properly represent Libya. Both parliaments soon became rather irrelevant, merely playing along with the agenda of their respective masters—Haftar and the Libya Dawn. In Tobruk, attendance shrunk to less than a third of its 200 seats. Journalists were not allowed to attend ses-sions because officials did not want them to see how few lawmak-ers took part in sessions. During a one-week visit to Tobruk in September 2014 I tried entering the assembly hall several times, but was blocked each time by an angry guard. Reporters were also not allowed to attend sessions of the rump GNC parliament made up mainly of elected HoR lawmakers who had boycotted sessions since its inauguration. Even Libya Dawn supporters admitted that there were rarely more than 30 attendees.

Fleeing and coming back

Most foreign journalists pulled out of Tripoli after the Libya Dawn attack. Before we did, my wife and I spent our leisure time judiciously, decamping from our office-cum-prison to Café Roma, an Italian-style café overlooking the old city harbour, enjoying coffee or dinner. You could hear the booms of artillery guns coming from the airport but otherwise life was deceptively normal. But each morning the booms seemed to get louder— the battle was moving closer to the city. It was time to leave, but the very nature of the battle meant you couldn't just hop on a plane. More than ten aircraft parked in front of the terminal had been damaged—among them two brand new long-haul Airbus models.

For days we tried to get a flight as Libyan Airlines struggled to get the remainder of their fleet in the air from Mitiga, which was quickly transformed into a commercial civilian airport. Foreign airlines stopped flying to Libya, leaving would-be travellers to rely on domestic airlines. The 175 km road link to the Tunisian border was still technically an option, but it had never been safe—kidnappers and robbers were long known to frequent the coastal road.

We spent hours every day at Mitiga airport, where tickets were sold on the spot two hours before departure. You couldn't be picky about destinations and had to buy whatever was on offer, with throngs of hopefuls handing banknotes through the ticket desk window. We had hoped to get a flight to Egypt, but ended up with tickets to Istanbul. The airline charged a premium and we had to change dollars quickly and at a very poor rate, but we were relieved to be in the air. Just some 30 miles away, a battle with artillery guns was raging at the now closed Tripoli International Airport.

The Libya Dawn militias made progress on the battlefront in August, but it would take weeks to fully take control of the capital. I yearned to come back, but it was impossible to get visas for Tripoli. I had used my old visa to visit the new parliament in Tobruk for a week before it expired, but was unable to get permission to enter the capital. The old, very cooperative head of the foreign media department did, however, try to issue visas to journalists. He wanted the world to know what was happening inside Tripoli, but couldn't enter his office as guards at the main gate—loyal to Libya Dawn—wouldn't let him through.

Instead, I covered Libya from the safety of Cairo, working with our local reporters but keeping hard-hitting stories to a minimum in the absence of a recognised government and worsening conditions on the ground. In Tripoli, militia fighters had torched the al-Asseema TV station as it had been supportive of the Zintan militia, now defeated by Libya Dawn. Houses belonging to journalists, activists and supporters of the new rulers were stormed, according to HRW and Amnesty International.[30] The flat of a colleague of mine was ransacked after he had fled. He had shared it with a Haftar supporter.

Many ordinary Libyans also left Tripoli, fearing reprisals from the new rulers. Their fighters had stormed houses of opponents, detaining some. During my Tobruk visit I met several contacts who had worked at embassies or for foreign firms who had fled Tripoli, often without packing. Some 80 per cent of my contact book now resided in Tunisia, Egypt, Europe or in eastern Libya—where the expelled premier now lived in a hotel. New in Tripoli, however, were some friends from Benghazi who had fled there due to their support for Libya Dawn. This included staff from the news website *Ajwa al-Belad*, whose offices and apartments had been ransacked by forces loyal to the eastern government. The conflict had also exposed another layer of division: Haftar's forces were, in 2014, mostly made up of tribesmen loyal to him. His supporters were gradually installing tribesmen in official positions to replace the old elites in Benghazi, who traced their origins to Misrata.

Some three months after the Tripoli attack, the Libya Dawn government finally invited the foreign media to showcase that life, at least as they saw it, was back to normal. Having won on the battlefield and set up officials in elegant suites, they yearned for international recognition, to receive ambassadors and represent their government abroad. I was eager to get back on the ground, as Libya is very difficult to report on from outside. I knew the reception for the new Tripoli rulers might not be friendly; their officials kept complaining about our stories, which (as in the rest of the foreign press) described the Tripoli administration as unrecognised by the international community. The tone of the emails from one official, who accused me of working for a 'media militia', made me wonder if I should go back to a country run by real militias. I had negotiated a visa to return, but as I was about to book a flight I received another hostile email after simply stating in another story that Libya now had two governments, with an unrecognised administration sitting in the capital. 'Hi Ulf,' the mail began. 'Look I always respect my promise and ... [will keep my] word about your visa ... but I cannot respect Reuters and its staff when they write rubbish stories about my country. I can write to our airport authorities that your visa is cancelled and send you back.' The next sentence said much about his understanding of rule of law and a deep suspicion towards foreigners: 'I'll never accept freedom or human rights (David Cameroon [sic]). Reuters staff cannot write such rubbish stories.'

I wasn't the only journalist facing intimidation. Right after the new Tripoli government had settled in and allowed foreign journalists to return, officials invited the bureau chiefs of foreign TV channels, news agencies and newspapers based in Libya for a meeting to discuss the new ground rules. The same senior official lectured the assembled media that the unofficial government was now the only government. 'How can you say we are the unofficial government?' he asked, exasperatedly.

The Tripoli foreign press corps had always been small, as few wanted to live in a warzone and could afford to pay for bodyguards. This meant that, aside from BBC correspondent Rana Jawad (who stuck up for both her organisation and Reuters' coverage), the meeting comprised freelance journalists, photographers and secretaries—hardly those involved crafting hard-hitting stories. We were represented by my photographer friend and our office driver, as the rest of the Reuters team had fled to

Cairo or Tunis, or had stayed at home. The invitation to bureau chiefs was a desperate cry for attention from a new government which had taken the capital by force and now—facing isolation—expected the media to play by its rules. The new powers also issued invitations to ambassadors, but they, like the journalists, were long gone and had no intention of recognising a parallel government occupying Tripoli's ministries.

So, I asked myself, was it safe to come back from my exile in Egypt? After agreeing to meet the foreign media office representative who had sent me the email, I booked a flight in November 2014. When I arrived in Tripoli life looked normal enough, with cafés and shops bustling with customers. Families were sitting on the beach when we entered Tripoli via the main coastal road, passing Mitiga air base. There were even traffic police trying to impose order on motorists ignoring traffic rules. But blackened holes in prefab residential buildings in the Fashloum district, one of the city's poorest, pointed to hits from rocket-propelled grenades during the battle for Tripoli. Some of the damage to residential buildings, government offices and shops was actually from the revolution, symbolising the country's steady descent into chaos, as no government had managed to clean up the war scars from 2011.

Still tired from the long trip, I began reopening the long-abandoned office when the same official told a Libyan colleague by phone about a news conference at the foreign ministry. I was a little reluctant to go, as I hadn't yet formally introduced myself to the new government (a condition for my visa), and I knew I was being watched. Within an hour of my arrival at Misrata airport an official had called our driver to confirm whether I had indeed arrived. But since the government had invited all reporters to the conference, I thought I might as well give it a go.

There was the usual high jinks—former fighters now working as guards and officials kept the reporters waiting, moving them around from room to room without explanation, and one guard shouting at a colleague, 'You just have to manage and wait!' The reporter pressed on, enquiring about the subject of the news conference, but the guard had had enough. He reached for a gun hidden in his jacket, loaded it and dragged the man out with the help of two others. They beat the reporter in a separate room, even putting the gun to his head. Despite hearing his scream, neither the ministry staff nor the other security guards interfered. The senior official responsible for inviting us all to the press conference rushed to downplay the violence, promising a punishment for the guards as the beaten reporter was brought back and hugged by officials and fellow reporters. 'This will be investigated,' he told the crying reporter. But I never heard of any punishment or formal charges launched against the guard.

In a final blow to the plan to stage a regular news conference, the government's Foreign Minister Mohammed al-Ghirani, dressed in an elegant suit, suddenly walked into the room in which we were waiting, looking confused. He quickly turned on his heels and asked three other officials who were standing behind him. 'So, what is the plan? Are we doing a press conference now? What do we have to talk about?' he asked, before disappearing again. He was, at the time, supposed to be at a cabinet session, a detail obviously made up to convince the press that this new government, boycotted by the world, was doing any work.

The press conference started two hours late and was a farce. The goal was to showcase that the unrecognised administration had peaceful intentions and was firmly in control. 'Many foreign journalists are now in Tripoli,' said the information minister, with a senior official translating for visiting TV crews from Germany and the UK who did not speak Arabic. One of the foreign reporters asked about the Tripoli government's relationship with Ansar al-Sharia, which the UN Security Council had just labelled as a terrorist organisation. Ghirani should have dodged the question, but he defended the group, confirming once and for all any suspicions about the Tripoli government's affiliations. 'Maybe some Ansar al-Sharia members are terrorists, but you cannot label the whole group as such,' he said. He was clearly under tremendous pressure from militias, the true rulers of the country, a fact which would make my life as a reporter very difficult too, as I found out when I reported to the official who had granted my visa the next day.

The new man in charge attacked me for an hour, complaining that Reuters wasn't supporting the new government, which was yearning for international recognition. On the table sat a coffee cup the size of a beer mug emblazoned with 'THE BOSS' on the side, while his phone rang constantly. His ringtone was gunfire, recorded from a Hollywood movie, and the first time I heard it I thought there was a real shootout.[31] The conversation dragged on: 'You cannot write that our boys are militias or that Libya is in chaos. This is now a country based on law,' he said. When I responded that efforts to build an army had failed, he insisted the forces were made up of regular soldiers, rather than militiamen. 'You cannot say we are Islamists. This is not true,' he insisted. I had met the same official in the run-up to the previous day's disastrous press conference. Then, he had been courteous, shaking hands and joking around with me and the other reporters. Away from the foreign TV crews his guards had issued a beating to a journalist, and here in my meeting he was combative. It was a taste of things to come.

Reporting from the west, reporting from the east

Relations improved as time went on, as the same official and others in the Tripoli establishment came to understand that they could reach the world via Reuters and other global outlets. I was issued with six-month multiple entry visas—which I had never been offered before—but it took several, painful weeks to establish that I would not bow to their pressure, which often came in the form of angry late-night calls.

Of course, I had run into trouble with autocratic governments before: in Sudan and Saudi Arabia—the latter expelled me in March 2011 over coverage of minority Shi'ite Muslim protests against the Sunni regime. State security agents had once stormed my hotel room in Khobar following my coverage of a protest in Qatif, the main settlement of Shi'ites, where residents complained that they did not benefit from the country's oil wealth, despite much of the oil coming from wells in their often very poor neighbourhoods. In Libya, things were more complex. Yes, it was tiring to explain to officials that, as a reporter, I could not ignore protests which upset the government. But in Saudi Arabia I dealt with a state; in Libya, detractors were ministers and militias, jockeying for a level of power that might one day match their enormous offices and couches.

It wasn't just government officials giving me a hard time as the country's split into two rival administrations divided normal people. The vast majority of Libyans were either with *Fajr* (as Libya Dawn is called in Arabic) or Haftar's Karama campaign. In a telling indication of who was really in charge, both sides would identify their opponents through their military leaders, not their prime ministers or parliaments. A normal meeting with friends would turn hostile when I did not immediately back the Tripoli side. 'It was necessary,' one of them said, coolly defending the attack on Tripoli airport. They were all journalists, Islamist-leaning, but still running one of the best local news websites. It was no surprise that, after four decades of political manipulation, emotions ran high during meaningful political discussions.

Libya's split into two administrations also ended a spell of relative freedom of debate that followed the revolution. From summer 2014, television news programmes were only about backing one side of the conflict or the other. On Tripoli-based Nabaa television, previously one of the best news channels, female presenters suddenly donned veils, while any sense of impartiality was skipped in favour of backing the Libya Dawn movement controlling Tripoli's ministries.

A typical evening news programme would start with a veiled lady reading out statements from government officials with pictures showing them sitting in the newly-occupied ministries, in the style of Gaddafi's Jamahiriya TV, or Saudi or Syrian state television for that matter. Then several videos would be played by a group of grim-faced men, a mix of civilians and soldiers from, for example, the Gharyan council (a small town south of Tripoli), announcing, 'We the revolutionaries of Gharyan affirm our support and solidarity with the honourable Libya Dawn revolutionaries in its heroic stance against Haftar the war criminal and the traitors in Tobruk.' Then the focus would switch to Benghazi, from where a video by the Islamist militant group Ansar al-Sharia would be shown. 'Today we captured two streets from the war criminal Haftar,' a man, his face completely covered, would say, accusing Haftar of shelling residential areas. Every hour, clips making fun of Ali Zeidan, his former cabinet ministers, the now eastern-based premier Abdullah al-Thinni or General Haftar would be played alongside videos showing the alleged shelling by Zintani or Haftar's forces. The Libya Dawn assault on Tripoli and its main airport that summer would go unmentioned.

Likewise TV programmes in the east underwent a similar transformation, with stations such as al-Awla or al-Wataniya, a state TV news channel set up by the eastern government with the same name as the original state TV now controlled by Tripoli. Statements by Haftar or Thinni would be read out alongside videos of 'spontaneous' support from various town council members. The former correspondent of the Saudi-owned al-Arabiya channel, who backed Thinni and opposed Libya Dawn, became editor–in–chief of a new state news agency, LANA, based in the east since the original LANA had become a tool for Libya Dawn. He had to flee to the east after his apartment, shared with a colleague of mine, was torched.

'We will be always fighting for our freedom,' a man who described himself as a human rights advocate from Zliten, a western coastal town largely associated to Misrata and Libya Dawn, told me during a public debate organised by Libya Dawn supporters.[32] It was a propaganda event, but I had gone along anyway to get a feel for the mood among regular Libya Dawn supporters—and to pretend I was covering such events to improve ties with the new Tripoli rulers. We needed them for permits to attend court sessions or films at government facilities and, most importantly, get help if militiamen arrested us. It was frustrating that the new rulers reinstated Gaddafi-era rules requiring journalists to attend state-organised events, transporting us in buses provided by the foreign media office. I insisted on defying this rule at the few state-sponsored events I chose to attend.

I struck up a casual conversation with the 'rights advocate' who accused the west of being responsible for the mess Libya was in. 'We will be always fighting because of you,' he said, getting agitated, before a round table discussion in which Libya Dawn activists and allied members of Libya's constitutional assembly agreed that constitution writing should stop because the venue in eastern Libya was controlled by General Haftar. It was dead boring, and exactly like one of the quasi-mandatory events staged by the Gaddafi regime for journalists staying in the Rixos Hotel during the uprising. I had strategically placed myself in a back row so my early departure wouldn't be noticed.

News and business conferences were held in ministries or the Corinthia Hotel, where a host of bankers, 'investors', ministry officials and owners of private companies friendly to the National

Salvation Government (the official name of the unofficial Tripoli administration) would pretend it was all business as usual to an unconvinced foreign media. Some officials were apparently forced to join in or risk losing their jobs, discussing infrastructure and other development projects that all amounted to wishful thinking, as the central bank, trying to stay out of the political conflict, had frozen all capital expenditures. As at the constitutional event, I played along sometimes, needing colour for feature stories and always aware that not showing up could have consequences. I didn't get an interview with the Tripoli-based Libya Dawn foreign minister because 'THE BOSS' complained that I had not attended a press conference announcing a new research institute set up to establish the causes of illegal migration. The institute was never heard of again.

Other reporters were threatened with having filming permits revoked for the court trials of former Gaddafi officials. For any story I filed, I could expect an angry phone call from the Libya Dawn government, the eastern government, a 'revolutionary' or some militiamen who read a story on social media. I stopped using the word 'militia' because the Arab translation has a more negative connotation, switching to 'armed group', 'former rebels' or 'faction'. Mere reference to the internationally recognised government in the east would give Tripoli officials a headache, despite objections from me and other reporters that we were merely using the UN definition. Later, the same officials dropped their complaints. It wasn't clear why, but I suppose they had managed to persuade the armed groups backing them that pressing the media would be counterproductive.

Interviews with top officials from mid-2014 were mostly lacking in real news value. The Tripoli-based oil minister, Mashallah Zwai, a rather junior engineer chosen mainly for his tribal roots in the eastern oil heartland and controlled by the opposing official government, was four hours late for our appointment on the top floor of the state oil firm's headquarters. When he finally appeared, Zwai said he wanted an invitation to attend the upcoming OPEC summit a few days later in November 2014 to discuss production quotas on behalf of his government before going to an investment conference in Turkey—or Libya would boycott all decisions taken there. As the Vienna-based oil cartel had only invited delegates from the east as the internationally recognised administration, Zwai never made it beyond Istanbul, quietly returning to Tripoli with no threats made. He was unfamiliar with detailed oil and gas production figures, always checking a spreadsheet in front of him, but became very friendly, inviting myself and two of my colleagues for dinner. We had to decline as it was past midnight and my security adviser was eager to get back to our villa. It took us a while to get home though. Having no Libyan colleague with me and without functioning street-lights, we took a wrong turn and ended up in wasteland in a southern district before finding the right way.[33]

One of the oil minister's aides took pictures of me and my colleagues interviewing his boss. I didn't notice at first, as I was busy asking questions, but to my shock I saw the photographs posted on the oil ministry's website. The moment I and my colleagues saw this we called the ministry aides, demanding they remove the pictures—which they did. This was a common trick by the unofficial government to—in their view—win international government support by taking pictures of foreign visitors to bolster their legitimacy. A few months earlier, the Tripoli government published a picture of a meeting with a Turkish official with the Libyan and Turkish flag hoisted in the background, celebrating the conversation as diplomatic victory on an official website while omitting the fact that the Turkish diplomat also travelled to eastern Libya to sit down with the internationally recognised government there.[34] Since that meeting, diplomats largely stopped visiting Tripoli, fearing a similar ambush.

Officials also forced the UN Envoy, Bernardino Leon, to hold a news conference right behind the logo of the unrecognised GNC parliament in Tripoli.[35]

Perhaps the worst example of a minister from the non-recognised administration having little to do was Foreign Minister al-Ghirani, who in November 2014 prolonged an interview for two hours, yearning for attention as his government sought international recognition. Only offices directly adjacent to Ghirani's were manned with newly appointed staff from Libya Dawn, as the existing ministry staff had not shown up for work—despite him claiming that thousands were busy working. He was proud to have occupied the office of the previous minister (who had fled to the east) but a dusty desk showed little work was underway despite several official letters lying on it. The tea lady, another new hire brought by the new rulers, was the only person to call during my visit. 'Why does Europe not recognise us? Why?' he trilled. Ghirani, who had been Libya's ambassador to Jordan before his switch to Libya Dawn, had a long list of grievances against the international community. I knew his government, with its Islamist ties, hated the new Egyptian President Sisi, a general who had removed by force the elected Islamist President Mohamed al-Mursi after a popular uprising against his chaotic rule. Enjoying the show of a career diplomat losing his temper, I asked what he thought about Sisi. At this he erupted: 'Sisi is a criminal who bombs us with Haftar. But he will be finished soon.'

When I met him again six months later he was even more ill-tempered, because the hope for international recognition, which would have brought the opportunity to host ambassadors and visit foreign countries, had failed to materialise. The only two countries that had received him were Turkey, with its Islamist President Recep Tayyib Erdoğan, and impoverished southern neighbour, Niger, which has a large expatriate community in

Libya, undertaking the cleaning and security jobs which Libyans refused. With the lure of Libyan aid money, Ghirani had won himself an invitation to Niger's capital, Niamey. He also had been to Malta, but not in an official capacity, as the EU was boycotting the Tripoli government. Not wanting to cut economic ties (many Libyans hold bank accounts in the island state), Malta had nevertheless allowed two competing Libyan embassies to open, run by the rival administrations. In the interview, he called Sisi a 'pharaoh' and a 'criminal' again, but had to cut things short because he had a rare appointment with a foreign diplomat, allegedly the Hungarian consul, who had come on a visit to Tripoli. Ghirani's office manager would later ask me whether I had a phone number for the Italian ambassador who was then still in town—Italy's mission is a short drive down the main coastal road, but the foreign ministry didn't even hold its boss's contact details.

The interview with the Tripoli foreign minister also exposed the double standards of post-revolution Libya, where officials have flexible political views. Under a political isolation law issued in 2013 banning former Gaddafi officials from taking political office, Ghirani should not have been minister as he had been a deputy ambassador under the old regime. That law, pushed through by parliament after pressure from militias, had contributed to Libya's divisions and polarisation. It was pursued by militias and Islamist-leaning factions who feared a counter-revolution of the old system as in the east, while in the western Zintan region former Gaddafi army officers made a comeback. But it also meant that Libya struggled to find qualified technocrats for the sovereign wealth fund, the central bank or other vital state institutions. Ghirani was never heard of again after the Libya Dawn government had quit.

Working in such an environment, it's hard not to question the wisdom of sticking around. Certainly, I needed to find the fine line between covering pointless exercises in state propaganda and getting myself in trouble. The state had disappeared: there was no police or security to call should someone threaten you over an article. The Tripoli 'police' was the Libya Dawn militia and its affiliated groups, who had no unified command as they patrolled each neighbourhood. There was no police hotline citizens could call. Once, when a nightly battle between armed groups was raging in 2015 near the Rixos, I lay in bed wondering if someone would ever come to the villa complain about our coverage in person.

Unfortunately, life for journalists dealing with the then internationally recognised government was as difficult as in Tripoli. The government of Abdallah al-Thinni fled the capital in mid-2014 to work out of rented villas and hotels in the small town of Bayda, a former tourist destination famed for its moderate climate and nestled in the Green Mountain hinterland. In Tripoli, despite all the restrictions and pressures, you could at least count on the foreign media office to get you a visa, as they wanted to showcase that they were running the capital. In the east, with officials working in hotels, that was much more difficult. Power and phone reception were often non-existent in Bayda, while political infighting and disputes amongst staff paralysed work.

I met the eastern Economy Minister Munir Asr in his modest hotel room, which had a small kitchen and washing machine, since he stayed there long-term. He had just finished his laundry when I arrived with a photographer and cameraman. He wanted to be seated behind a Libyan flag in the hotel manager's office on the ground floor, to look more official on camera. I had hoped to get some insight into the economic crisis paralysing much of Libya, but he kept going on about optimistic growth projections and investors' interest. 'There is no need to worry at all about Libya. We have everything: touristic sites, agriculture land, industry,' he told me, rather unconvincingly.[36] He also denied the fuel crisis, which had been evident for two weeks, as only Tobruk was still receiving fuel imports. During my Bayda visit I saw dozens of people waiting in freezing temperatures in front of petrol stations after rumours emerged that a tanker had docked at Tobruk. While Asr spoke, not a single petrol station was open in Bayda.

Our intrepid reporter Ayman al-Warfalli had bought petrol from Benghzai, where he lived, on the black market, but he had only managed to get enough to pick me and our security adviser up at Labraq airport, some 20 km outside the city, and to drive to Bayda. We spent the next day trying to meet the staff of Husni Bey—one of the country's most prominent businessmen, who got along with Gaddafi officials and post-revolution politicians. Bey runs Libya's biggest private firm, the HB Group, and kindly agreed to open his company's storage tanks to refill our car. From his exile abroad he sensed I was despairing at not being able to get any work done.

Perhaps the most bizarre element of the late-night interview was that the economy minster had no knowledge of a statement his ministry had issued weeks earlier—that a flour crisis was forcing authorities to open Libya's emergency wheat reserves.[37] We and other media outlets had carried it, since it signalled much worsening economic conditions, though it was clear that the statement would have no practical meaning as the state agency distributing flour was based in Tripoli, outside the control of the eastern-exiled government. I was surprised that even the minister himself had no knowledge of it. The head of the Tripoli agency also hadn't heard of the statement—he said dryly in an interview that his agency was taking orders only from the Tripoli rival parliament, the resurrected GNC, which had also fled east to oppose the elected recognised parliament on its own turf.

Meeting the eastern Prime Minister al-Thinni was so similar to sitting with his Tripoli counterpart Omar al-Hassi that it was as if they had worked together on their manuscripts. Thinni's comments about fighting terrorism and accusations of betrayal were almost identical to al-Hassi's: you just needed to replace 'GNC' as the recognised parliament with 'HoR' or say 'Tripoli' instead of 'Bayda' when it came to terrorists. Both made use of vague slogans borrowed from the 2011 revolution on achieving 'freedom' for Libya to justify their actions in the same way Gaddafi had used opaque phrases from his Green Book to claim legitimacy for his regime. Freedom was the mantra for most political factions and militias wrangling for power in the new supposedly democratic Libya.

Thinni demanded airstrikes against Tripoli, saying: 'The Tripoli militias are in contact with Islamic State. It is the same.' A day later, Egyptian fighter jets bombed Derna, a jihadi hotspot to the east of Bayda, which sent hundreds of fighters to conflict zones from Syria to Afghanistan, after IS had published a video showing the beheading of 21 Egyptian Copts.

I had planned to travel to Benghazi after the Bayda trip, but after the gruelling IS video emerged late at night I decided to pack up. I headed the next day to the tiny Labraq airport, hoping to catch a flight to Alexandria in Egypt from where I wanted to go to Cairo where my wife was waiting anxiously. But in Libya getting an air ticket is a gamble, especially after the exit of foreign carriers in 2015. Libyan Airlines are overbooked on popular destinations. Even if you managed to get a ticket or a boarding pass there was no guarantee there would be a flight, or that you will be allowed to board. Once, during a visit to Benghazi, the Libyan Airlines staff at Benina airport checking in angry passengers on two overbooked evening flights to Tripoli threatened to refuse to work after long shouting matches with desperate would-be passengers. A German scholar told me that airline staff in Benghazi, beleaguered by a mob, once threw boarding passes into the crowd—if you caught a boarding pass, you were able to catch a flight.

Once a sleepy provincial airport with an adjacent air base, Labraq International turned into Libya's busiest hub in 2014 as

Benghazi's Benina airport closed when Haftar's war against Islamists kicked off in May. Several countries, such as Egypt and Tunisia, banned flights to Tripoli's second airport Mitiga, which had replaced the damaged main airport, since the government in the capital was not recognised by the international community. Suddenly anyone flying from Mitiga to Amman, Tunis or Egypt needed to make a detour via Labraq, which has just a single small building as terminal. Arriving passengers sometimes search for their luggage, dumped on the tarmac by handlers whenever the power in the building itself went out.

While the flight to Alexandria was delayed for 15 hours, I managed to get on with the help of our reporter Ayman, who knew the airport director, helping to secure a ticket to Istanbul. Ironically, while Tunisia and Egypt had said they did not trust the sloppy passport and check-in procedures at Tripoli and Misrata airports (controlled by Libya Dawn), checks at Labraq were even lighter. There was no computer at the passport control desk—the officer just stamped a blank passport page without looking at the visa or the photo page. Handing over the fee of 440 dinars (and being issued with no receipt), I received a blank boarding pass without my name or a flight number.

The day before the Thinni interview, he had not shown up as initially planned because protesters angry about economic hardship and chaos had stormed his office, a former Gaddafi government building next to the historic parliament where the country's constitutional commission now sits. 'It's not safe here,' said a guard outside the main gate in police uniform after civil servants had run out of the sprawling white building perched on a small hill, some carrying files and bags. When Thinni was back at work the next day we waited for seven hours to interview him, with his media manager apologising as an army of deputies, ministers, civil servants, bodyguards and even the parliamentary speaker bullied their way in. I placed myself next to the door, hoping to gain entry between meetings. Finally, Ayman and I, plus a cameraman and photographer, were allowed to enter, walking a corridor floor occupied by some 20 guards leading to Thinni's office, the building's only heated room amid freezing temperatures of the rest of the compound. 'Is he a spy?' a guard asked Ayman, as we walked.

Thinni's office compound was packed with aides who had previously been based in Tripoli and a private team of journalists who would film his speeches to spread his message to the whole of Libya. Otherwise, there were few signs of work being done, apart from the signing of fantasy instructions to ministries now run by Libya Dawn in Tripoli. Sitting behind a Libyan flag in a room much smaller than his old Tripoli office, Thinni told us about the annual budget his cabinet was busy preparing, a meaningless document which would only exist on paper as the central bank in Tripoli controlled oil revenues, the budget's only source of income, and froze infrastructure expenditures. He also claimed that his government had created a new state oil firm handling crude oil exports. But buyers of Libyan oil continued to pay through existing payments systems via the central bank and the state oil firm in Tripoli—the new eastern oil firm to be based in Benghazi didn't even have a building in which to begin work. How little real work was done became clearer when we left his office: Thinni's deputy foreign minister was fixing the battery of his car, parked outside the palatial seat of government.

I met an official who occupied a small office in Thinni's compound in Bayda who had told me a year before about an initiative to launch a petrol card system and other ambitious plans aimed at ending fuel and food subsidies that cost the state $3 billion annually.[38] He had then been full of hope that Libya could make it as a country ruled by law. The sad look on his face when I entered his small office now showed that this was no longer the case. He asked us not to quote him by name any longer—he still had family in Tripoli, which was now like a city in a foreign, and hostile, country.

* * *

Thinni lost his internationally recognised status when Fayez al-Serraj, an architect from a wealthy family, was named head of a new Presidency Council in a UN-brokered deal after month of talks between rival factions in December 2015. Neither the Haftar camp nor the Libya Dawn government accepted the deal, which meant that Libya briefly had three governments. Serraj boarded a boat in southern Tunisia to arrive at a Tripoli naval base, from where he worked and lived until July 2016, as allied militiamen first struggled to take control and expel the Libya Dawn ministers to Misrata. Some officials resisted.

I was then based in Nigeria but followed with amusement the news that the foreign media official under Libya Dawn, who had sent me the aggressive emails, was one of the last to leave— camping out in his office until he finally realised it was game over for his regime. His Prime Minister, Khalifa al-Ghweil, claimed for over a year to still be the legitimate prime minister, issuing statements on official letterheads from exile in Misrata.

Conditions for foreign journalists trying to visit the east worsened in 2016, when visas were rarely granted and only then with Gaddafi-era strings attached, like the requirement to be accompanied by a minder. I was not able to return to the east until February 2019.[39]

The new Tripoli government did not end the country's split into east and west. The eastern-based HoR never approved the nominations for the Presidential Council as the deal was torpedoed by hardliners and Haftar's camp, which expanded parallel institutions and the LNA with the help of Arab partners. Haftar's position was boosted by progress on the battlefield in Benghazi, where his troops pushed out Islamist fighters district by district until declaring victory in July 2017 (though isolated fighting continued for months). France had sent special forces to advise the LNA on urban warfare, seeing the general as a stabilising force. The UN and Western powers had first tried first to work around and isolate Haftar but, having become the dominant force in the east, they began to include him in their solutions. Haftar never accepted the UN-brokered deal (the Libya Political Agreement), and he dodged a clear position about the UN efforts before declaring both the Skhirat deal and the Serraj government obsolete on 17 December 2017. He used the day the deal was meant to expire to dismiss the UN mediation talks as having failed, demanding elections in which he would run. Pro-Haftar rallies were already underway. 'We declare clearly and unequivocally our full compliance with the orders of the free Libyan people, who are our guardian,' Haftar said in a televised speech. The eastern camp and the Tripoli-based government co-existed for years with no major confrontation, but in 2019 Haftar made a move on the capital. Misratan militias from the former Libya Dawn government rushed to stop his offensive, plunging the capital into war for a third time and killing any hopes for national elections.

5

TRIBE VS. REGION VS. TOWN VS. FAMILY

If anyone knows about Libya's divisions, it is Farraj Yassin, the former mayor of Tobruk, Libya's easternmost city. For six months he was trying to end a blockade organised in 2013 by his brother-in-law, Mansour al-Salhin, of the oil port of Hariga, located on the outskirts of the town. Sitting in his office on the first floor of the once grand Dar es-Salam Hotel in February 2014, Yassin said he agreed with Salhin on regional autonomy as a way to combat systemic neglect from Tripoli. But he warned Libya might collapse due to the port protest drying up vital crude exports. 'We are against it. We understand the grievances but blocking oil we reject because Libya only has oil [for its] income,' Yassin said.

His brother-in-law met me shortly afterwards in the ground floor café of the same hotel. 'Our oil feeds corruption,' Salhin said, sitting opposite his son who, dressed in an army uniform, acted as his secretary and bodyguard. 'We will not open the port until we get our share of oil revenues and a federalist system.'

The next day I met a geology graduate called Mohammed who was also campaigning for autonomy for Libya's neglected east.

He wanted jobs at the state oil firm for young people like him, and had joined an earlier port blockade with other graduates who had later agreed to give negotiations a try. 'If we don't get jobs in the oil sector then we will do another protest,' he said, dismissing Salhin's armed guards as rough; damaging to the cause of federalism.

And so, here you have three Libyans—all from the same city and all desirous of a political system that could give the east more power—but they cannot agree on a strategy. Libya is a divided country: families, tribes, regions and towns with their intersecting and overlapping secular, religious and political rivalries are in conflict over how to shape the post-revolution transformation. There is hardly a family whose members do not argue every day over the country's future—some were then fighting in Benghazi for Islamist militants like Ansar al-Sharia, while others backed General Haftar and later found themselves disillusioned. Libya has splintered into small power centres run by local militias in which governments have only limited control, if any.

Many of the terms applied to Libya by the international media feel moot on the ground: things are never so black and white. Islamist. Secular. Liberal. Nationalist. Many of the players fit more than one of these descriptions, and political affiliations in post-revolution Libya are necessarily fluid: the country lacks any of the political institutions familiar to functioning democracies, as well as a proper debate language.[1] Indeed, pinning down the country's divisions was the most difficult task I faced during my time in Libya. When I asked fellow Libya-watchers for advice on mapping out the divisions, the only agreement was that it's impossible to define the multiple factors keeping Libyans apart. I don't claim to know the truth, and can only base my analysis on having lived in Libya, travelled across the country and met hundreds of Libyans—many of whom have become friends.

TRIBE VS. REGION VS. TOWN VS. FAMILY

Revolutionaries vs. the old guard

What makes Libya different to other Arab countries is that community control is limited, and several layers of division make it difficult to build a state or carve out a national identity. The country's two governments compete for legitimacy, but both control only limited territory as they work with different armed groups, tribesmen and former rebels, often with competing agendas. There are layers of division between regions, tribes and towns that are rooted deep in history; others have developed only recently. Alliances change, and even scholars and journalists who follow Libya struggle to keep up with its shifting loyalties. The divisions reach into families, like Yassin's in Tobruk.

Lawmaker Fathi al-Gabasi, from the small eastern town of Aoudjila, likened Libyans to a herd of goats locked up for decades and then suddenly set free in 2011: 'Having been imprisoned so long, they take freedom into their own hands,' he said, sitting in the same hotel. 'They do what they want without any limits,' he said, adding that he was still hopeful people would see reason and resolve conflicts through dialogue.[2]

One important historic division is between tribes, or 'Bedouins' and sedentary people, or *hadar*—peasants and town residents.[3] Describing the situation at the start of the 16th century, Lisa Anderson writes: 'Tribes or the more distant eastern and southern regions had very regular intercourse with the settled regions along the coast.'[4] Nowadays, urban elites dominate western cities such as Tripoli and Misrata. Gaddafi sharpened divisions by curbing the power held by the tribal elders key to Idris's rule, and then fostered ties with tribes sympathetic to him. While Gaddafi comes from the Qadhadfa tribal home in central Libya, his second wife, Safiya Farkash, belonged to the Barassi—a large tribe in the east. 'Gaddafi always used the tribes to dominate the cities,' writes Atif Bukra, a Libyan Islamist-leaning blogger from Tripoli. The dictator played on divisions and competition between tribes, some of which are thought of as more noble than others based on power accumulated through centuries of alliances. Put another way, 'the disruptive nature of Libyan state formation allowed tribal loyalties to survive,' wrote German researcher Wolfram Lacher.[5] In any case, loyalty to the tribe has always been stronger than to the state.

Our Benghazi-based reporter Ayman al-Warfalli comes from the biggest tribe—the Warfalla—based in the western city of Bani Walid, one of several which made up the security apparatus under Gaddafi.[6] People like Ayman are invaluable to reporting in Libya: through his tribal connections (you can find a Warfalla member living in every town, or working in every oil port or gas field), he can confirm almost any story. Many times he was able to do so, to the dismay of the National Oil Corporation (NOC), which often complained about our breaking news of protests and pipeline blockades based on local sources they could not control. Although based in the east and unable to visit Tripoli (his tribe is still seen as close to the Gaddafi regime), he maintains good relationships with sources in western Libya. He even found residents in Sirte willing to talk about the brutal occupation by Islamic State (IS) militants in 2015 and 2016.

The division between tribes and cities was reinforced by a political split that occurred during the 2011 uprising. Islamists having languished for many years in torrid prisons wanted to erase the former state and ban its officials from participating in the new Libya. Other rebels, including former soldiers, Gaddafi officials and defected army units from the western mountain regions, joined the Islamists in the uprising, but did so with some of their old state loyalties intact. This group wanted to avoid the chaos of post-invasion Iraq, when millions of members of Saddam's Ba'ath party and national army were barred from participation in the new regime. Former regime soldiers also wanted to retain their privileges, which antagonised those from the western city of Misrata, who saw themselves as the truly revolutionary camp.

This conflict worsened when several militias besieged ministries in 2013 to force the General National Congress (GNC) to approve a so-called political isolation law banning former Gaddafi officials from public office. Though phrased only vaguely, the law was a blow to reconciliation and the country's transition to democracy as it excluded a large number of those who had joined the uprising. Many former regime officials had thrown their weight behind the initial protests in the east, giving the revolution momentum. Because of the damage done to state institutions and the exile of thousands of dissidents under Gaddafi, the country desperately needed anyone with experience in public service, the military or the oil industry. It was impossible to have a career in Gaddafi's Jamahiriya without at least paying lip service to his ideology—meaning any senior executive from the NOC would have been excluded from public life in the new Libya.

When Libya Dawn, made up of militias from Misrata, attacked Tripoli in July 2014, the motive was to stop a counter-revolution from former regime and security officials such as General Haftar, who was trying to control the capital with a tribal force from Zintan. But there were strong social ties, too: Libya Dawn had an Islamist component, but it also included more Western-minded businessmen whose only common ground with the Islamists was that they also came from Misrata.

On the day of the Libya Dawn attack, several journalists I had known as liberal and anti-Islamist were suddenly backing the Tripoli attackers simply due to their provenance. Seemingly secular reporter friends from Benghazi suddenly supported the Islamist militant group Ansar al-Sharia. I had wondered for a while why a female colleague (and women's rights activist) would always side with a reporter known for his piety; a man who had once complained that she wasn't wearing a headscarf during

Ramadan. I had first thought there was some secret romance between them, but then I realised—both came from Misrata. Their joint heritage trumped their opposing political views.

Regional identity would often transcend more fundamental boundaries. The Misrata forces sent in 2015 to confront IS fighters in Sirte would maintain contact with the extremists' local leader, Hassan al-Karami. He was also from Misrata, and while now on the opposite side of a violent conflict, would keep a line open about prisoner exchange and other issues.[7] Some Misratan fighters had gone to school together and even teamed up to topple Gaddafi in 2011, but then, like the rest of the country, fell out.

As per the true nature of Libya's ever-growing divisions, there would also be exceptions. The Libya Dawn militia attracted support from the Amazigh (plural Imazighen), or Berber, minority: they were tribesmen—the natural rivals of Misrata's coastal elites. The Amazigh had sought protection from their neighbours, the Zintanis, who had allied themselves with Haftar. He himself had help from Salafists, though Haftar declared war on other Islamist groups. A whole Salafist militia brigade called Tawheed fought at Haftar's side—they were part of a group of Islamists in the east who Gaddafi had invited in the 1990s to counter the influence of the Muslim Brotherhood and the other jihadist groups who opposed him. They follow a 'quietist' movement founded by Saudi cleric Rabee al-Madkhali, which tends not to oppose rulers who allow them to control their mosques.[8] At the outbreak of the revolution, Libyan Salafists spoke out against anti-Gaddafi protests. In that sense, they were as much Islamists as they were regime loyalists. This group lost influence at the hands of other Islamists who joined the rebels, gaining access to weapons and power. By backing Haftar, the Salafists hoped to regain influence and managed to become, in 2019, a key component of the general's fighting force. In a Benghazi fast food restaurant, I once bumped into the top Salafi Madkhali leader, Haftar Abdul-

Fattah ben Ghalboun, who was enjoying a meal with a fellow fighter, both splendidly dressed in army uniform. Meanwhile, Tripoli residents living on the airport road and its surrounding districts grew tired of the Zintani militias treating Tripoli airport as their bounty, and so many of them joined the Misrata-led Dawn offensive.

Haftar's battle to oust the Islamists in Benghazi shows another layer of division which makes understanding the Libyan conflict so complicated. His camp framed the struggle as a mission to rid Libya's second city of jihadists and terrorists, and it is true that many of his opponents were part of Ansar al-Sharia. But there was another rift between the opposing camps. Haftar based his Libyan National Army (LNA) faction on a 'web of tribal alliances'[9] in eastern Libya, including his own tribe, the Ferjani. The Islamists and many other forces opposing him were urban elites, many from families who had once migrated from Misrata. When Haftar declared victory over what he called terrorists in July 2017, he appointed tribesmen to control Benghazi. In 2018 these tribal forces seized much of Derna, another eastern city with a significant jihadist presence.

Misrata vs. Libya

The most prominent example of an urban elite 'revolutionary' camp opposing former regime officials was to be found in Misrata. The city produced some of the most powerful rebel groups, capable of stopping an assault by Gaddafi forces, who surrounded the city for months, leaving only the port open (for supplies). It is also the best organised and safest city, with a close-knit community that distrusts outsiders, and it is this discipline that helps explain the temporary success of the Libya Dawn militia in Tripoli.

The former Misratan rebel groups were integrated into police and security forces and paid by businessmen in mutually beneficial arrangements. There are traffic police and even cameras monitoring the roads, something almost unheard of in the rest of Libya, where few motorists bother using number plates. That gives Misrata a bit of an atmosphere: as if it is located in a special zone, away from the rest of the chaotic country. Whenever I went there it reminded me a bit of my native Germany.

I visited Misrata in 2014 to gauge the mood after Haftar's jets had bombarded the port. The unrecognised government in Tripoli, which had seized the capital in July 2014, insisted I submit a list of interviewees ahead of the trip. I could have sneaked into the city on my own, but with a TV cameraman in tow I decided to play by the rules. Upon arrival at the city council I was given a piece of paper listing my meetings, with almost all interviews actually starting on time. In the rest of the country you would just walk into an office and see what happened. Officials might see you right away or tell you to come back *inshallah bukra* (God willing, tomorrow).

The presence of the militias and the city's special identity made colleagues from other regions wary of Misrata. During visits, Libyan colleagues who were not from Misrata would let me do the talking. 'They are so difficult here,' a journalist from Tripoli kept telling me during a visit. Many in the capital can't stand people from Misrata and see them as Islamists—suspicions they felt were confirmed by the Libya Dawn attack led by hardline commander Salah Badi. The city's relative stability has translated into a special pride often perceived as arrogance—at least that's what many non-Misratans say. 'Misrata is trouble,' you hear from people in tribe-dominated cities such as Zintan and Bani Walid. Relations have worsened since the revolution, as Misratan rebel groups conquered Bani Walid in 2011.[10] Zintan, a region in the western mountains bordering Tunisia, then emerged in 2014 as its most powerful opponent allied to the then internationally recognised government that fled to the east after the Misratan militias conquered Tripoli.

TRIBE VS. REGION VS. TOWN VS. FAMILY

Misrata always felt somewhat independent, a fact which can be explained by its history. Between 1918 and 1922 it was the capital of the short-lived Republic of Tripolitania, emerging from the void as Italy invaded parts of Libya in 1911. Its previous ruler, the Ottoman Empire, backed the resistance against the Italians, who nonetheless crushed the first republican government in the Arab world. During the revolution many rebel fighters brought pictures of the republic's leader, Ramadan Suwaihli, framing their anti-Gaddafi fight in the same tradition of self-reliance in the face of an unfair fight.[11]

Many Misratans feel other cities were slow to help them in 2011, and this has added to a sense that the city must lead the country—though, in fairness, Misrata was only able to resist the assault because of the arms, food and aid shipments sent from rebel headquarters in Benghazi. That feeling is supported by the fact that the city is the country's biggest non-oil trading hub, and plays host to the biggest steel firm, the largest commercial port and tax-free zone, a dairy company and harissa factory, both also the country's biggest. For centuries the city has lived off trade with Turkey, Arab countries and Europe, adding to inhabitants' sense of a mission to lead the rest of the country.

'We in Misrata started already in July 2011 a plan for future industrial development of Libya', said Mohammed al-Tumi, spokesman of a local business council in Misrata that calls itself the 'Libyan council' to hammer home the message that it speaks for the whole country. 'In Benghazi, the revolution was over in three days, but they didn't plan anything for long,' he said, outlining his 'economic vision' of attracting foreign investment when, in December 2013, the country was falling apart. The meeting started on time (I was actually a few minutes late) and we didn't waste any time exchanging formalities. Tumi got right down to business.

While unwilling to discuss the Misratan militias who had just a month before killed more than 40 people in Tripoli by opening fire on a peaceful protest, he had no shortage of business pitches. He spoke at length about plans to build a shopping mall and hotel with the help of investors from the Gulf and Turkey. He was also full of hope that German airline Lufthansa, flying to Tripoli at the time, would add Misrata to its global network. 'Lufthansa has told us that Misrata airport is the best in Libya,' he said.[12]

The city's reputation was hit badly during Libya Dawn's attack on Tripoli in 2014. 'We have a problem with Misrata and the Muslim Brotherhood and other Islamist groups there,' said Mohamed, my landlord in Tobruk, who I stayed with for a week when the hotels were packed with lawmakers and their entourages. Tobruk, 1,200 km from the capital, wasn't involved in the Tripoli clashes, but the violence triggered by Libya Dawn, a group with Islamist links, had given fresh momentum to widespread belief in the east that Misrata was a bastion of Islamist extremists.

As the enormity of the Tripoli attack's impact became clearer to the ever-active business council—which had banked on the Misrata container port weathering the trouble in Tripoli—life continued as normal, at least at first. There were none of the fuel or food shortages gripping much of the rest of the country. Some ambitious businesspeople even hoped for growth as Tripoli and Benghazi harbour were now warzones. That stability—however illusory—was shattered when Haftar's air force started bombing Misrata's commercial port and a nearby steel plant in a successful attempt to scare away shippers and Turkish Airlines, the last large foreign carrier still flying to Libya. Sure enough, the airline pulled out after jets attacked the airport for the third time, just before the morning flight to Istanbul took off. Cargo turnover at the port also collapsed; a senior official from the port's tax-free zone timidly asked me not to write about the fall in numbers while showing me a warehouse hit during an airstrike.[13]

TRIBE VS. REGION VS. TOWN VS. FAMILY

Libyans' aversion to Misrata since the Libya Dawn attack in July 2014 has made many of its residents more introspective, switching from ambitions to lead the country to general complaining. 'It's always Misrata that needs to solve all problems,' said Mohamed Bala, a prominent businessman, commenting on a story about Misrata-based coastguard ships being asked to help out in Zuwara, a region near the Tunisian border that lacked proper boats. This attitude was bolstered when forces from Misrata took on IS in Sirte in 2015, and hundreds of poorly trained Misratan youths were killed in their bid to drive out IS. Misratans complained that the rest of Libya wasn't helping, but they were assisted by US airstrikes the following year.

In yet another division, Islamists and businessmen from Misrata and other western coastal cities opposed a movement demanding a federal political system, popular especially among tribal circles in the east. Worried about neglect in the new Libya after Gaddafi punished the east for dissent by denying development funds, the federalists wanted to return to a power-sharing agreement from the early days of King Idris. They especially wanted to return to a sharing of oil revenues between Libya's three historic regions (west, south and east) based on the 1951 constitution. But it wasn't long before the first cracks in the federalist front appeared after the unseating of Gaddafi: a few campaigners called for a boycott of the 2012 parliamentary vote, which went down badly even with people in the east. The boycott call was later withdrawn.

For Jathran, our oil port rebel, getting Mansour and his men blocking the Hariga port on board simply meant more power in his talks with Tripoli. Shutting off Hariga maximised damage to public finances. At the same time Jathran also broadened his base beyond his own tribe. For Islamists and people from Misrata and other coastal cities, the federal cause was just an excuse to give tribalism a political cover. 'I don't mind federalism. It works in

80 countries,' said Ahmed Zlitnee, an Islamist, sitting in the Tibesti Hotel, the once premier, but now much rundown, venue in Benghazi (it, along with every other hotel in Benghazi, closed down when Haftar launched his war against the Islamists in 2014). 'But I am against it if it's only about tribes.' Zlitnee's name suggests that his family is from Zliten, a city near Misrata, another instance of intersectionality in divided Libya: an Islamist member of the western coastal city hemisphere.

A shopping mall proprietor in Benghazi, Ghanem Sheikhi complained to me that people in Misrata had ripped off the east by lobbying Gaddafi to include eastern oil wells in a central administrative area to which Misrata belonged. 'They are clever, but we want our share,' he said, drawing a rough map of the old administrative zones for me. In fact, this system had made little difference in an administration where state resources were controlled by Gaddafi's inner circle, but it was of symbolic importance to the east, which was otherwise marginalised by western Libya.

Interviewer vs. interviewee

For journalists covering Libya, the existence of its two administrations was a nightmare—it was a daily challenge to work out whether an official you interviewed had any power or knew what he was talking about. It was nearly impossible to run a story based on one official's account, as he might be misleading you to bolster his profile. Visiting a ministry in Tripoli could bring many surprises. After meeting a department head in 2014, his deputy called me:

> 'Do you want to meet? The guy you met before does not represent anything. I can meet you to tell you everything what's going on. Let's meet in a supermarket café so my boss won't get suspicious if he bumps into us.'

TRIBE VS. REGION VS. TOWN VS. FAMILY

You could go to one ministry, get a paper—like a visa request—stamped, and go to the next office in the same ministry where someone would not accept the stamp, questioning its legitimacy or having his own rules, often depending on his mood on that particular day.

As there was no functioning state, officials—often acting in a private capacity—uploaded official documents and sensitive materials such as central bank account statements, state oil firm contracts and bilateral agreements regarding the overseas training of Libyan soldiers to social media. You would even find military orders to buy weapons from countries like Belarus or Ukraine. There would always be someone with a smartphone taking pictures in a government office or during a high-level meeting. Just minutes after a car bombing, the shelling of an oil tanker or a military aircraft crash, a video would be posted online. Such media helped to fill coverage gaps; travelling inside Libya was often too dangerous, but every video or document needed to be checked against eyewitness accounts and other sources, as activists and militias sought to manipulate public opinion by recycling old pictures and forging documents. It wasn't hard for militias to gain access to ministry letterheads and stamps.

While officials, relishing their newfound freedom, were open to meeting with me after the 2011 revolution, there were limits and consequences for journalists and interviewees. Meetings with government officials would follow a certain routine: for the first five to ten minutes the interview would be rudimentary, with interviewees unwilling to divert from the prescribed government line. Interviewees would claim everything was fine, *mia fil al-mia* (100 per cent). Once I gained their trust—showing an interest in the country, complimenting them on the transition and talking in Arabic—they would open up. Having covered the secretive regimes of Sudan and Saudi Arabia (where the highest profile interview I could ever score was with an assistant education minister), post-Gaddafi Libya was a breeze. You could walk into a ministry, police station or municipal building and ask to see whoever was in charge. The prime minister, oil officials and hardcore Islamist fighters—everybody in the initial years after Gaddafi's overthrow, spoke openly. Top officials sometimes treated interviews like therapy: an opportunity to vent their anger and frustration at being bullied by militias to put them on the state payroll and do whatever they demanded.

The trouble only started after the interview. Deputy central bank governor Ali Salim al-Hibri, in the middle of a November 2013 interview about the rapidly worsening economic situation, suddenly started to shout about the public's unrealistic demands for state oil jobs. 'Each person is looking only after his interest and not working as a nation,' he said, sitting in his large office in the bank's headquarters in Tripoli's old city.[14] He went on to disclose that the bank had been forced to burn its foreign reserves to offset a slump in oil production caused by public protest. It was a great scoop, but the interview took its usual turn in Libya—officials get cold feet, often after a complaint or threat from a militia. Hours after the interview had run, the central bank issued a denial, claiming foreign reserves had never been mentioned and warning foreign media to adhere to professional standards and accuracy when reporting news.[15]

Such denialism was common in Libya. I started to evaluate the potential for trouble for the interviewee and myself by omitting certain disclosures and adding an extra layer of balance as cover. At the Zawiya refinery, I managed to land a permit to meet its managers at a time when there were widespread fuel shortages. The managers tried to hammer home the message that queues at petrol stations were caused not by a real supply problem, but by a lack of trust in the post-war state. At the same time, they admitted that the refinery was running at half capacity. 'New petrol imports are on the way,' said Hassan al-Haj, the refinery's operations manager. But when an engineer pointed out that output was actually 10,000 barrels a day lower than Haj had said, I realised both the interest it would generate among international oil traders and the difficult position it would put both me and my respondents in. I tried to bury the snippet further down in my report, but it still proved a focus for the ordinary Libyans who read the story online. By nightfall, queues formed at petrol stations in Tripoli. An angry refinery official called, first shouting and then pleading with me to remove the remark. 'Please, people have lost their head. They queue because of that what the engineer in the control room said,' he said. Even my own colleagues were worried that angry militiamen might turn up at our villa. We agreed to update the story, adding yet more assurances from the refinery that everything was under control, a claim already made in the initial report.[16] With armed youths roaming around the capital unchallenged, journalistic ethics sometimes have to take a backseat.

The Tobruk bubble

There is no doubt that Libya's divisions were deepened by the post-Gaddafi power struggle. The 2014 battles for Tripoli and Benghazi displaced some 100,000 people and forced another 150,000 to flee abroad.[17] In Benghazi, more still had to leave their homes as they were no longer welcome by the forces of General Haftar.

It was never easy to win the trust of officials suspicious of foreign journalists, but the events of 2014 made things much worse, adding an extra layer of paranoia which I noticed when travelling to Tobruk in September 2014. I left Tripoli in July, setting up shop in Cairo to cover Libya remotely when the capital and Benghazi became too dangerous. Our Tripoli team also evacuated, while reporters in Benghazi and Misrata were also laying low as battles with artillery, tanks and aircraft raged on.

The stress of leaving our Tripoli villa was complicated by Tripoli International Airport being taken out of action as Libya Dawn troops attacked the entrenched Zintani forces. Authorities scrambled to open the air base of Mitiga for civilian traffic, moving the remaining fleet which had survived the battle there. We spent days at the crowded ticket counter competing with hundreds of others trying to get out. One morning, my wife stood next to a closed Libyan Airlines counter, when suddenly an employee shouted, 'Tickets for Istanbul!' She convinced him to hand over two tickets and we were on our way just a few hours later.

As the internationally recognised government headed by Thinni had set up shop in the east, I flew from Egypt to Tobruk—where the House of Representatives (HoR) was now based—in September. Benghazi would have been more interesting, but was too dangerous—the battle between Haftar and his opponents was still in full swing. Tobruk had turned into a new home for those who had fled Tripoli—Libya Dawn militias threatened those accused of opposing them, basically anyone who didn't support them: militias attacked the Zintan-backing Alassema TV station and kidnapped three members of staff.[18] In the east, opponents of Haftar received similar treatment and fled to Tripoli.

The Tobruk bubble fuelled frustrations and divisions, as those who had until a few months ago enjoyed power and a large government office in Tripoli were now stuck in a small town, closer to Cairo than the capital. Tobruk, with its skyline dominated by rundown prefab multi-storey buildings with once obligatory green windowpanes, was dead at night, with only one decent Syrian eatery and a fish restaurant to dine out in. Like other eastern cities, Gaddafi had neglected Tobruk, which was then served by just one weekly flight to the capital.

Tobruk was a prison: it was impossible to go by road to the main eastern city of Benghazi as the jihadi hotspot Derna, a no-go zone, lies halfway between the two cities. That fostered a bunker mentality, and the few foreign reporters who made it through the nightmare of getting a special eastern visa on top of the regular Libyan visa, were treated with suspicion.

An official in the parliamentary press department wanted me to clear interviews with him 'for security reasons'. He would then advise the lawmaker I wanted to approach not to talk to me, claiming my questions would get them in trouble. I protested to his boss, who denied there was such a policy, but with no real state in place this particularly intimidating official was free to create his own, private rules. He would hassle me and other journalists and even listen in to television interviews. Spending my days in the lobby—the only place in town with reliable internet—I would approach lawmakers coming out of the assembly, discreetly asking whether they could talk to me, all the while watching out for this official.

That wasn't the only breakdown in authority there. The parliamentary media department issued me a pass to enter the Salam Hotel, the city's biggest, which was then housing lawmakers and their families. But every morning, travelling by taxi from my rented apartment, I made my way to the first of two checkpoints at the gate, where the soldiers refused to let me through. 'This pass is not valid. I don't recognise this,' the commander at the makeshift checkpoint said. When asked which permit he would accept, he said: 'My commander ordered me not to let anyone through without his permission and a valid pass.' His comrades, wearing a mix of army and police uniforms and civilian clothes, were sitting on camping chairs enjoying cappuccinos and playing with their smartphones while one of them manned the gate. Every time I had to call the press office, ask staff there to call their commander and send a minibus to get me in, often after a shouting match between the officials.

Ironically, inside the building lawmakers would go on interminably that the east had established a 'proper army' based on the rule of law, compared to the militias controlling western Libya and in contrast to Tripoli with its rival government. 'The men at the gate are soldiers of the Libyan army,' Ali Tekbali, an anti-Islamist lawmaker from Tripoli, told me over tea. He also insisted the situation in Benghazi was improving, despite some districts having been turned to rubble after weeks of airstrikes by Haftar's forces. In the end, the guards at the outer gate were typical militiamen who only took orders from their commanders, who in turn had their own rules.

The hotel bubble certainly contributed to a mismatch between reality and imagination. Lawmakers lived and worked in the hotel: one hall had been converted into an assembly hall, with no journalists allowed to visit, even when it was not in session, as the administration was embarrassed attendance had fallen to less than half of the supposedly 200 members. By 2015 there were around 60 lawmakers left and later attendance dropped to 40 or so. Their families spent the day mostly by the outdoor swimming pool, though nobody actually dared use it, as it hadn't been cleaned for a long time.

During the day there were sessions like in any parliament—discussing the budget, laws to regulate telecommunication or education—but the main focus was still on pumping out political statements like in the old GNC assembly, with little time for legislation. Not that it mattered: authority did not extend beyond Tobruk or some other eastern cities secured by Haftar. It wasn't long until divisions erupted between the pro-Haftar federalist factions led by the son of Haftar's air force commander and those who were afraid of Haftar trying to reinstate Gaddafi's old police state, with Haftar at the top. But in the end even those against Haftar would have no choice to back him for their own survival. 'Without Haftar [the militant Islamist] Ansar al-Sharia would have attacked parliament,' said Fathi al-Gabasi, another lawmaker. Deputies then argued long about getting jobs in the toothless cabinet of Prime Minister Thinni, based in Bayda some 250 km away. Lawmakers were shouting and even throwing chairs at each other one night in September 2014,[19] reviving the arguments in the GNC assembly about getting access for various groups to state money. The Zintan factions wanted the defence ministry in Thinni's cabinet to force authorities to hire their youth.

It was difficult for me cover events during the visit because much of parliament's activity took place late at night, in line with the rest of Libya where many take a nap in the afternoon. My rented apartment was around 15 km away and I was reluctant to get a taxi from the streets. My Arabic is good enough to pass as a non-Westerner, but still I preferred to walk instead of using a taxi, passing state buildings abandoned since the revolution or rundown residential houses on my way home. I often waited until a friendly employee at the press department would head home, throwing myself at his mercy to get me home safely. Walking back late one night over a flyover—littered with discarded plastic bags—I almost dropped 15 metres through a huge hole in the tarmac that I hadn't seen, as streetlights were not working.

Late at night, emotions often ran high when, over a waterpipe or tea, lawmakers and their aides complained about what a forlorn place they had landed in. Imagine you were an official sitting at night in your hotel room, watching the former state TV news channel Wataniya, which now belonged to Libya Dawn and whose officials were giving interviews from a ministry you had been working in until summer 2014. Libya Dawn's first Prime Minister Hassi made a point of giving every visiting foreign journalist an interview in Thinni's former office to hammer home the message about who was now in charge.

'NATO left us with these militias and terrorists like Ansar al-Sharia,' the Tripoli lawmaker Tekbali told me one night late in the Salam Hotel. He was picking on me as a citizen of a NATO member country. 'You want us to negotiate with these terrorists,' he said. By 'terrorists' he meant Libya Dawn, which had seized Tripoli, not the former rebel groups in the east which Haftar had united as the LNA. 'We need weapons to fight.'

For him, Tobruk was like political asylum. A professor in a geology university department, he had fled Tripoli, leaving his house behind after Islamists had burned his effigy on the central Martyrs' Square. 'We will win militarily over these people,' he said, referring to Libya Dawn. I met him months later in a café in Cairo, where he was taking a break. He was still convinced that the UN talks to end the conflict between the two governments were going nowhere. 'This is just talk from both sides,' he said. He showed me pictures of his face next to women, which he said Islamists had forged to discredit him with alleged girl-friends. 'I wish it was true,' he said with a chuckle, while looking exhausted at the same time. He suffered a massive stroke a few months later.

Tobruk's division from the rest of the country hasn't healed. Some I met there in 2014 haven't gone back to Tripoli since, even though the Libya Dawn government was replaced by a UN-backed administration in 2016. They fear they will be targeted as Haftar supporters, though many have fallen out with the general and so cannot return to Benghazi either.

* * *

Lawmakers from the HoR long resisted pressure by the UN to approve legislation for elections to unify the country and create a national government. It was obvious they feared losing their jobs, having become cosy in Tobruk. For months, lawmakers postponed sessions to approve a law to hold a constitutional referendum and then later elections, making excuses. 'It is now clear that the postponed sessions and contradictory public statements were simply intended to waste time. The body calling itself Libya's sole legislature is largely sterile,' UN Special Envoy

Ghassan Salamé told the UN Security Council in November 2018. Two weeks later, parliament finally agreed on a law, but competition has seen divisions erupting between its President Aguila Saleh and Haftar. Saleh helped Haftar gain legitimacy by signing a decree reinstating him as a retired general in 2014, but later got his own taste for power with the other lawmakers based in Tobruk. Saleh rarely travels to Benghazi, where Haftar is based in a barracks just outside the city.

As Libya's conflict evolved, new divisions appeared—often on top of existing ones. When I travelled to Tripoli in April 2018 after three months of waiting for a visa, I met a group of women exiled from Benghazi. They had backed the Islamists and other groups fighting Haftar but had to flee in the middle of the night to escape the revenge of Haftar's forces. Here you had the previously mentioned divisions of former army soldiers in the form of Haftar's troops and those from the 'revolutionary camp' who feared a coup from the old regime. There was also the question of tribes versus community dwellers and divisions between east and west. Haftar's forces are mostly eastern tribes, while his opponents historically come from Misrata. Now a new layer was added: the Benghazi exiles who found themselves almost foreigners in Tripoli.

They tried to start a new life but struggled to legitimise their stay, having left behind vital documents from their so-called family books (which every Libyan has)—without these it's nearly impossible to get identity cards or passports. Tripoli authorities refused to issue new papers, referring them to the central registry in Benghazi. But eastern authorities did not issue replacements, not even for relatives or friends who went there to vouch for the Tripoli exiles—security and Haftar's forces labelled them as 'terrorists'. Twenty-one-year-old Fatma was one such example.[20] Her family couldn't even access her bank account after fleeing to Tripoli from Benghazi. The Tripoli branch of the same bank refused to access her Benghazi holdings. One would think you could sort it out—Benghazi is just a 50-minute flight away—but such things are impossible for those who are seen as terrorists. 'My family was fighting Haftar, so we had to flee after the LNA attacked our house in the middle of the night,' she said. 'I can't go back because I would get arrested.'

She struggled to continue her studies because her exam results from Benghazi University were missing and she could not get them replaced, and Tripoli University wouldn't enrol her without them. Her father could not access the salary payments in her Benghazi account, while one of her brothers was unable to marry as he had lost his birth certificate, which he could not replace in Tripoli—a problem encountered by other Benghazi exiles. One of my colleagues, who had nothing to do with the Islamists, spent years trying to get a new passport because the Tripoli passport office refused to serve him. This policy changed in 2016, but many issues remained, such as the lack of marriage certificates. Some 13,000 families, roughly between 60,000 and 70,000 individuals, were stranded in exile.[21] The exile council, made up of former elected municipal members sacked by Haftar and replaced by a military governor, lobbied the Tripoli government, but got no financial support and hit walls when it came to lost documents which could only be replaced in Benghazi.

I wanted to meet as many Benghazi exiles as possible, but it took time to win their trust, even after a Libyan friend had introduced me to the group. I only had limited time as my security adviser had been turned back at Mitiga airport for a visa issue. I couldn't fly back with him to Tunis because the flight was full. Luckily it was high season, and with Libyan carriers struggling to keep the shrinking fleet in the air, I managed to stay for five more days. There wasn't much time to take security preparations. I didn't want interviewees to visit our office villa, so after making contact by phone I visited them in cafés or in a private home doubling as the office of the Benghazi exile council. My worries were unnecessary—thanks to Libyan hospitality, strangers I had only communicated with via text messages and phone calls received me.

It wasn't only opponents to Haftar who couldn't go back. Another person I spoke to was an oil engineer called Mahmoud who hailed from the same tribe as Haftar, but had lost both his house and an apartment—the former having been hit by an airstrike by Haftar's fledgling air force and the latter by rough gangs affiliated to the LNA, who seized houses from opponents as revenge.[22] I don't have a problem with Haftar, but I fear going back because everyone who left Benghazi in 2014 is seen as 'Daesh', he said. With Haftar entrenched in the east and eyeing a national role, it seemed unlikely that his former opponents would go home anytime soon. Their worst nightmares came true when Haftar's forces launched an offensive to take the capital in April 2019.[23] A 26-year-old female friend of Fatma, who only gave her family name of Saghili, sent me this text message: 'I'm so sad that Haftar comes to Tripoli. I guess we can never run away from him.'

6

FUELLING CONFLICT

When interior ministry officer Ibrahim al-Mumin comes to work in a rundown white cubicle building in the eastern town of Musaid, he usually stares at an empty office. He has 120 border guards on the payroll to patrol the porous desert border with Egypt, but his employees often don't show up. 'Maybe 30 come to work,' Mumin said, sitting at a large desk in his office on the first floor. 'The rest goes on the 30th to the bank to collect their salaries.'[1]

Libya has one of the world's largest public services. Around 1.8 million adults, almost a third of Libya's population, work for the state.[2] The country never had much of a private sector as oil production has dominated the economy since the 1960s, providing little incentive to build up alternatives when everything was so easily imported. Gaddafi followed Idris's example, expanding the latter's patronage system after his coup, using the public sector to buy political loyalty and offering Libyans a salary in exchange not so much for work, but for putting up with his revolution. In his Green Book, Gaddafi talked of creating a 'stateless' society, but he needed an enormous public service to make his revolution work, and resorted to creating meaningless jobs in overstaffed ministries in order to keep the peace.

He had another, related motive: he deeply distrusted private firms, viewing them as a source of dissent. Even now, very few people work for the private sector, and many of those who are in business often get a salary from the state as well. If there is one thing its multiple players agree upon—from radical Islamists to secular forces and former Gaddafi-era soldiers—it is that in Libya, you must not try to reform the welfare state.

By 2017, Libya had upwards of an estimated 1.5 million civil servants, but a third of them were further exploiting a breakdown in state authority by claiming two salaries, says Husni Bey, chairman of the HB Group, the largest private sector firm.[3] Diplomats put the number at 1.8 million in 2019, as the eastern parallel administration hired its own staff, adding thousands more civil servants. Reliable official data does not exist in Libya: I often asked officials about the number of civil servants, but even the central bank, which processes their salaries, and the head of the parliamentary budget committee were unable to provide a reliable figure—part of the legacy of secrecy under Gaddafi. Gaddafi officials are also thought to have destroyed any records from Idris's reign that might otherwise have survived.

The Tripoli-based foreign minister of the unrecognised Libyan Dawn administration, Ghirani, who I interviewed in November 2014, had no idea how many people were employed by his ministry—he only said 'thousands'. By the end of the 1980s there were only 120,000 civil servants, but this number rose to 800,000 by 2010, according to Bey. Gaddafi boosted the number of civil servants to discourage dissent, a trend that continued throughout the post 2011-chaos. As state institutions started to disintegrate and with violence spreading, a meaningful supervision of public salary payments ceased to exist, opening the door to massive corruption as people started to claim multiple salaries.

Others even continued receiving salaries long after their work ceased, as in the case of staff at the Ougadougou conference hall complex in Gaddafi's hometown, Sirte, where the leader staged summits hosting foreign leaders, requiring hundreds of security and administrative workers. The buzz of activity stopped in 2011, after which the sprawling complex was largely unused until Islamic State (IS) turned the complex into their headquarters when they seized the town in 2015. 'I stopped going to the Ougadougou hall in 2011, but kept collecting my salary every month,' said Ali Miftah, who I met in October 2017 during a visit to the city. At that point, the city was again under the control of Libyan forces who had expelled the jihadists. 'My salary was cut from 800 dinars to 400 dinars but it never stopped,' he said, showing me his house, which was destroyed during the military campaign to oust IS. Like many Sirte residents, he had never accepted the fall of the old regime, complaining his hometown had been neglected, which is partly true. Many Libyans cast Sirte residents as traitors to the revolution, and the weak governments in Tripoli had done little to rebuild city districts heavily damaged in two periods at the centre of the conflict: in 2011 after rebels from Misrata seized the city during the revolution, and in 2016 when US airstrikes flattened whole districts in the campaign against IS.

A major difficulty in the fight to curb such instances of fraud is a lack of a centralised payment system for public servants. I've met Libyans living abroad who had relatives picking up their salaries on their behalf. Several governments and the central bank tried after the revolution to introduce a national identity card to avoid people claiming multiple salaries, but the scheme was not applied throughout the country, especially since eastern parallel authorities allied to Haftar built up new state bodies and ministries. Prime Minister Ali Zeidan (2012–2014) knew about this problem, but lacked any real power or competent advisers who might have been able to act on his concerns. For all the complexities of the problem, there were also more straightforward boundaries: when a militia or tribal leader arrived at a branch of Jumhuriya State Bank to collect salaries for his own heavily armed men, with some of them waiting in trucks mounted with anti-aircraft guns outside, what bank clerk would challenge the request, let alone refuse to pay out the salaries?

'There is no need to beg.'

When the first signs of unrest appeared in 2011, Gaddafi quickly administered pay rises in a futile attempt to discourage those on the public payroll from joining the protests.[4] That left Libya's rulers too afraid to reverse the pay increases, with a soaring public servant bill which made it impossible to use state funds to overhaul the country's dilapidated infrastructure and build schools, roads and hospitals. In 2014[5]—the last year in which Libya had a nationwide, parliament-approved budget—the public wage bill was some 24 billion Libyan dinars ($17 billion), out of a budget of 57 billion dinars.[6] Without the double salary payments, the figure should have been closer to 18 billion dinars, said Bey. 'Libya definitely has the highest per capita civil service/population ratio, of over 17 per cent, if not considering public owned companies,' he said. In 2011, Libya spent only 14.8 billion dinars on public salaries.[7]

Facing a slump in oil revenues from when militias and tribesmen began to block crude oil export terminals, oilfields and pipelines in 2013, officials used the budgets earmarked for development projects to pay the massive wage bill—a short-sighted solution that only exacerbated Libyans' frustrations, finding that no money was available for schools or roads. Oil revenues improved from 2017, with crude production hovering at around a million barrels a day for much of 2018. That boosted oil revenues by 78 per cent—to $24.4 billion—but the pattern of spending remained unchanged: some 75 per cent of the budget was still being squandered on public salaries and subsidies.[8]

Under Gaddafi, there was no doubt that the living standards of Libyans were much lower than in other oil-producing countries, as much of the oil and gas revenues, the state's only source of revenue, enriched Gaddafi's family, funded his security apparatus, financed development projects in Africa and otherwise disappeared in his inefficient Soviet-style state economy. Still, Libyans were much better off than Egyptians, Moroccans or Tunisians, who had no cradle-to-grave welfare state to support them. Gaddafi once admonished poor women in Libya, arguing that they had no reason to beg as they were entitled to *mash asassi*, or a basic living allowance provided to those in need. 'Why do you beg? You humiliate us in front of the world!' he fumed at a woman during a public appearance in Tripoli, broadcast by state TV. The woman was asking for medicine she alleged was not available in state hospitals, in order to treat her sick son. 'Where is your son? Go with your son to the state hospital. He will be treated there for free. Why do you beg? Why do you beg?' he repeated. 'There are thousands of people who will receive you at hospitals,' he told a Tunisian lady living in Libya. 'Your husband works at the post office. So you have a salary. There is no need to beg.'[9]

I reported for Reuters from seven oil producers (Kuwait, Saudi Arabia, Sudan, South Sudan, Iraq, Libya and Nigeria) and have seen how difficult it can be to force people to make changes by hiring fewer state employees. But in the case of Libya, the consequences of spending almost all available resources on an unproductive public service was even worse than in other countries, because it strengthened militias who managed to put their men on the public payroll. The focus on the state as the country's principle employer also prevented the establishment of the private sector, which would have been possible had more funds been used on alternative job training or to encourage private investment.

Gaddafi's Green Book called on workers to take over private firms. 'No records were taken, so there was no trace ability of funds, stocks, machinery,' Bey told me. 'Overnight, employers and owners were chased out of their businesses, and banks changed personal accounts.' Gaddafi claimed that these moves freed workers at dairy or soft drink firms from 'capitalist exploitation'.[10] But in reality he turned them into unproductive state employees, as firms were increasingly required to fill hiring quotas in exchange for loyalty, rather than to boost their productivity. That left the country with very few private firms which, although terribly overstaffed, produced little. Whenever I went shopping I was surprised that basic food items such as cheese, milk, juice and cookies came from Germany, Italy and other European countries, paid for with Libya's hard currency reserves. At best, there was one local cheese product, dwarfed on the shelves by 20 higher quality offerings from abroad. In western Libya, even eggs sometimes come from Tunisia. 'We've never had dairies,' Tarek, a policeman and friend told me over a picnic in the eastern city of Tobruk. Most of Libya's industrial plants have not reopened since the revolution due to the instability, or because they ran out of spare parts and functioning machines. Driving through Libya, you will often see deserted entrances to factories, overgrown with weeds—nature making its bid to reclaim these once productive spaces from the state.

Exploration, extraction and extortion

Libya's economy depends on oil and gas exports to fund its extensive welfare state and to earn hard currency to import almost everything it needs. It does not pump as much crude as Saudi Arabia, Iraq or Kuwait, but its oil is prized for its quality, and the country's proximity to European markets means lower freight charges than the Gulf. Libya has crude reserves worth some 48 billion barrels, making it Africa's biggest oil producer. It is also the fifth-largest holder of natural gas reserves on the continent. Half of its gas production is used to generate electricity, while the other half is exported to Italy via the 520 km Greenstream offshore pipeline.[11] Crude oil exports alone account for 80 per cent of state revenues, but gas exports—less affected by oilfield grabs by power-hungry militias—have become increasingly important.[12]

Oil production, carried out by foreign companies, started in 1961 at just 20,000 barrels a day, surging to 3 million by 1969. Libya's 1955 petroleum law attracted some of the biggest oil firms and some smaller, independent companies, providing a mix which later helped the Gaddafi regime to continue producing when US firms pulled out over the Reagan administration's conflict with the 'mad dog', Gaddafi. Libya rose to become the fourth-largest oil producer in 1971 when output peaked at 3.7 million barrels a day. Output fell again as Libya ordered oil firms to make cuts to avoid overpumping and forced them to agree on higher prices per barrel—a strategy so successful it has even helped other producers to negotiate better terms.[13] Since 1973, so-called production-sharing agreements came into effect, in which the state oil company, the National Oil Corporation (NOC), partners with a foreign company. Various European and American firms have operated in Libya, some leaving and others entering since exploration started.

Thanks to the historic ties between Italy and Libya, Italian energy firm ENI is one of the biggest players, operating the Mellitah gas complex west of Tripoli, the Greenstream gas export pipeline and offshore operations alongside NOC. Germany's Wintershall has also long been present in Libya, although it never signed a production-sharing agreement. US firms Marathon,

Conoco Phillips and Hess are also active, as well as France's Total, but their production in the Sirte basin in the so-called Oil Crescent has been affected by militia fighting and Islamic State (IS) attacks. Around 12 Libyan and foreign workers were killed in 2015 when IS militants attacked the Mabrook oilfield, in which Total has a stake.[14] There are also some smaller foreign oil firms and a Norwegian fertiliser company active in Libya. The instability in the central Sirte basin meant that the biggest active field since the uprising has been El Sharara, cooperatively run by Spain's Repsol, France's Total, Austria's OMV, Norway's Equinor and the NOC, deep in the southwestern desert. The field, which pumps around 315,000 barrels a day, has been repeatedly shut down by gunmen, guards and tribesmen seeking to blackmail the weak Libyan state for financial gain.

Oil and gas infrastructure wasn't significantly damaged during the uprising, but it has never regained its former production levels of around 1.6 million barrels a day before 2011, as oilfields have become key political (and actual) battlegrounds for the country's warring and would-be leaders. It started on a large scale with the seizure of eastern oil ports by Ibrahim Jathran, but blockages have continued to this day, as the state is too weak to protect facilities. Output comes only from existing fields; there is hardly any oil exploration taking place due to ongoing instability. Foreign firms have largely moved their expatriate staff out of the country and halted projects that go beyond regular, well-established activity.

NOC, with its headquarters in Tripoli, has survived as an entity despite attempts in the east to form a separate oil firm with the power to sign its own contracts—for legal reasons oil firms, foreign buyers and banks have preferred to deal with the existing NOC structure under its current chairman, Mustafa Sanallah. NOC is by far the most professional state body, and even Gaddafi spared it from his revolutionary zeal, recognising the importance of oil and gas exports to his welfare state. Many of its staff studied abroad, and the organisation is very efficient: appointments are usually kept, a total contrast to the situation found in government ministries. Even the headquarters themselves look different to the rest of the city, with its shiny blue shaded glass wall a stark contrast to the decaying buildings that make up the rest of the Tripoli skyline. Entering the tower-shaped building feels a little like leaving Libya altogether.[15]

But dealing with NOC brought its own, very specific challenges. As with other official data, it has become very difficult to get accurate technical information on the hydrocarbon industry. Tired of the pressure exerted on it by militias, in 2014 NOC became increasingly reluctant to publish production figures, or even to announce when an oilfield had reopened following a protest. Officials feared the good news of a field going back online would encourage others to form a new blockade, and not without good reason. If production approached 800,000 barrels a day, protests would sometimes begin, and civilians would seize oilfields to press for jobs at the NOC. In an act of transparent bribery, some would demand jobs as security guards, tasked with protecting the oil facilities from the selfsame occupation. Foreign news agencies reported the resumption of extraction at the El Feel oilfield, which in 2015 was blocked by a protest which caused almost a month's delay. NOC didn't announce the reopening in a bid to avoid unwanted attention. Reporters calling oil officials would often be greeted by shouting, sarcastic jokes, or laughter when they inquired about oil production figures—often the phone was not answered at all. I sympathised with the NOC spokesman and other senior officials working out of NOC headquarters: the oil sector was the only professional institution in Libya, save for the central bank, but they were pawns in the hands of armed groups and tribesmen who made a business of seizing oilfields. The NOC spokesman was often annoyed when I called, but when I visited him in his office in Tripoli he was extremely welcoming (if a little stressed out), and talked at length about how tired he was of his firm being blackmailed by militias.

In 2018, oil production rose to 1.3 million barrels a day, its highest level since 2013.[16] Some oilfields put out of service in 2014 were finally back online. It wasn't long before various groups, state guards, and even NOC staff, demanded salary increases—the latter hit hard by inflation as they were paid in dinars, which had lost heavily against the dollar on the black market in recent years. In 2013, authorities promised a 67 per cent pay increase that was never implemented, as oil revenues fell sharply due to port blockades.

In 2017 NOC made a push for further transparency by more regularly publishing production, oil revenue and fuel consumption data. Its chairman, Mustafa Sanalla, is widely seen by analysts and diplomats as a competent technocrat trying to serve the whole country. He is welcomed at business conferences, embassies, universities and think tanks like Chatham House in London. But away from the glare of such public events, NOC has its own way of dealing with journalists seeking information about oilfield closures. The company hired communications specialists in the UK. I had become accustomed to pressure, intimidation and shouting from Libyan officials—these things are simply part of the job description when covering Libya. But this was different: suddenly foreigners were doing the job of 'handling' journalists on behalf of the Libyan state. Often when I called NOC for comment on an oil workers' protest, I was discouraged from writing about it as the firm feared the stories might inspire more to join future protests. When I wanted to confirm that a pipeline or oilfield had been blocked, I was asked to hold the story back until an official statement had been issued, which would sometimes come hours later—too late for the oil markets. The PR specialists—under pressure from their angry clients in Tripoli—provided timely information only to those who cooperated, parroting their line that any blockade was instigated by armed militias. That was often true, but in Libya the picture is often not immediately clear, and rarely so black and white.

A lack of maintenance and investment took its toll, as NOC only had access to emergency funds to repair and fix oil and gas fields, and habitually failed to pay its share of the costs it shared with foreign firms. With reduced oil production and a protracted era of low prices between 2014 and 2017, it became increasingly difficult to fund the welfare state, and not just because of the country's enormous public service salary costs.[17]

Where bread is cheaper than water

Apart from public salaries, the Libyan budget is spent mostly on subsidies and other forms of state assistance—from medical treatment and study abroad to household electricity. In 2018, 7.8 billion dinars were spent on subsidies.[18] The biggest chunk of this is spent on fuel subsidies: the central bank spent $4.7 billion on imports, offering motorists one of the world's lowest pump prices. Much of Libya's fuel is imported, as the country's refinery capacity is around 130,000 barrels a day. The biggest refinery in Ras Lanuf in the east, with a capacity of 220,000 barrels per day, never resumed work after the revolution due to a legal battle with its venture partner, the Ghurair group of the UAE. The Zawiya refinery, some 40 km west of Tripoli, operates well below its capacity of 120,000 barrels a day, as protesters regularly stop crude flows from the El Sharara field deep in the south to make political or financial demands. There is also a tiny refinery in Tobruk.

The low fuel prices present a major opportunity to engage in fuel smuggling. In 2018, some 46 per cent of locally produced or imported fuel was smuggled abroad, causing damages of $750 million, according to NOC.[19] Much of the smuggled product goes to Tunisia (by truck) and Malta (by boat) but also to Libya's southern neighbours, involving militias, tribesmen and other armed groups. Southern Tunisia benefits greatly from smuggled Libyan petrol, which is sold openly in the streets of border towns. NOC has repeatedly tried clamping down on smuggling, but with little success. In 2018, militias stormed the offices of the Brega marketing firm, which is in charge of importing and distributing fuel, and tried forcing the new chairman (who had instigated a campaign to fight smugglers) to resign. They even ran a campaign on social media against him.[20] More recently, fuel is increasingly sold on the black market inside Libya. 'As much as one-third of the supply of some fuels—such as petrol and diesel—is believed to be diverted to the black market each year, totalling around 1.3 million tonnes. This is enough petrol to fill 178 Olympic-sized swimming pools,' wrote Tim Eaton, Libya analyst, in a research report for Chatham House.[21]

The one area in which authorities began tangible economic reforms was in food subsidies. From 2019, Libya had budgeted to stop subsidising wheat and other basic food items, having gradually reduced them over a period of several years.[22] I am sceptical that authorities are able to implement this fully, given that Libyans are used to receiving free bread from the state. Like other Arab countries, Libya has long subsidised bread, which made it the largest bread consumer per capita, according to the agency charged with the distribution of wheat imports. The average Libyan consumes 15 kg of flour per person, per month—or 180 kg annually. The closest runners-up are 5 or 6 kg a month, said Jamal El-Shibani, head of the state Price Stability Fund (PSF) organising flour production across Libya until subsidies got lifted.[23] In the United Kingdom, for example, the annual consumption per person is around 59 kg.[24]

Even if there are no more direct subsidies, bread prices are still kept low as the central bank allocates hard currency at an exchange rate lower than that of the black market.[25] When I visited Tripoli in June 2019, you could buy four large loaves for 0.250 dinars, less than 20 cents. There is still more bread on offer than needed, though the move to end bread subsidies was long overdue. Six million Libyans couldn't possibly eat all the bread the country produces without suffering extraordinary levels of obesity. Much of the bread, therefore, gets wasted. When you order food in a restaurant, waiters put piles of baguettes on the table, even if you order a pizza. Often not touched by diners, the bowlful of bread will then go straight to the bin. When I first came to Libya I tried to refuse the bread, but gave up, as most restaurant owners would just shrug or say that bread was cheaper than mineral water. Bread is also the main side dish—rice and potatoes are almost non-existent in Libya.

Libyan farmers, lacking rainfall but also modern equipment, produce only 10 per cent of the country's wheat. The rest is imported at high cost, as shipping insurance risk premiums are added to persuade foreign shippers to call at Libyan ports. The flour is shipped to more than 16 state-owned mills. Some of it is, as you would expect, is used by bakeries, but much of the staple was creamed off by workers and sold via the same smuggling network that ships African migrants and weapons. Subsidies were lifted in 2019, and it remains to be seen if this will put a stop to flour smuggling. 'These countries do not need to import wheat,' said Idris, the chairman of the biggest Tripoli mill, Matahan. 'The whole subsidy system doesn't make sense. It doesn't help the poor, it helps black market traders,' he said in 2013, sitting in his office in a tower-like office complex where adverts for the firm's products, such as macaroni, are from the Gaddafi era.[26]

Authorities also ended subsidies for other basic food items in 2019, but again, the decision came years too late. The Matahan mill was, until recently, producing a host of other basic food items—from rice to pasta—sold at a fraction of production prices in a nationwide network of cooperative supermarkets. You can get 12 packets of macaroni for only $2. Gaddafi introduced the retail chains to guarantee cheap basic food items, while the regime restricted imports of higher quality food. The new rulers lifted these restrictions, which made the dusty coop markets superfluous. My photographer friend still uses them, but just once or twice a month. 'The quality is not great,' he says.

Nowadays, people head to new, private supermarkets offering French cheese, Italian pasta and Swiss chocolate. These stores are springing up everywhere—we had three well-stocked supermarkets just around the corner from our office villa. A large hypermarket, the Mahari, was close by. I often stocked up there for my wife, as they had European food products that were hard to get in Cairo, where we lived from 2014 to 2015. Even while based in Tunisia from 2017 to 2019, I bought Austrian juice, Italian pasta sauce, British porridge oats and Italian shoes whenever I visited Tripoli.

Arrested development

The state never had much left for development and infrastructure projects under Gaddafi, a trend that drastically worsened in 2011. In 2010, the public wage bill accounted for just 17 per cent of the budget, but has surged ever since the revolution, as militias recruited more fighters.[27] In 2014, the public wage bill was around 24 billion Libyan dinars ($19 billion),[28] out of around 56 billion dinars, while subsidies cost around 12.7 billion dinars.[29] Practically nothing (apart from emergency funds) was spent that year on development projects as oil revenues fell to $20 billion, down from almost $52 billion a year earlier.[30] What had been budgeted for overhauling dilapidated public infrastructure, roads and schools was used to pay the salary and subsidy bill and to pay for other state assistance programmes, including medical treatment abroad. No politician would have dared touch either one.

In 2014, the central bank even had to tap into a $10 billion future generation fund, started in the Gaddafi era, to make up for losses of $68 billion in oil revenues from the various blockades of oil ports since 2013.[31] 'The development fund is used for other purposes,' said Abdel-Salam Ansiya, former head of the budget committee in the General National Congress (GNC) parliament. 'Unfortunately, Libya will always spend the budget on salaries and subsidies.'[32]

When that was not enough, the bank was forced to burn its foreign currency reserves, shrinking from $132 billion in August 2013—when Ibrahim Jathran's oil port blockade in eastern Libya started—to less than $60 billion two years later. A quarter was burned in 2014 alone, according to a state audit report.[33] By 2017 the reserves were estimated by the World Bank to stand at around $70 billion, though it was impossible to get hold of a final figure. It was never clear to me how central bank reserves were calculated: a central bank document from 2013 included the value of foreign reserves the foreign holdings of the Libyan sovereign wealth Libyan Investment Authority fund, such as bank holdings in Italy or Bahrain, which distorts the picture, as many of these assets have been frozen since 2011. Since ownership of those overseas assets is mostly disputed (some were registered in the names of Gaddafi officials and family members), it didn't make much sense to include them in the accounting of foreign reserves. Central bank officials rarely grant interviews, but however hard I pressed for answers about how the reserves were calculated and why figures that excluded these disputed assets were never supplied separately, I never received a satisfactory response. I got the impression that, with the country's chaos and the bank splitting in 2014, it was very difficult for officials to obtain exact figures themselves—throwing the validity of all the figures into doubt. It wasn't just the central bank that struggled to assess Libya's reserves—the World Bank stated in its 2015 report that reserves were around $35 billion, but changed this to $60 billion in 2016, even after the country's economic crisis had worsened.

Public finances were deteriorating from 2015 as oil revenues remained volatile. The central bank was forced to print money to fund salaries paid in local currency, while inflation kept rising as the black market value of the Libyan dinar dropped massively.[34] With no sizeable food industry, anything from yoghurt to pasta, shipped in from Germany, Italy, France and Turkey, got more expensive. With dollar inflows disrupted, the Libyan dinar fell by 60 per cent on the black market as hard foreign currency at state banks became scarce. This increased the import bill once again, and the dinar's value dropped further in 2017, with one dollar buying 9.6 dinars on the black market. Banknotes became increasingly scarce as wealthy Libyans were afraid to put money in banks, whose employees might leak information of their holdings to kidnappers.

In September 2018, under pressure from Western powers and the UN, the GNA effectively devalued the dinar to 3.9 by slapping a 183 per cent fee on private hard currency transactions in a bid to bring down the spread to the black market rate at 6. That eased the black market rate to less than 5, with officials hoping to unify the rates. This effort did bring down prices, but Tripoli residents dismissed the reform as achieving too little.

The 2014 split also hit public finances as the east built up its parallel administration and Haftar's forces. The Tripoli-based central bank refused to pay salaries for the new appointees, forcing the eastern government and its parallel central bank to issue loans from eastern banks and bonds issued outside the official financial system.[35] They were partly paid out with banknotes and coins printed in Russia, which has started to back Haftar, but the debt has not been recognised by Tripoli. Still, under any political settlement between west and east, the debt will have to be paid. By 2019, the east had amassed 35 billion dinars ($25 billion) in debt in addition to the 65 billion dinars of debt accumulated by authorities in western Libya, as the country cannot afford its welfare state and ballooning public sector salary bill. There will be few funds to build new schools or hospitals anytime soon, but officials distracted by their various power struggles seem unconcerned about the debt 'time bomb'.[36] 'The law allows me to delay payment of the principal for 15 years,' the eastern central bank governor Ali Salim al-Hibri, whom I had first interviewed in Tripoli in 2013 when he was deputy governor of a then unified central bank. 'So there is no problem,' he shrugged, when I visited him in his office in Benghazi in February 2019.[37]

Even before the split, Libya was badly in need of the help of professional banks to build up a functioning banking industry, as its existing lenders are state-owned, with a range of products as limited as those found in the former Soviet Union. The banking system is largely isolated from the rest of the world, making international transfers complicated. I travelled to Cairo and Tunis every six weeks or so during my time in Tripoli to pick up cash from our local offices to the pay salaries of our local reporters. To avoid questions, especially at Cairo airport—Egypt was becoming another police state after the army-led ousting of the Islamist president in 2013—I hid the cash in books or underwear stashed in my hand luggage. Upon arrival in Tripoli, Misrata or Tobruk I needed to get the cash past nosy militiamen and roadside checkpoints. Still, the risk was worth it as bank transfers rarely worked out. Even if salary payments arrived, the Libyan bank usually didn't have dollar banknotes for recipients to withdraw.

Libya has very low external debt as there hadn't been a need to borrow much given the abundant oil revenues during Gaddafi's regime, but officials and the central bank floated the idea of selling Islamic bonds (*sukuk*) from 2013, when a seizure of oilfields saw oil production fall to a quarter of 2010's output. But Islamic bond issues are much more complicated than conventional debt, because the ban on interest payments forces lenders to back up bond issues with profit-sharing schemes invested in real estate or business, which need to be approved by a *sharia* (Islamic law) board. Designing such structured financing deals requires a lot of experience, and there was no time to train Libyan staff as the transition was supposed to happen in just 18 months. For clerks at Libya's existing banks, the challenge is to be able to make a transfer abroad in time, given the often slow internet.

The only major economic bill approved was pushed through by Islamist factions: the mandatory conversion of all banks into Islamic lenders by 2015. It was never implemented, but its initial success sent shockwaves through the industry, as Libya had no experience with sharia-compliant banking that would require the banning of interest rates. Libya would have been the only country to outlaw conventional banks, apart from crisis-torn Sudan. Bankers were warned that Libyans lenders needed more time for such a bold move. 'I don't think it makes sense just to have Islamic banks,' said Hibri, the then deputy central bank governor. 'The experience from other countries shows that conventional and Islamic banks complement each other.'[38]

Islamist lawmakers were having none of it. 'The world is moving towards an Islamic economy,' deputy GNC parliamentary speaker, Saleh Makhzoum, told an Islamic banking conference in the Corinthia Hotel in January 2014.[39] He claimed the conventional banking model was in decline due to the 2008 banking crisis, but offered no advice on how the ill-equipped banks should make such a quick conversion. We reporters covering the Islamic banking conference asked economy minister Mustafa Abu Fanas how the conversion of the banking system would work, but he had no answers. 'Regarding a starting date, this will need studies,' he said, while the senior GNC lawmaker stood nearby. The Islamic banking law shows the political gameplaying and lack of vision among post-revolutionary politicians.

Lawmakers relished their dreams of imposing their views, but had little practical sense of what was needed to create stability. But even the most basic laws, such as the outdated investment legislation or passport rules that made it difficult for foreigners to obtain residency permits, would not be overhauled. Some blamed the inaction on inexperience, having lived in a police state where every small detail was decided by the Gaddafi inner circle. Others clearly had an Islamist agenda. Among the first decisions taken by the National Transitional Council (NTC), which took over after the defeat of the Gaddafi regime, was to reintroduce polygamy (without having to consult the first wife) for men in October 2011.[40]

Complaints about rundown hospitals, schools and universities were an important motive for the uprising against Gaddafi. 'Here, see: Gaddafi never invested anything,' a rebel fighter told me in August after the fall of Tripoli, walking through a rundown residential area near the Bab Aziziya compound. 'He never gave us anything,' he said, echoing what dozens of rebel fighters would tell me in different cities. After the revolution, this righteous indignation gave way to a sense of entitlement among the rebels, who felt it was now their turn to get their hands on state resources, winner-takes-all. This pattern is seen in many post-conflict societies, such as South Sudan, where the former rebels running the country after the 2011 secession from Khartoum squandered much of the budget in the first years of independence.

Things were getting worse in Libya from summer 2014, when the split into two administrations sent state institutions into decline. It wasn't a question of launching projects, despite both governments making much of their alleged innovations, but of keeping the status quo. State institutions such as refuse management, hospitals and road maintenance firms stopped working, while hospitals were running out of drugs due to closed ports and a shortage of foreign currency. Any national-level infrastructure planning stopped. From 2015/16, the central bank managed the budget by booking the oil revenues and paying out what was needed for public salaries and subsidies, which became more and more difficult with the country's economic meltdown amid unstable oil revenues.

This had severe consequences for the daily lives of millions of Libyans, as even government-funded maintenance work mostly stopped. When I first came back to Libya in July 2013, power cuts of two to three hours a day were normal. But with oil production falling—fuel is, of course, needed to power electricity plants—and violence spreading, outages of up to 12 hours became the norm. First, banks struggled to provide dollars to customers as oil revenues dried up, but by 2015 even Libyan banknotes became scarce. The central bank was no longer able to print new money—for a lack of funds or willingness of foreign firms to assist—and delivery of banknotes to branches across Libya was hampered by security concerns. Even inside Tripoli the bank cut down on cash deliveries due to the high risk of robberies by militias or criminals (who are, of course, one and the same). Worse was to come: as oil revenues paid in dollars were parked in bank accounts abroad, the central bank faced a major challenge to find insurers for shipments to Libyan ports.

Public institutions disintegrated because of the violence of power-hungry militias—tragically, armed groups undermining the state were the biggest winners. As state institutions disappeared, more young people took up arms or joined armed groups seizing oilfields because they saw it as the only way to get a share of the oil revenues and access to basic state services. Militias would regularly force the state power firm, the General Electricity Company of Libya (GECOL), to give preferential access to electricity for residential areas under their control.

In the race to the bottom, militias backed by foreign powers benefited most—Egypt and the UAE gave support to forces led by General Khalifa Haftar for fighting Islamists in the east.[41] The UAE, Egypt and Saudi Arabia—three Arab Muslim countries opposing Muslim Brotherhood activities in western Libya—even gave humanitarian support such as medical supplies to the eastern government, which was essentially under Haftar's control.[42] That sent the message to ordinary Libyans in the east that Haftar and his Libyan National Army (LNA) was the one rebuilding Libya, when in fact he—like other militias—was destroying the state.

The only positive impact from dedicating some 70 per cent of the budget to public wages was that consumer spending in the first years after the revolution got a fillip, as people had more money. That lured some Libyans who had spent the Gaddafi era in exile to come back home to offer their skills and tap into investment opportunities. In Tripoli's upmarket Gargaresh district, restaurants and shops selling foreign suits or sneakers opened up in 2012, when there was a glimmer of hope Libya might see some stability. Higher incomes—approved by Gaddafi in a failed attempt to discourage dissent—and the end of import restrictions for luxury goods meant that business for retailers and restaurant and café owners was good until 2014. Even in the notorious Benghazi, new shopping malls with Western-style fast food outlets and sports fashion retailers opened. But by 2016 the devaluation of the dinar and galloping inflation were eroding the living standards of ordinary people. All the while, militiamen were thriving.[43]

* * *

You can see the disastrous results of spending state funds on an inefficient public service—and food and petrol subsidies—in every Libyan city. Libyans are fond of the (likely apocryphal) tale that when the founder and then ruler of the UAE, Sheikh Zayed bin Sultan Al Nahyan, visited Tripoli for eye surgery in 1972, he had a dream that one day Dubai would be as modern as the Libyan capital, admiring the rows of newly-built multi-storey residential buildings, government offices, schools and universities. The new buildings went nicely with the elegant Italian palaces clustered around the old city and the seafront in Tripoli's centre.

Dubai transformed into a major trade hub and travel destination because oil revenues were used to diversify the economy and end reliance on oil. The shiny new buildings of 1972 were the result of Libya's last major development scheme. Gaddafi used the project to bolster his rule, but the credit was not rightfully his: it had been planned by King Idris in his last Five-Year Plan. Today, the Italian palaces are run down and in many cases derelict. The central bank is an exception: its headquarters occupy a more-or-less intact palace on the corniche, next to an Ottoman castle from where Gaddafi gave one of his last public speeches. Nowadays, much of the public infrastructure is from the 1970s and 1980s, making Libyan cities, with their potholed main roads and unpaved streets, look more dilapidated than those of its much poorer neighbour, Tunisia, which produces no oil. Elevators in public buildings have been out of service for years, while stairways and balconies look as if they might collapse at any time.

The situation is especially bad in the east, neglected under Gaddafi as punishment for its long-standing dissent. In Benghazi, once the country's main port and trading hub, shell-pocked buildings still have scars from World War II, when it was bombed by British and German warplanes. General Haftar's use of Soviet-made jets from the 1980s in his campaign against Islamists has turned whole streets into rubble with very little reconstruction, even years after he declared victory—in July 2017. Haftar's opponents, including Ansar al-Sharia, also contributed to the destruction by shelling residential areas.[44]

Spending under Gaddafi focused on securing his regime by boosting security forces, paying patronage to tribes and other supporters and filling weapons arsenals across the country. His other focus was his dream of winning recognition abroad, mainly in the Middle East and Africa, where mosques, roads and other infrastructure projects were executed, but that his own country desperately needed. While independent reporting was impossible without running into trouble, the regime generously invited journalists to cover Gaddafi's speeches and congresses. An Egyptian reporter and activist friend of mine, Nour Zaki, knows most of the five-star hotels in Libya, where foreign reporters were accommodated and showered with expensive gifts. 'A chauffeur would pick you up at Tripoli airport, or there would be a VIP flight to Sirte from Tripoli,' she said.

European, US and Gulf Arab investors came to Libya after the UN lifted sanctions on Libya in 2003, when the country handed over the prime suspects in the bombing of a PanAm aircraft and Gaddafi made his comeback on the international stage. Western oil firms signed multi-billion dollar contracts, while skyscrapers shot up in Tripoli and Gaddafi's son, Saif al-Islam, opened up the economy just slightly. But many building projects were never finished, including two five-star hotels in the city centre and a huge mosque in the Ben Ashour district, close to our office villa. Most building cranes you see in Tripoli are from projects started before the revolution, on which work never resumed. In the city centre stands the shuttered construction site for the five-star Intercontinental Hotel.

Authorities even failed to turn the Bab Aziziya compound, the most potent symbol of Gaddafi's 42-year long rule, into a memorial or museum (as initially planned), leaving the destroyed buildings to rot, inhabited by stray cats and dogs. Ghoulish foreigners, such as businessmen hunting for relics like army uniforms, were the only visitors to the site after the revolution.

7

THE STRUGGLE TO SECURE LIBYA'S BORDERS

I could hear the weeping of women long before arriving at the quay at Tripoli's naval base. A group of 11 Nigerian women sat hugging each other. They were part of a group of 45 survivors of an overloaded inflatable which they had hoped would deliver them to Italy, but which sunk off the Libyan coast a few hours after setting off. The migrants had been rescued by Libya's coast-guard, thanks to a new vessel they had just received from Italy. 'Rescued' was not really the right word to describe the situation of the mostly female survivors, since their dreams of a better life in Europe had been shattered and having endured months of abuse and violence at the hands of human traffickers who had brought them via Libya's southern neighbour, Niger, to the coast. The women came from Benin City in southern Nigeria, a major hub for smugglers to coax women—who are often lured under false pretences—and then sell them to prostitution networks to pay off the price of their passage.[1]

Having been intercepted and brought to Tripoli, navy officials allowed UN staff just 30 minutes to give food to the survivors and treat their injuries. After this, militiamen in police uniforms shoved them inside a truck, transporting them to one of the country's state detention centres, where up to 10,000 illegal migrants are held across different locations.[2] 'I never wanted to go back to Libya. Where will they bring me now?' asked a terrified 23-year-old from Benin City, before an official cut short my interview and led her away. I had many more questions, but I was relieved I didn't have respond to hers, knowing she might face rape, beatings and overcrowded cells with little food in the months ahead, thanks to the complicity between the European Union and Libya's militia-driven rulers.

Libya had fallen off the Western policy agenda once Gaddafi was removed, with officials hoping the country's former rebels would somehow work out a peaceful transition. There were attempts by Western countries, as we saw in the first years after the revolution, to build an army and police force, but these had failed as the country plummeted into further chaos. When the Government of National Accord (GNA) arrived in 2016, Western countries did not resume training camps for regular soldiers in NATO countries, working instead to support the Tripoli administration. Meanwhile, some were quietly putting out feelers to Haftar, who was building up his troops with help from the UAE and Egypt.

But there was one issue that brought European countries back into the fray, and saw them resume and boost military cooperation: the flow of migrants who had begun to travel by boat from Libya to Italy. With arrivals of migrants in the European Union jumping to more than a million in 2015[3]—most of them Syrians and Iraqis arriving via the so-called Balkan route through Turkey, Greece and the Balkan countries, but also via the Mediterranean Sea—the European Union took a much greater interest in Libya. Europe seemed to realise at last that chaos in Libya meant good business for smugglers bringing desperate migrants from sub-Saharan and Arab countries to Europe. In just three years, from

2014 to 2017, some 600,000 had made the crossing, setting off from various spots on the coast of western Libya.

European officials were in panic mode, unsure how to stop the influx. There was talk among officials to open 'reception centres' or 'hotspot camps' in North African countries, including Libya, to assemble migrants, process their asylum applications outside Europe and send them home if rejected—a plan that was buried in October 2018 after countries in the region unanimously rejected it.[4] The European Union agreed instead on a package of measures, among them providing funding for African countries to help them cope with transiting or returning migrants.[5] But most importantly, Europe wanted to stem the influx of migrants by better securing its borders and assisting the Tripoli government in what diplomats call 'capacity-building' for the coastguard and other government bodies like the judiciary, police and administrators of assistance programmes—several million euros have been spent towards this goal since 2016.[6] That looked like a solid plan on paper, but in reality it only strengthened the dominance of militias, as the GNA depended on them not just to guarantee security in the capital but also in staffing the coastguard and running detention centres—the maintenance and construction of which the EU also helped fund. There were plenty of opportunities for militias to benefit from European funds.

The cooperation with the coastguard went back to 2008, when Gaddafi and the then Italian Prime Minister Silvio Berlusconi agreed that Italy would help Libya tackle illegal migration with training assistance and vessels. In 2011, Gaddafi visited Italy to foster economic cooperation (major oil deals were signed), while warning Europe would 'turn black' unless it contributed $5 billion.[7] The following year, part of the Libyan navy was destroyed or damaged during the revolution, hastening the force's decay. Libya's armed forces were already in need of repair when the revolution erupted, as boats, jets, tanks and trucks were badly outdated. Vehicles mostly dated back to the 1980s (or before), prior to the imposition of UN sanctions after Libya refused to hand over suspects in the bombing of a PanAm plane over the Scottish town of Lockerbie. Spare parts and maintenance have been scarce ever since.

Tripoli-based coastguard spokesman Ayoub al-Qassem said Italy had agreed in 2010 to overhaul six navy ships and equip them with better technology, such as radar.[8] The repairs were not finished by the time of Libya's split in 2014. The trouble that followed ended the official cooperation between Libya and Italy, which only resumed in 2016 when the UN-backed administration arrived, docking at Tripoli's naval base and expelling the unrecognised Libya Dawn government. Until the end of 2017, Italy sent four navy patrol boats and six smaller navy vessels to enhance Libya's capacities, and there were even more deliveries planned for 2019. Italy also offered millions of euros to the Tripoli government and local authorities in 2017 to persuade militias to clamp down on human trafficking—some were themselves engaged themselves in the lucrative trade.[9] Sources said that Italy reached out directly to one major group in Sabratha, a smuggling hub, west of Tripoli, paying them off to end the practice. While this arrangement was never confirmed and Italian officials denied any payments to militias, departures fell sharply after it was said to have taken place. When I visited Sabratha in November 2018, officials and a minder from the GNA showed me the naval base and an abandoned boat the smugglers had used, pointing out that departures were now close to zero.[10] However, this may not be a lasting solution as other groups will doubtless emerge and use alternative ports. In fact, two weeks before the Sabratha trip the old smuggler group had tried to come back, battling with local security guards for days.

Italy has also set up an operations room on an Italian navy ship in Tripoli.[11] The goal is to coordinate search and rescue operations conducted exclusively by the Libyan coastguard in a 30-mile zone off Libya's coast, deep in international waters, outsourcing tasks previously carried out by the Italian navy and aid organisations. The latter group are increasingly being denied access to ports in Italy and other southern countries to disembark migrants they've rescued. Even cargo ships that have rescued migrants are sent to Libya.[12]

While the coastguards intercept more inflatables, survivors are been put through 'hell', as Human Rights Watch (HRW) said in a report in 2019. Overcrowded detention centres are nominally under the control of the GNA and its department to combat illegal migration, but are actually run by militias, who often have ties with human traffickers and are paid by the administration. Migrants already face mayhem on their journeys from the southern borders lasting sometimes for months, as they get held up by armed groups, militias and smugglers (it is often hard to distinguish between them), beating them until their relatives wire the funds. There are also reports of migrants being forced to work as slaves.[13] 'They treat us like animals,' said 24-year-old Eritrean Mussie Tolde, standing in a former school-turned-prison outside Misrata—home to several hundred of illegal migrants sitting on the floor. He shared a cell with some 80 fellow migrants when I visited the facility in 2015. 'This place is not fit for human beings. We don't get fresh air in the cell and many are sick.'

HRW and other rights groups denounced the European action to beef up the Libya coastguard to stop migrants, saying it risked 'condemning migrants and asylum seekers to violent abuse at the hands of government officials, militias, and criminal groups in Libya' as the coastguard was bringing captured migrants to overcrowded prisons.[14]

Nevertheless, the assistance provided to the Libyan authorities got the results the EU sought to keep migrants from its shores. On some days, hundreds of migrants who might have made it by boat to the Italian island of Lampedusa are picked up less than 300 miles away from western Libya.[15] In 2018 the Libyan coastguard stopped some 15,000 migrants who might have safely made the journey or been picked up by rescuers.[16] But the new vessels could not alter the fact that the Libyan coastguard and the department to fight illegal migration, which is part of the interior ministry, were far from professional state bodies and remained dysfunctional and effectively run by militias. The European efforts in the area are further evidence of a hesitant approach towards helping Libya getting on its feet: a quick fix that ignored humanitarian issues. The massive European push from 2017 also showed that if Western countries had shown more interest in Libya after 2011, they could have made much bigger impact in helping build a state.

The dinghy coastguard

When the new rulers set out to rebuild the navy and coastguard after 2011, they needed to go back to the drawing board. Thousands of navy and soldiers refused to return to duty after the revolution. Having worked for Gaddafi's military, many were afraid to resume work—rebel groups which had fought against them were now calling the shots as commanders. The new rulers filled the ranks with former rebels, most of whom had never been to sea before. 'We don't have a problem with the number of people ... but the lack of training,' said Qassem, a coastguard spokesman who is actually a career navy soldier, sitting in Tripoli's navy base, located close to the commercial port. The Misrata coastguard alone had some 1,000 people on the payroll in 2015, but few among them had any prior sailing experience before their recruitment.[17]

That left authorities turning to fishermen—the captain of one coastguard boat also runs a popular fish restaurant in Tripoli.

Most of the crew interviewed during a patrol monitoring the east of Tripoli in May 2015 were fishermen who had been asked to join the coastguard in the absence of real sailors. They were using a single 12-metre inflatable to monitor 120 km of coastline—a vessel that elsewhere might be used for white water rafting.

The whole western coastguard sector based in Zuwara, a smuggler hub town right next to the Tunisian border, had until 2016 just two small inflatables like the ones in Tripoli, and not a single proper boat, forcing them to beg other command centres for assistance. 'We have been asked to help out in Zuwara,' said Colonel Essa, the Misrata commander. 'But we also don't have the capacity.' His forces had just three boats as recently as 2017.[18]

The Zuwara coastguard used to have several speed boats, but they were snatched by a militia from the Amazigh minority during the anti-Gaddafi uprising, which refused to return them—they needed the boats (which were mounted with machine guns) to seize the Mellitah oil and gas port in October 2013. A former rebel fighting unit from the revolution, its fighters stormed the port quay, sporting their Kalashnikovs and expelling frightened port staff from administrative buildings they then turned into barracks. They pressured parliament to have their language guaranteed in Libya's future constitution: 'We will not lift the blockage until our language will be guaranteed by the constitution,' said Adel al-Falu, an army officer who had joined the protest in the terminal. 'From tonight on, gas exports to Italy will stop,' he said, standing in front of the one-storey administration buildings the group was using as a temporary headquarters.[19] Three speedboats were moored at the quay next to oil tugboats when I visited the terminal in 2013. Other Amazigh fighters, wearing army or police uniforms, were lying on mattresses on the floor, smoking shisha, discussing politics over green tea with mint. 'Wouldn't you be willing to use weapons to get your rights?' one of the fighters asked me. I dodged a response—with battle-hardened fighters it's best to stay out of trouble by avoiding frank conversation. A separate crew manned the front gate, denying engineers access to the control room unless their loyalty was guaranteed. Around 40 occupants were all in fighting units from the 2011 uprising, which had never been dismantled and were instead put on the state pay roll afterwards. They ended their protest (without having reached their goals) after the National Oil Corporation (NOC) warned the loss in gas production was causing electricity outages. Such a threat is the only language militias understand.

The Misrata Commander Essa promised to take us on a night patrol to showcase efforts to fight boat smugglers, but over two weeks in 2015 all planned trips were called off due to poor weather. There was a bit of a breeze, but by European standards fishing expeditions would have gone ahead. For the nascent coastguard, with its ageing boats and inexperienced sailors, this was a no-go. That left 800 km of Libya's coast unguarded at a time when smugglers, exploiting the breakdown in security, were launching boats filled with hundreds of migrants and refugees every day. One day, 500 people were rescued by the Italian navy.

'Our possibilities are very, very limited,' said Essa, sitting in his office.[20] His desk was packed with sales brochures from European firms offering navy boats, though with no budget he admitted it would take years for any deal to be finalised. When a boat packed with migrants capsized off the Tripoli coast in July 2015, European navy and rescue boats rushed to save the survivors. Navy spokesman Qassem, when contacted by reporters, had no knowledge of a sunken boat. Officers like Essa seemed motivated to rescue migrants despite their limited resources.

HRW and UN reports have extensively documented how officers in the coastguard and other forces run by militias work hand-in-hand with human traffickers.[21] Migrants who make it to Lampedusa alive often report that the smugglers had help from militiamen-turned-coastguards who turn a blind eye when boats are launched, or who actually arrange the passage. Like other reporters, I was never able to prove links between smugglers and former rebels working in the security forces, but it was an open secret. 'I warned that anyone will be prosecuted according to military law,' Essa said, wearing impeccable navy uniform, a contrast to the often unironed or randomly assembled uniforms worn by Libyan soldiers. But in the absence of a functioning judicial system and amid widespread corruption, few sailors are punished or even caught when doubling as human traffickers. There are stronger state institutions in Misrata than in Tripoli or in other cities, but the port is not really a launchpad for smugglers, being too far away from Lampedusa.

Capacity-building, the European way

Europe was, at first, slow to help the Libyan coastguard. Trying to stem a flow of illegal migrants and stopping Islamist extremists travelling to Europe via Libya, the EU set up a training mission called the EU Integrated Border Management Assistance Mission in Libya (EUBAM) in May 2013.[22] It took Brussels two years to form the mission, though it had become immediately clear since the toppling of Gaddafi that Libya needed help fast—the number of Europe-bound migrants transiting through the country had risen since 2011. The mission had an annual budget of 60 million euros to train Libyan sailors and other security officers to help build up functioning passport controls at land crossings and at Tripoli airport. In reality, much of the funds were spent on security advisers and accommodation for expatriate staff in a high-security compound in the five-star Corinthia Hotel.[23] They later moved into the luxury Palm City compound in a western suburb, home to most Western diplomats based in the capital.

A European ambassador told me EUBAM was a failure because senior management never helped build up structures in the navy or the defence and interior ministries. 'It is not successful. They should be focusing on first getting the defence ministry organised, to get different departments before starting training courses,' he said. But that was only partly true. Many EUBAM trainers I met were dedicated, but security restrictions forced them to stay indoors for much of the day. Even worse, the lack of technical knowledge among Libya's sailors, most of whom had never sailed before, limited the training efforts. When the training mission began, shocked coaches realised the Libyans didn't even have life vests, let alone boats. They needed to drastically lower their expectations of what was achievable, dedicating much of their time on basic skills such as man-overboard rescue drills or how to detain people respectfully—a novelty for the new recruits as well the old timers from the military trained in Gaddafi's police state. Some sailors couldn't even swim.

'I admire these young men. They are very bold to go out in such boats so far,' said David Aquilina, a trainer from Malta working for EUBAM.[24] 'They want to work, but need training and equipment,' he said as he watched coastguard officers in 2013 practicing how to rescue a comrade who had gone overboard. 'First they need to learn how to stay safe before they can rescue migrants.'

Earlier that day I observed one of his courses, during which he had shown slides on an overhead projector of how to conduct first aid and other basic instructions for sailors—the final session of a training class. Since most sailors didn't speak English, every slide needed to be translated into Arabic, which slowed down communication. 'You are no longer my students, you are now my sailor comrades,' he said at the end, shaking hands with some of the men. It wasn't clear that this cumbersome training style had engaged many of the students.

I asked officers how many men they had in the coastguard, but as like with the other armed forces, it was hard to get a reliable figure. The Tripoli base employs some 600 men, most of whom never go out to sea.[25] However, many don't show up, but still collect their salaries at the end of the month like other unproductive civil servants. Others just work out of overstaffed port offices, drinking tea and whiling away the hours

The other reason the EU trainers didn't make much of an impact was the lack of a centralised command structure—exactly the problem NATO faced when trying to build up a functioning army. In 2013, the coastguard had administrative regions which tended to operate independently—another legacy from Gaddafi, who fostered distrust between different army units and security services to prevent them from teaming up against his rule. There is little coordination, as each unit has its own command and base, a fact exacerbated by the split in the country. When EUBAM held a training course in Tripoli, participants would come from the local base, not other command centres. Libya's split into western and eastern governments in 2014 exacerbated these divisions.

Another declared goal of the EU training mission in Libya was to get the security forces to treat detained migrants with humanity, in line with international laws and customs. Detained people were supposed to have access to their embassies, lawyers and visiting relatives. But racist attitudes, even towards black Libyans, meant these efforts didn't go far. Several detained migrants from Eritrea I met in detention facilities told me of ill treatment and beatings at night when guards were drunk.[26] During a visit to a school-turned-prison east of Misrata, guards, wearing the typical mix of army, police and interior ministry uniforms, were parading some 150 Egyptian workers who had just been arrested for entering the country on forged visas—all so the press could film them. Afterwards they were brought back to an unlit warehouse where they spent the night sleeping on the floor, again with much shouting. The workers were only allowed to use the bathroom once a day—one, shared between 750 inmates.[27]

It was not just individual behaviour but state policy that made the life of the detained migrants so miserable. Authorities did not provide medical services in detention facilities, despite the high prevalence of disease. Faraj Abdullah, deputy director of the Gharboulli detention facility east of Tripoli, said there was no budget for a doctor on site, but on the drive to the prison I spotted a fully equipped state hospital very close by.[28]

The EU mission pulled out its staff in 2014, having just moved into a new base which was quickly looted by militias. After 2014, the mission was mothballed, though it retained an office in Tunis with two staff as part of the mission of the European Commission's delegation, but no further training courses were organised.

The coastguard and other Libyan officials bitterly complained in interviews that Europe and the US had let them down, as Western firms were not providing much-needed equipment. In addition, Libya is under an arms embargo imposed by the UN Security Council in 2011 when the uprising broke out—this has, to date, still not been lifted. The embargo was eased in 2013 to allow non-lethal equipment for humanitarian and other purposes to be brought in, but any deals need to be approved by a sanctions committee. The embargo has been broken for years by various states, shippers and Libyan and foreign businessmen, as the sanctions panel was established but made official supplies of arms difficult. Italy, whose right-wing government has led the European action to curb migration, called for the embargo to be lifted in 2018 to combat smugglers.[29]

But even before, when there was some tentative stability, few deals surfaced, despite Western security firms offering equipment such as x-ray machines for airports showing up at a trade fair in an army barracks in Tripoli in 2014. Authorities had hoped for more, but a worsening security situation had reduced the number of companies willing to make the trip. Officials allocated a smaller showroom in the barracks than initially planned. The only major arms deal signed after 2011 was with Italian defence contractor Selex to deliver a radar system to monitor the country's border, but a worsening security situation and lack of training meant that it was never implemented.[30]

Contractors blamed unattractive terms going back to laws from the Gaddafi era, which the General National Congress (GNC) parliament of 2012–2014 did not change, meaning that Tripoli held the court of arbitration. Contract language was in Arabic, a policy that harked back to the time when Gaddafi banned English, and foreigners visiting Libya needed to have their passports translated into Arabic before they could apply for a visa.[31] These terms, and the absence of a functioning court system, help to explain why foreign companies were reluctant set up local operations and train staff. The GNC parliament was paralysed much of the time, spending weeks on political declarations such as making Islamic law the only source of legislation, or endless debate about the future of Libya.

EUBAM made a comeback in 2017, thanks to the renewed interest in Libya as part of the migration measures. But the approach was again hampered by security concerns and the lack of a clear strategy, so its impact was limited. EU member states were, until 2018, unsure what EUBAM's mandate should be, leaving an office with more than ten staff from 2016 to make proposals about what they could do—called 'mapping'—as several frustrated EUBAM officers told me.[32] They were mostly grounded in Tunis, visiting Tripoli on day trips to meet Libyan officials tired of having discussions about the kind of assistance EUBAM might offer in the future. 'I'm tired of doing nothing and so are the Libyans,' said one EUBAM officer. The unit settled on border management assistance and training law enforcement as well as judiciary officers, a highly problematic area which means dealing with militias and detention centres where inmates are abused. The idea looks solid on paper, but the training was not very efficient, and amounted to lecturing militiamen on human rights. In December 2018, the EU finally mandated EUBAM to resume its capacity-building work, granting a budget of 61.6 million euros for the 2019 to June 2020 period.[33] But just as the mission was beginning to function again, war broke out over Tripoli in April 2019,[34] forcing EUBAM officials to return to Tunis. Some were back in Tripoli by autumn, but most activities involved flying members of the Libyan security forces (mostly the GNA's militiamen) to Tunis, putting them up in five-star hotels and delivering workshops. Some of these, like training in how to detect forged passports, were effective. Others, like human rights awareness training, were not.

Bordering on disaster

Like the coastline, Libya has also been unable to control its land borders with Tunisia, Algeria, Niger, Chad, Sudan and Egypt—stretching almost 4,300 km deep into the desert. This is the main gateway for migrants arriving from sub-Saharan countries as far away as Gambia, Senegal and Nigeria, hoping to make it to Europe with the help of smugglers who bring subsidised Libyan products such as petrol or flour on their way back.[35]

There has never been much of a state in Libya's south, known as Fezzan, which saw little development under King Idris or Gaddafi, despite being home to the country's biggest oilfields. The latter provided some modest development such as hospitals, schools and universities in the main cities of Sabha, Ubari and Ghat, but otherwise showed little interest in the sparsely inhabited region. Gaddafi's main interest was to use tribesmen like the

Tuareg based in the south to integrate their youth into the security forces. Many Tuareg joined his forces during the revolution in the hope of getting citizenship and other benefits, while others worried they would lose out if the regime changed. 'Most Turaeg had jobs as drivers or guides for tourists who were coming in the past so they thought, 'Why would I join the revolution?' said Ahmed Sarhan, who had picked up some German from showing tourists prehistoric rock carvings near his hometown of Ghat.[36] Many of the sites, which include a huge elephant carved on a rock as well as cows, giraffes and ostriches, have been destroyed by vandals since then.

Gaddafi's welfare state also existed in the south, but to a lesser extent than in the more developed coastland. Many in the south had no papers, having slipped into Libya over the porous border seeking work—action that was tolerated because Gaddafi welcomed Africans as part of his attempt to style himself as 'King of African Kings'. Gaddafi made promises of citizenship, especially during the 2011 uprising, to lure fighters into his forces, but he didn't fulfil them in the end—a major source of dissent in the years that followed. Many Tuareg, as well as members of the rival Tebu tribes who had joined the uprising in the hope of gaining Libyan citizenship as a reward, were frustrated that those promises were not kept. They started occupying oilfields in the south, demanding to be hired by the state.

Since 2013 the south had descended into turmoil, shutting down the main southern airport of Sabha for more than two years. There wasn't much the southern communities could expect, as decision making in Tripoli was paralysed due to political infighting. With little employment alternatives and militias exploiting a rapidly growing security vacuum, many joined a surging cross-border smuggling of subsidised goods in exchange for weapons, migrants and consumer goods. The tribes had lived for centuries on informal trans-Saharan trade routes, and fighters joining a Tuareg advance in northern Mali, repelled by French army forces in 2013, came the same way.

When I visited Ghat in May 2014 I met a depressed but very candid town council head, sitting in a rundown cubicle townhouse built in the typical socialist style you find across Libya. 'We don't get any support from Tripoli,' said Mohamed Abdel-Qader. Anything from fuel to basic food items such as cheese comes by truck from Tripoli, but only with long delays as drivers, fearing kidnappings at fake checkpoints, were increasingly reluctant to make the 1,000 km trip. The central bank was, for the same reason, delivering less and less cash to local banks who needed to pay civil servants. State mobile phone operator al-Madar had stopped working in Ghat and other parts of the south as it could no longer bring in spare parts due to the security situation. Instead, people bought Algerian SIM cards, climbing a hill outside the city where reception was available.

The town's mayor had requested several times for EUBAM to hold training courses in Ghat for the understaffed border security guards, but to no avail, despite relatively good security for foreigners in the close-knit tribal city where outsiders—including Islamist militants—are quickly spotted by locals. I felt safe staying almost a week with a former tour guide in Ghat. 'I heard so much about training and support from Europe, but we never got any help,' Abdel-Qader said bitterly, but the EU training delegation rarely left its luxury accommodation in Tripoli, holding training courses only as far as the main crossing to Tunisia in Ras Jdir and some 450 km to the southwest in Ghadames, which borders Tunisia and Algeria. Ghadames, an ancient city and former tourist magnet, was still more than 700 km from Ghat.

Abdel-Qader also blamed corruption in Tripoli for the failure of border guards in the south, where 150 interior ministry troops have to monitor a border stretching 600 km, from Niger to Tunisia. 'We requested four-wheel vehicles for the border guards, but officials preferred to drive them in Tripoli,' he said. Even worse, a wave of oilfield grabs by militias meant that oil revenues were being squandered. As a result, Tripoli stopped sending funds to the local interior ministry in Ghat to run a detention facility for illegal migrants. 'We cannot pay contractors anymore for laundry or to provide food,' said the town's top security official, who did not wish to be named. He showed us around the modern one-storey prison, which stood unused—bunk beds lined up in cells with neatly folded blankets. Migrants from Niger, Mali, Chad and other sub-Saharan countries who were supposed to be detained after crossing the border were now wandering around Ghat unchallenged.

Most migrants stood by the road hoping for a day job on construction sites or farms, trying to raise money for the onward travel to the coast while police or army drove by, having given up on chasing them a long time ago. 'I didn't see any soldiers,' said Abdulkadir, a man from Niger who had come via the nearby Algerian border. When I drove by with a cameraman he was resting under a palm tree just 2 km from Libyan passport control. Soldiers, some wearing police or army uniforms or a combination of both, were dozing there on dusty chairs and smoking. Even Libyans and Algerians, who need visas to visit one another's countries, were just walking across the border to visit family on the other side.

Abdul-Qader, the senior security official, drove us around the border in his white jeep following a dirt track to a post of the Libyan border guards, made up of interior ministry troops and regular soldiers. Sitting with him in the back during the 30-minute drive, he would talk endlessly of how Tripoli had abandoned him and his men. 'We cannot do our job. We've got no equipment, no modern guns,' he said, getting agitated. He had just one satellite phone and no binoculars for his men, who would work in a group of 15 out of a hut with a corrugated iron roof next to the unmarked border, invisible in the sand. 'This is where people cross,' Abdul-Qader said as he was walking a tarmac road jointly used by Algerian and Libyan border guards. An Algerian truck delivering water to the army passed by. 'Here, look at the shoes and water bottles they left behind,' he said, pointing to a shoe left by a migrant on a dirt track leading from the tarmac road into Libya. Five metres further down the track there was a discarded water jug. 'This is the main route the smugglers are taking,' he said. 'They use it every night.'

The soldiers at one border observation point, just 500 metres from the dirt track, had the standard weapons shared by army and former rebels in Libya: Kalashnikov guns and pistols, but no heavy guns or four-wheel cars. A unit would cover an area of 20 km, but they avoided confrontation with the better-armed smugglers. There would be little point trying to stop them, as migrants would just cross the long border at another desert stretch. They even offered us the opportunity to watch migrants escorted by smugglers crossing at night while they sat idly in their huts to showcase their frustration, hoping we could tell someone in Tripoli about it to get them better equipment. Two hundred migrants crossed this part of the border every day, according to Ghat's mayor. In 2018, EUBAM again floated the idea to send trainers for Libyan border guards to the south, but for security reasons, nothing happened.

So relaxed are the smugglers, that one of them even agreed to let us film him as dozens of migrants, mainly from Niger, climbed in his Toyota four-wheel truck for the drive to Ubari, the next large city on the main road to the north, after having crossed via Algeria in Ghat. Before heading off with his passengers—each of whom had to pay around $30 for the four-hour drive—he took the time to ridicule the state forces in an interview on a sand dune overlooking Ghat, a picturesque oasis town which has a Turkish forest on a hill in the centre. When asked whether weapons or militants from Al Qaeda were crossing alongside the migrants, the smuggler, covering his head in the traditional Tuareg headdress, said, shrugging: 'Look, the border is open. Anything can come, migrants, Al Qaeda. There is no state.' Even if he was caught by one of the rare patrols, he had little reason to worry: 'I have friends in the police and army.' With European tourists long gone, cross-border smuggling offers the best employment opportunity for locals. He is a cog in a vast machine: a network shipping migrants Libya's coast, where they hope to catch a boat to Italy.

That was the situation in May 2014, when there was still some sort of unified government in Tripoli, though fragile and with little power. With the country splitting into two halves months later, and tribes and militants more than willing to exploit the vacuum, the smugglers expanded their networks, routing migrants via Sudan or the Ghat–Algeria crossing to the north. 'We are helpless. We know the routes smugglers use but cannot do anything,' said Colonel Mohamed Abu Breeda, assistant director of Libya's anti-immigration police force based in Tripoli. On top of shortages of weapons and qualified soldiers, a budget crisis had frozen payments for anything from salaries to stationery. 'What do you want me to do? There are delays everywhere. I am a boss but with no power,' he said, getting worked up and raising his voice.[37]

While the EU's push from 2017 to assist the coastguard helped to stem the flow of inflatable boats, there was no progress in curbing the trafficking of migrants from the southern border to the coast. 'Along the migration routes, armed groups exact passage taxes and provide protection services to the smugglers' convoys against payment. These schemes generate significant revenues for armed groups and presumably for tribal and state actors,' a UN report from September 2018 stated.[38]

The Tripoli state prosecutor wasn't aware of a single smuggler who had ever been caught and put on trial. 'To fight illegal immigration you need an efficient coast and border guard,' said Sadiq al-Sour, head of the investigations department at the Tripoli prosecutor general. 'We need a proper police force, not just some revolutionaries, so we cannot enforce any arrest warrant.'[39]

The courthouse where he has a small one-room office is a showcase of Libya's chaos. I had been waiting with a colleague for half an hour in the modest reception room where guards were trying to impose order. First, some 30 handcuffed prisoners were marshalled by rebels-turned-soldiers carrying guns to an upper floor. Then, a crying woman demanded to see a prosecutor to get access to her jailed son, shouting at the reception staff who had turned her away before slumping into one of the uncomfortable metal benches in the crowded waiting room. 'I want to see my son,' she kept shouting until she finally left.

Despite their shortcomings, authorities managed to detain 16,000 migrants who had entered through the open sub-Saharan routes by May 2015, according to the Tripoli government, who let them languish in makeshift prisons with no hope of relief: their embassies had long left Tripoli.[40] Some missions would not cooperate with authorities in Tripoli, including those of Eritrea or Ethiopia. Their nationals also did not want to be deported, fearing reprisals or a return to the poverty from which they had fled in the first place.

While doing very little to stop the mistreatment of migrants or improving conditions in overcrowded prisons, the unofficial Libya Dawn government running Tripoli from 2014 to 2016 sought to exploit the rise in the number of smugglers' boats setting sail for Italy to win international recognition. Foreign Minister Ghirani had almost no diplomats willing to meet him, save for some African envoys. He told me in May 2015 that the EU was, of course, free to deal with the official government in the east. He knew well that the government of Prime Minister Thinni in Bayda, working out of hotels and rented villas, had effectively lost power. In addition, the main launchpads for smugglers were in western Libya, under the control of Ghirani's government. From eastern Libya, the distance was too far to reach Italy in makeshift boats. 'Let [the European Union staff] go there. But if they want to do something they will have to deal with us, the de facto government,' he said. The government was willing to help, but if Europe wanted to stem a flow of migrants it needed to work with Tripoli, said Ghirani. 'If Europe does not support us then the continent's skin will turn from white to black. It will be an African Europe,' he said, paraphrasing Gaddafi.

8

THE ARRIVAL OF ISLAMIC STATE

Islamic State (IS) militants seized much of Iraq and Syria in 2013, with its bearded fighters driving Toyota pickups and waving rifles as they overran Mosul and other major cities. After all, a country in chaos with weak state security forces, depots full of weapons and a huge pool of Islamist gunmen looked like the perfect place for the Sunni extremist group to expand into.

Exploiting the porous Egyptian-Libyan border, a delegation of foreign fighters arrived in September 2014 in Derna, halfway between the border and Benghazi, to make a formal pitch to the local jihadist community, some of whom already held ties to Al Qaeda-type groups and other battle-hardened fighters. The coastal city was a logical first stop as a hub for jihadist activity, and had been through much of the Gaddafi era. Finding no public space outside official channels in Gaddafi's tightly controlled Jamahiriya, hundreds of fighters from Derna had gone abroad to fight on foreign battlefields, especially in Afghanistan against the Soviet invasion in 1979. The biggest of these groups was the Libyan Islamist Fighting Group (LIFG), whose members tried to topple Gaddafi when they returned. Waging a campaign in

179

eastern Libya using the Green Mountain region with its hard-to-monitor caves and valleys, they rejected Western democracy and saw Gaddafi as an apostate. Hundreds were jailed in the Abu Salim prison when the regime cracked down on them.[1] The jail time was a bonding experience for many who joined the uprising a year later, including members of other outlawed Islamist groups such as the Muslim Brotherhood. There were also Salafist groups who had first sided with the regime as part of their 'quietist' policy. Once Gaddafi was toppled, prominent members took positions in ministries or other official capacities in the Interim Government that followed. In the following years, younger fighters were recruited and radicalised in Derna and Benghazi.

Benghazi descended into instability after Gaddafi's ousting—Western assistance to build functioning state bodies (like in western Libya) was largely abandoned when foreigners moved out and consulates closed after the assassination of US Ambassador Christopher Stevens in 2012. A wave of assassinations against former regime security agents followed, mostly blamed on Ansar al-Sharia and other groups in a score settling from the Gaddafi era, making the city a no-go zone for foreigners. Though Reuters always strives to be close to the news, I only managed to visit Benghazi twice in 2013 and early 2014, locking myself in my hotel room after conducting carefully arranged interviews in the hotel or in private houses while my nervous security adviser waited outside, texting me reminders not to stay too long.

In the chaos, Islamists asked groups friendly to them to join Syria's civil war against forces loyal to President Bashar al-Assad. One of the few foreign airlines still flying to Benghazi was Turkish Airlines, whose daily flight to Istanbul was regularly used by fighters who, once in Istanbul, took a domestic flight to Gaziantep and slipped over the Syrian-Turkish border from there. By the end of 2013, Libyans were among the top five nationalities heading to Syria.[2] Having gained credentials on the battlefield, many came back to fill the security vacuum at home, exploiting the absence of a rule of law, easy access to weapons from the Gaddafi era (and those illegally imported afterwards) and porous borders, setting up their own groups or joining others. 'The experience of returning from Syria to Libya allowed the "graduate" to branch out on his own, and attempt to recruit others to work with him in Libya's political vacuum,' said a report by the Atlantic Council.[3] At the same time foreign jihadists were coming to Libya, particularly from neighbouring Tunisia, where rampant unemployment and poverty as a result of economic crisis were driving many abroad. Many Tunisians worked in Libya until 2011, but then lost their jobs due to security risks and the lack of job opportunities. Even at the tail end of 2013, you could still see many Tunisians working as waiters, construction workers and in petrol stations in Tripoli and other western coastal cities, but many left afterwards. Some Tunisians used their old connections to come back as jihadists. The government in Tunis estimated that some 3,000 Tunisians went to foreign battlefields, most of whom were killed or otherwise never returned.[4] They joined Ansar al-Sharia or other groups in what was then a vibrant jihadist scene.

Derna was the natural choice to set up an IS branch, given its global jihadist links and its reputation as a hub for various Islamists groups. The planned post-democratic transition never made it to Derna. In the 2014 elections, officials were unable to open ballot boxes due to threats and attacks. Unfortunately, I have never been able to visit Derna: my bosses deemed it too dangerous after a Reuters team reporting the aftermath of the 2012 killing of the US ambassador ran into trouble there with Ansar al-Sharia. They made it out thanks to the help of our Tripoli-based reporter, Ghaith Shennib, who hails from the city and has provided us with insight from Derna whenever we needed it, even after he left the agency in 2014.

IS's official launch in Libya was in October 2014, when a little known group called Majlis Shura Shabab al-Islam (the Islamic Youth Shura Council) announced its presence and allegiance—with young men holding guns driving around in pickup trucks in videos posted online, similar to those already seen in Iraq and Syria.[5] Our Cairo bureau had a month earlier reported that several foreign IS preachers from Yemen, Egypt and Saudi Arabia, among other countries, had slipped over the Egyptian-Libyan border to make their pitch to local groups.[6] More declarations of allegiance followed, some from fighters linked to Ansar al-Sharia, with IS's leader Abu Bakr al-Baghdadi, then based in Iraq, announcing the formation of three *wilayas* (provinces) in Libya for the west, east and south. The group has used similar structures in other countries.

Slow progress

But IS's expansion was not as rapid as it had been in Iraq and Syria. There, the group thrived on a hate campaign against Shi'ites, who dominate both governments—Assad is a member of the Shi'ite Alawite sect and Iraq's Prime Minister Haidar al-Abadi, is also Shi'ite. That sectarian division does not exist in Libya, a Sunni Muslim country with no history of religious violence or division between different branches of Islam. In Iraq and Syria, IS had seized territory from weak national armies, but the group faced greater resistance in Libya, where it was just one of dozens of major armed groups.

Since the revolution, other Islamist groups had established themselves, gaining access to state resources and attracting former rebels, meaning the field was crowded from the start. In addition, the Islamist community was close-knit and suspicious of newcomers, as many had formed bonds while languishing in the Abu Salim prison. Most crucially, IS did not help to unseat

Gaddafi—a minimum requirement for militias trying to establish legitimacy.

Nevertheless, to win members outside Derna, the group posted a recruitment video in the Tuareg language to target a marginalised tribe in southern Libya in January 2015.[7] Many Tuareg from neighbouring countries had joined Gaddafi's forces in 2011 hoping in vain to be granted citizenship. The south had never seen much development, and life would get much worse from mid-2014 when the battle over the Tripoli disrupted domestic flights. Libya's had been one of the most extensive domestic flight networks in the Arab world, but from July 2014 there were hardly any flights going south, cutting off supplies of everything from banknotes to medicine and food. The main road from Tripoli also became insecure, turning the southern Fezzan into a humanitarian crisis zone almost as bad as in sub-Saharan countries. 'It's incredibly bad. There is no electricity. Hospitals are closed and people cannot fly to Tripoli for treatment,' said Abdullah Karfanuda, a lawmaker from the south I met in Tobruk.[8] He asked me whether I could put him in touch with UN aid agencies. The recruitment video played on anger over neglect of the south, and some Tuareg were believed to have joined IS in Sirte, but the overall reception was far less rapturous than the group had hoped.

Most other Sunni or religious extremist groups saw IS as competition to control territory and recruit capable fighters. The influx of hardened foreign fighters and preachers from Tunisia, Yemen, Egypt, Sudan and Syria troubled locals from the start. While an unruly and conservative Muslim country, many Libyans were appalled by the group's infamous beheadings and attacks on oilfields, such as the al-Mabrouk facility in 2015, where IS fighters had fired rocket-propelled grenades at warehouses and wells with the sole purpose of damaging state income, affecting ordinary people dependent on public sector salaries.

The arrival of foreign fighters also hit a nerve in a country where, thanks to Gaddafi's regime, foreigners were generally distrusted. In my own case, I was regularly accused of being a spy. It greatly helps if you speak Arabic in a country where few can speak English, but in the eyes of many of the Libyans I met, this was just part of an elaborate ruse to cover for my real work as a Mossad agent.[9]

The help of NATO and Arab countries such as Qatar in toppling Gaddafi also reinforced suspicions that foreigners were trying to control Libya. That sentiment got another boost when Western countries, Qatar, Turkey and Arab neighbours such as Egypt and Sudan tried to influence the post-revolution era, especially after the breakup in 2014. Then, Egypt backed the east openly, while some Islamists sought inspiration from Qatar and Turkey.

In most interviews, even with respondents with exposure to the Western world, I would, often out of the blue, be asked: 'What do you think the West is planning for Libya?' All leaders who had spent time in exile to escape the Gaddafi regime—Ali Zeidan, Abdulrahman el-Keib, Mahmud Jibril and even eastern commander Khalifa Haftar—failed to quash rumours that they were in fact foreign agents. When Zeidan was briefly kidnapped in October 2013, his abductors accused him of having a German passport (since he had lived in Germany and Switzerland)—something he denied.[10] I encountered even more paranoia during a visit to Tobruk in February 2015, when a middle-aged man asked me: 'Why is Ali Zeidan travelling so often to Europe? That must mean something.'

Another reason for the slower expansion of IS was that it was relying on different local players travelling under the banner of the Sunni group. It appears there was no central leadership for IS in Libya, as the militants only controlled limited territories, located hundreds of miles apart. Nawfliyah, a small town southeast of Sirte, had always been a jihadist hotspot, which made it an easy target for the IS fighters arriving in February 2015 in their four-wheel pickups.[11] They paraded in the streets and staged several attacks on oilfields in the area, kidnapping foreigners. But they quickly withdrew from the oil facilities after brief attacks as they only felt safe in remote locations where they had already a presence, like Derna and Sirte.

The Tripoli attack

While IS didn't cause as much havoc in Libya as in Iraq and Syria, the group did scare away the last resident foreigners— myself included—when it struck in the heart of the capital Tripoli in February 2015.

It started with a car bomb that went off around noon at the entrance of the Corinthia Hotel, a 40-storey tower overlooking the sea where I had spent a few nights after 'embedding' with the rebels when they took Tripoli in August 2011. At least six fighters stormed the lobby cafeteria, spraying it with bullets. In the past there had been two checkpoints: one at the compound's outer gate and another on the ramp leading from the parking lot to the revolving doors, but security rules had been relaxed with the overall deterioration of state and security institutions. At least five foreigners were killed—one US security adviser[12] and crew members from Libyan private airline Buraq[13]—in the attack, which lasted several hours. Security forces loyal to Libya Dawn gathered outside, unsure of what to do, but eventually moved into the ground floor. Highlighting the difficulties faced by reporters trying to check facts in Libya, authorities never gave a final death toll and failed to provide any details of the attack.

I was on my way back from Misrata (where I had conducted several days of interviews) when news of the attack broke. I stayed in contact with our Tripoli bureau during the car ride, helping to file stories, but I didn't want to believe that the extremists had made it to Tripoli—which in those days had been peaceful. The hotel attack was the moment I realised I would not be able to continue living full time in Tripoli, despite the advantages of being on the ground without having to rely on social media postings or phone interviews. The lobby café—now covered in blood—had been one of my favourite hangouts to meet contacts or just to enjoy a cappuccino, as they served one of the best in town. By January 2015, I had found a way to work around the pressures of competing governments in Tripoli and the east, while still getting our often controversial stories out without too much hassle or intimidation. Getting shouted at by angry officials or militiamen had become part of life in Libya in the same way I had to pay my electricity bill in Germany.

But dealing with foreign suicide attackers hunting for the last foreigners left in Tripoli was a different thing. The Italian embassy, the last European mission still open, closed days later. Foreign staff at the Corinthia and some oil and aviation firms also left, and the hotel shut down for a few months. It was the final blow to my pretence that life was normal. The city's other luxury hotel—the Radisson Blu—had closed months earlier due to a lack of business and expatriate staff. The Rixos, the base for foreign journalists in the final months of the Gaddafi regime, only briefly reopened after the revolution and was used afterwards to house lawmakers from the General National Congress, which met next door.

After the Corinthia attack, most of the remaining foreigners packed up, and those of us who stayed behind a bit longer kept a very low profile, venturing out only rarely, and only ever to buy food or conduct interviews. I hardly ever met friends or contacts in cafés anymore, and when I did, was careful to only sit for a few minutes. Was the waiter or a customer who sympathised with IS making a phone call to alert the group of my presence? Most kidnappings in Libya are random—someone with ties to an extremist group spots a foreigner and makes a call from his smartphone. That's why, even before the arrival of IS, I never walked for more than 200 metres, and usually just from a car and into a restaurant or ministry.

After the attack on the Corinthia I went with two friends to a shisha café in a historic building in the old city, opposite the fish market. I had been there with my wife many times before, even watching World Cup matches on a large screen surrounded by Libyans, without worry. But this time it was different. 'Let's talk only Arabic. We don't know who might watch us,' one of my friends, Umar from Pakistan, said as he parked his car at the deserted square in front of the building, where maybe six customers were enjoying mint tea or a waterpipe. (The place used to be so packed that you couldn't get a table in the evening.) We went to the first floor, away from the street, so passers-by wouldn't spot us. Still, we stayed for less than 45 minutes before nervously heading off.[14] Back in the relative safety of the villa, my wife begged me in late-night phone calls to leave Libya.

Since the storming of Corinthia, the foreigners still living in Tripoli had been bracing themselves for the worst. But militants loyal to the group focused on small-scale attacks on Western and Arab embassies: Algeria, Egypt, Spain, Morocco and Iran, striking sometimes several times in one week to maximise the embarrassment of Tripoli officials who had claimed that life in the city was back to normal and had urged diplomats to return.

The reality was much less spectacular. For a start, the attackers were hitting empty buildings, as almost all countries had evacuated their missions—a fact we were careful to make clear in our stories. I forgot once to make this clear during an attack on the vacant Iranian ambassador's residence in February 2015, and my editors got in touch to remind me not to leave out such a detail, which put the limited impact of the attacks in contrast to the group's action in Iraq or Syria.[15] The militants mostly came at dawn when the city was asleep and with few security guards around, in hit-and-run missions. One would fix a small and usually low-impact device to the front door, while a second person would be filming: the video uploaded on social media would always give the impression of a larger scale operation. It was still scary—many of these attacks took place in the vicinity of our villa in the upmarket Ben Ashour district, home to many missions. But it was clear that IS had only a small presence in the capital: otherwise their militants would have focused on bigger targets such as the Italian embassy, based in a former palace overlooking the Mediterranean.

The Tripoli government had stepped up security in the city after the Corinthia attack, and had staged 'business conferences' and other events in the best Gaddafi tradition—to falsely claim that life was back to normal. Senior officials I interviewed after returning to Tripoli in November 2014 would ask me: 'So, you agree that life is totally normal in Tripoli, right?' The Libya Dawn government had always downplayed the IS threat as Western spin. Since some of the militias backing Tripoli were jihadi-like Islamists, the emergence of IS was, due to their overlapping ideologies, a sensitive subject. They blamed Gaddafi loyalists from Libya, even when a video showing foreign fighters emerged.[16]

IS was more successful after the Corinthia attack in eastern Libya, especially in war-ravaged Benghazi, where it orchestrated suicide bombings against Khalifa Haftar's forces. A drone filmed one such attack in February 2015, showing they felt more comfortable in the eastern port city than in their dawn attacks in Tripoli. The suicide bomber was identified and filmed before he set off in a jeep laden with explosives. Another bomber also blew himself up in Qubbah, a small town between Derna and Bayda and the seat of Thinni's government, killing 42 people, among them five Egyptians. This attack was filmed for maximum media coverage.[17]

THE ARRIVAL OF ISLAMIC STATE

By the time of the Corinthia Hotel attack the first fighters had arrived in Sirte, moving from Derna and other spots in the east. The city, home to around 150,000 before 2011, lies halfway between Benghazi and Tripoli. Only here did IS win support from locals, though it seemed that this was of a more tactical, temporary nature—the group offered a way to strike out at the country's new rulers.

Why Sirte? The city had been favoured by Gaddafi, who staged foreign summits and moved government bodies there from Tripoli, turning it into an unofficial second capital. Many Libyans told me he wanted to make it the capital at some point, but feared people would not accept it. Located on the coast, Sirte is home to a dozen or more tribes, among them the Warfalla and Gaddafi's own, the Qadhadhfa. The city had formed the main base for his regime along with Bani Walid, a town located some 175 km southwest of Tripoli. Gaddafi had hidden here in the last days of his rule, and it was from here that he tried to flee with his entourage before being captured and killed by a mob who dragged him unceremoniously out of a drainpipe, south of Sirte. Misratan fighters later ransacked the city in revenge, having already reduced it to rubble in weeks of shelling. NATO airstrikes also contributed to the destruction. The Misratan forces looted houses and took prisoners, many of whom were held in special jails run by militias operating outside proper judicial channels. Human Rights Watch (HRW) said in a report issued in December 2015 that almost 2,000 people were being held on unspecific accusations, such as being pro-Gaddafi or facing torture and ill treatment.[18] Most were released in 2016 and 2017.

Security and state control slipped in Sirte after 2011, making it very dangerous for outsiders. When I arrived in Tripoli in 2013, much of Libya was still accessible for reporters, as long as you trop with caution and had trusted contacts guiding you around. Sirte, in contrast, was nearly impossible to visit. I told my security advisers several times that I wanted to see the city, but they were reluctant to let me go. In June 2014, just as I had won tentative approval for a reporting trip, gunmen killed a Swiss national working for the International Committee of the Red Cross (ICRC). He was based in Misrata, which was more secure, and came for day trips to Sirte. He was shot after leaving a meeting in a government office in the city. My reporting trip was once again cancelled.

The authorities' handling of the aftermath of the killing was typical. The Swiss ambassador, a neighbour of my wife and myself in Tripoli, kept asking for a report of what had happened, hoping also for some signal of regret from the Libyan state. Only weeks later, the Libyan embassy in Berne managed to send a short letter confirming the death, but failed to provide any insight into who might have been behind the killing. According to the ambassador, the name of the victim, 44-year-old Michael Grueb, was spelt incorrectly in the letter.[19]

The arbitrary detentions and overall decline of state institutions left many in Sirte bitter, pining for the good times—when Gaddafi showered his hometown with development projects such as new roads or residential districts. 'Before the revolution, life was so much better,' said Mohamed Ali, an 18-year-old student. 'Schools were always open.'[20] Many of Sirte's younger residents never mentally arrived in the new Libya, which helps explain why at least some didn't mind IS taking over their city. 'They don't bother you unless you come to fight them,' he said. That sentiment would change a few months later, when IS brutally crushed an uprising by a rival Salafist Muslim group.[21]

A Misratan commander at his group's last road checkpoint before IS territory began told me that some officers from Gaddafi's security services had joined IS, similar to former Ba'ath party officials or army officers in Iraq's Mosul. Cases like this seemed more like tactical support. The main fighting force consisted of foreigners, said Commander Tuhami Ahmad, listing the Sudanese, Tunisians, Egyptians, Yemenis and Syrians his men claimed to have seen. 'There have been hundreds,' Ahmed said, speaking to me only after a relative of another commander had called him to vouch for me. 'They have 106s,' he said, referring to high-calibre guns. The bearded commander, in his 30s and wearing standard army uniform, had first refused to talk, banning me and my team from taking pictures or talking to his men, who were scattered around a road checkpoint and giving most cars only a cursory glance. They took shifts, sleeping on mats in an abandoned fast food restaurant. Residents from Sirte, cut off from the water supply, sometimes stopped by to fill their bottles. A long row of shops and cafeterias was shut when I came in May 2015.

Since then, IS fighters had placed themselves between Ben Jawad and Misrata by moving into Sirte from the south, arriving via desert roads and taking over the city one building at a time over a period of weeks, until they even controlled the airport located to the south—exploiting a vacuum while Misrata and Jathran's forces were further east, fighting amongst themselves. This hampered supplies to the Misratan troops, adding to their growing frustration—they had not been paid for months.[22] The Tripoli-based central bank kept salaries back for up to two months to try and slow down the burning of its reserves. I met fighters like Mohammed Abu Shager, who was exhausted having fought Jathran's troops for three months over control of Es Sider, suffering heavy casualties without seizing the port. 'Every night they open fire at us,' he said, pointing to another house some 300 metres away.[23] What had started as an offensive where commanders promised a quick victory against Jathran had turned into a disastrous defence mission with a slow and painful retreat: first from Ben Jawad, then from Sirte when IS arrived, leaving the city centre, then the airport and even the power plant,

191

located on the western edge of the city. This only encouraged IS fighters to deploy suicide bombers as far as the eastern end of Misrata, sending shockwaves through the city. 'We need to do something about Islamic State,' said Ali al-Mahdy, owner of a bookshop on a central Tripoli street, the main battlefield during the 2011 uprising in the port city. 'They are dangerous,' he said.[24] Misrata had mostly escaped turmoil since the toppling of Gaddafi, becoming Libya's most prosperous city thanks to its port business and foreign trade. Now it found itself faced with car bombs for the first time. Even during the fighting in the capital in summer 2015, little impact had been felt in Misrata, where petrol stations never ran out of fuel and shops remained well stocked. Its civilian airport became the main gateway into western Libya.

IS kept pushing, seizing the road from Sirte where Gaddafi had fled before being sodomised with a stick, beaten and finally killed by a mob. Misratan fighters didn't have enough resources to reclaim Sirte in 2015, nor did they manage to hold on to the power plant located in a suburb 20 km from the city centre. At the same time, IS kept them busy with suicide bombings, but made no attempt to move further west. They focused instead on moving south, where they attacked oilfields, kidnapped foreigners and set up shop in Nawfliyah.

But it wasn't long before IS ran into trouble. In Derna, the group was expelled by a rival Islamist militant group, the Abu Salim Martyrs Brigade. The Abu Salim fighters had much better ties with Derna residents (owing to the shared experience of the 2011 uprising) than the foreign IS militants trying to impose their austere religious doctrine on the town. At least seven people were killed when IS opened fire on a protest against their presence in Derna following the killing of an Abu Salim commander. Trouble had been building up for weeks when IS sought to pressure locals and other Sunni groups, some with ties to Al Qaeda, to swear allegiance to caliphate leader Baghdadi.

THE ARRIVAL OF ISLAMIC STATE

It was very difficult to get reliable information out of Derna, where the state never gained real control after the 2011 uprising. There was no police or Libyan army spokesman to call. Our Benghazi-based reporter, Ayman al-Warfalli, kept calling residents, who were often too afraid to talk, to get an idea of what was going on.[25]

In a show of force, one of IS's Yemeni leaders had occupied the landmark Pearl Hotel overlooking the Mediterranean, kicking out staff and setting up a new headquarters.[26] The state-owned hotel, the city's biggest, had been closed anyway, though some staff were still going to work. The move was meant to expand IS's grip, but it backfired, triggering clashes with other armed groups. In the end, the Abu Salim brigade had the better network and roots in the population, which resented the presence of foreign fighters. IS moved out in June 2015 but vowed to take back the city. Military officials later blamed a series of suicide attacks and car bombs on IS, which started just days after the group's withdrawal from Derna. This wasn't the last of their ambitions to reclaim the town: they easily hid in the Green Mountain hinterland, where national hero Omar al-Mukhtar sought refuge when fighting the former Italian colonial rulers before he was caught and executed.

The second setback was in Sirte itself, where a group made up of members of the Ferjan tribe and the Salafists tried to expel IS, who they accused of killing a Salafi preacher, Khaled al-Ferjan, in August 2014. More than 40 people were killed before IS regained complete control of the city. In retaliation, IS torched private homes and executed Salafi fighters, putting their bodies up on public display.

Militants claiming loyalty to IS also struggled to fund themselves—an effort that was complicated by their lack of central leadership. Unlike in Syria and Iraq, they were unable to sell crude oil or petrol as the smuggling routes to Niger, Chad and

Malta were dominated by long-established Libyan networks which saw them as competition. IS also never controlled a border area suitable for petrol smuggling, while the Mabrouk oilfield and other facilities in the central Sirte basin had all closed due to fighting between Jathran's troops and Operation Sunrise. Oil wells had long been turned off by the time IS arrived.

That left IS focusing on kidnappings to obtain ransoms from foreigners or motorists on the main coastal road, and 'donations' from the group in Syria and Iraq. Suicide bombings were not expensive—the explosives or cars were often stolen from military bases—but there was no money to run state services, like in the towns the group had seized in Syria and Iraq.

Tripoli-based state prosecutor Sadiq as-Sour said that militiamen had captured 50 million dinars in Sirte in a bank heist in 2013. Sour claimed this had boosted street gangs and militias, some of whom had joined IS when they conquered Gaddafi's hometown some 18 months later.[27] They also raided a passport office. I had my doubts that many locals had actively joined IS in Sirte, but when IS arrived in spring 2015 they found cash in state buildings, a university campus and banks they had taken over in the central city. They also got petrol from stations in the city and searched houses for weapons. The flow of money ended with their takeover, as the Tripoli-based central bank stopped sending banknotes to the embattled city. State oil firm Brega, in charge of supplying Libya with petrol, also halted shipments to Sirte. Residents like Mohamed Ali, who lives in the western outskirts, would go to nearby villages which would still get fuel from Tripoli or Misrata depots supplied by the National Oil Corporation (NOC).[28]

Another, albeit modest, source for funding was the state salaries from Libyans who had defected from other militias but were still on the payroll. There were reports of members from local groups switching allegiances as IS, with its brutal beheadings, provided Islamists with a more attractive platform than Ansar, which was focused on combating Haftar's troops. When fighters left Ansar (or other groups) their salaries were still paid by the central bank under the militia-funding scheme set up by the transitional government in 2012. Members who had never been affiliated with another militia still received salaries if they had been in the public service, or had received help from a state programme such as the social insurance fund.

In December 2016, the Misratan troops, now operating under the banner of the new UN-brokered unity government (boycotted by the east), managed to retake Sirte after months of heavy street fighting. The US flew some 500 airstrikes against ammunition depots and other targets after a request from Tripoli, while Western special forces on the ground helped advise the Libyan troops how best to enter the city—just as they had helped with intelligence when taking Tripoli from Gaddafi. The airstrikes flattened entire residential districts, especially the El Manar and Giza Bahriya areas where IS made a last stand—both districts are located on a hill, so fighters used them as vantage points. Some 700 men, mostly from Misrata, fighting IS were killed.[29]

Around 2,500 to 3,000 homes need to be rebuilt so families who fled to Misrata or other parts of Sirte can return, Siddeeq Ismail, a municipal official said in an interview in October 2017 when I visited Sirte. 'They are suffering from a lack of services, and we don't see any real efforts or results on the ground at any level,' he said. When I visited the two destroyed quarters there were rows of piles of concrete, metal and doors—showing where residential houses used to be. Inside what was left of the buildings were skulls and skeletons—residents were unsure whether they belonged to the fighters or their own relatives, and with unexploded ordnances buried in rubble, it was too risky to retrieve them. While some parts of the city were back to normal, with supermarkets buzzing with customers, there was no sign of any reconstruction activity or support from Tripoli to rebuild the destroyed districts. Anger and frustration was rising, providing a new breeding ground for radicals. 'If the situation continues like this then *Daesh* will come back, no doubt. That was the reason why they came. People felt angry, felt sidelined,' said Ali Miftah, a civil servant and father of five who took me and some colleagues on a tour through his destroyed district, which had been one of the city's most affluent areas. 'Now we don't get any support from the government. Look at these ruins. We lost everything.'

While he was talking, other bombed-out residents joined in, complaining that their houses had not yet been rebuilt, forcing them to live in rented apartments in Sirte or even Misrata. They were struggling to pay their rent, as public salaries had been delayed by the country's cash liquidity crisis. Some were open about having supported Ansar al-Sharia fighters who had established a strong base in the city before IS arrived. Ansar al-Sharia had set up checkpoints on the main road crossing Sirte from Misrata to the east, but they had also done charitable work, such as distributing food and medicine, which had won over some marginalised residents. IS used Ansar al-Sharia as a springboard, recruiting some of its members when they arrived. 'Daesh took over the city in stages. They recruited members of Ansar al-Sharia, which was popular because they were running charities, helping the people,' said another resident called Ali Suliman, standing in front of his destroyed house. 'I also supported them. Then some Ansar members joined *Daesh*, there was a split and the repression started when they imposed their harsh rules. It was terrible.'

Many residents recall with horror the executions and hard rules imposed by the group, fearing that they or another radical group would make a comeback and recruit from the angry pool of residents—something that could happen with a largely absent state. Salafists have started to fill the vacuum again, with an affiliated group called the 604th Infantry Brigade having emerged as a major security force.[30] The group follows the Madkhali Salafist school, mentioned in Chapter 4. 'While Madkhali doctrine emphasises obedience to a sitting ruler and political quietism, as constituted in Libya, Madkhali followers are anything but apolitical,' wrote Libya researchers Frederic Wehrey and Emad Badi.

I tried returning to Sirte during my two reporting trips to Libya, but there was no time, no security clearance from Reuters and none of the necessary paperwork—the usual mix of obstacles that put paid to most of my travel plans. I stayed in contact with residents, though: a member of the Sirte municipal council told me in December 2018 that the Salafist brigade controlled most primary schools, had replaced imams and was acting as a police force, arresting at people will. They also set up a technical college and took control of local media.[31]

Security remains poor, as IS has staged several suicide bombings in Sirte and even Misrata, attacking a courthouse in October 2017 and sending shockwaves through the port city which has been spared much of the country's violence. Sirte residents are particularly exposed because the city sits between the country's rival forces: the Misrata-based militias linked to the Tripoli government and General Haftar's forces in the east. There is very little coordination between the rivals, neither of whom has done much to deter IS from establishing camps south of Sirte. Even security officials are unsure they will be able prevent any new attacks on the city. 'We contain the threat, but we cannot chase them in their camps because we lack the right equipment like four-wheel cars we need to drive in the desert,' said Taher Hadeed, an official with the main Misrata force in Sirte, the Bunyan al-Marsus (Solid Rock) brigade. 'It won't be possible for *Daesh* to take back the city, but there is a risk of attacks.'

By mid-2018 there were signs IS was making a comeback in the deserts of central and south-eastern Libya. With Libya's porous borders, the group can ship in new fighters or weapons with ease, due to the lack of an oppositional Shi'ite community, which is part of the reason they lost the strongholds of Mosul and Raqqa in 2017. During 2018, IS staged several attacks on desert towns deep in the southeast, occupying no territory but sowing terror by kidnapping locals. In October, they killed four and wounded ten when driving into the desert town of al-Foqha, south of Jufra, kidnapping at least six residents who were later executed.[32] The group also claimed several high-profile attacks in the capital, with gunmen and bombers attacking the national election commission's premises in May 2018, the NOC headquarters in September and the foreign ministry three months later, shattering the illusion of relative safety in Tripoli just as Serraj's government was trying to woo embassy staff back from Tunis. As long as unemployment, poverty and the absence of the state persists, the revolution's losers will struggle to find their place in the new Libya, and more fighters will join IS or other extremist groups.

9

A COUNTRY BEYOND REPAIR?

In August 2017 the UN made a new push for a political settlement to unify the rival governments and main power blocs in western Libya and the east, in a bid for stability. A new UN envoy, the sixth mission head since 2011, Ghassan Salamé, took office and outlined an ambitious plan to negotiate a deal to pave the way for parliamentary and presidential elections the following year. The main difference between Salamé (a Lebanese national) and most of his predecessors is that he is a native Arabic speaker, which gave him better access in a country where even top officials rarely speak foreign languages. He also had an advantage over his Spanish and German predecessors, having experienced civil war in his home country (between 1975 and 1990), providing personal insight into the challenges of resolving conflict in a deeply fragmented country.

For the first round of talks in September 2017, Salamé invited delegations from the east and the west to a luxury hotel in Tunis, having returned to Libya after two years in Nigeria. The event was strikingly similar to one in 2015, when then UN envoy Bernardino Leon invited rival camps to a luxury hotel in the

Moroccan resort town of Skhirat, offering almost identical platitudes about state-building that were somewhat divorced from the reality on the ground. Leon had begun to mediate after the country split in 2014. Then, talks started in Libya but moved to Morocco, where delegates agreed on a shaky power-sharing deal that produced a weak new Tripoli administration called the Government of National Accord (GNA), headed by a presidency council with Fayez al-Serraj as prime minister. His administration was never accepted by the east, where the House of Representatives in Tobruk, linked to Haftar, refused to give its approval. The UN agreement also created the Tripoli-based state council, a quasi-parliamentary body advising Serraj's government in an effort to broaden power by including as many figures as possible. The names of the new institutions all looked impressive, but you'd need a dictionary to remember all the official titles and abbreviations for Libyan state bodies created since 2011.

Leon quit late in 2015 following a job offer from the UAE, the main foreign back of Haftar and his Libyan National Army (LNA), support which undermined a solution at the negotiation table by giving the LNA a military edge. The more Haftar grew his military and territory, the less reason his camp had to compromise. A German UN envoy, Martin Kobler, followed Leon but also made little progress in bridging the differences between the rival camps. Now trying to revive the stalled process, Salamé wanted to expand the state bodies created under the 2015 deal to create a government that could prepare the country for elections—an impossible task given the fractious situation on the ground.

Delegates' opening speeches in Tunis were also similar to those made at previous talks: full of vague pledges to overcome divisions and take responsibility to end the country's crisis. After one month, the show was over. Neither side could not agree on the role Haftar, who was testing the ground to run for president in the upcoming polls, would play: the Tobruk faction didn't agree on a proposal to put the commander of a future unified army in charge of the Presidential Council, the top body in Tripoli. On the last day, Salamé's media team invited the press, hoping to announce some sort of interim deal or at least the parties' commitment to continue talks. They invited us hours before a planned news conference and had us wait in the courtyard of the UN compound while talks were ongoing inside. Salamé, flanked by the two delegation heads, made a brief statement that talks would be interrupted as further consultations were needed in Libya.

I learned just how unprepared Libya was for a peace deal when I returned in November 2017. The capital was highly dysfunctional (and highly repressive for reporters), despite having a UN-backed government in place which was meant to restore order and build up a functioning state. Serraj's challenge was even greater than that of previous administrations: he had to make do without use of a real army and police force. Security remained poor, with Mitiga airport regularly closed during shootouts between rival groups. The only Western embassies reopening were Italy and Turkey. The UN mission and some other European embassies had reopened their compounds, but diplomats rarely spent time there, preferring to parachute in from the safety of Tunis. Power cuts and interruptions to the water supply were frequent, which made life difficult for residents tired after years of chaos.

The welfare state bites back

There was little sign of real activity from the Serraj government, apart from the familiar sight of ministry staff coming to work but doing very little. The prime minister spent much of his time on foreign trips to western European, Arab and African capitals—even meeting US President Donald Trump as Western powers tried to bridge the gap between his administration and the eastern camp to bolster a new attempt to unify the country. There was a constant flow of photos of Serraj meeting one foreign minister or another, but little concrete action as security in Libya remained too poor for substantive support or investment on the ground. Another blast from the past was ministries' hiring of foreign PR agencies to document the meetings and activities of high-profile government officials. Journalists would be emailed up to five statements a day, with titles like this one from 17 December 2017: 'The head of the Presidential Council (Serraj) returns home after a work visit to Algeria.'[1]

At the same time, the Serraj government did very little to deliver basic services. Tripoli residents were drilling water holes through pavements when I visited in November 2017, after an armed group had cut off water supplies from southern reservoirs via the Great Man-Made River system after a rival faction had arrested one of its members in Tripoli. The GNA was helpless and had little to offer beyond appeals to restore the supply. With my colleague Aidan Lewis, I met the totally frustrated head of the water authority, Naji Assaed, and while he was talking, a private water truck brought fresh supplies to his own building. For him, this latest gap in service provision was just the latest in a long line of frustrations. With the central bank spending oil revenues to pay for the welfare state, his authority had only received emergency funds since 2011, meaning his engineers had been unable to carry out maintenance work for years. 'The technical state of the water pipeline system is poor as we haven't done enough maintenance,' he said. That explains why water supplies remained unreliable even after officials persuaded the armed group to turn on the water, after three long, dry weeks.

At least Asaed was trying to get something done. By contrast, there was Abdelrahman Swehli—head of the state council—and a familiar face from the post-2011 turmoil. Having been a member of the General National Congress (GNC) in 2012, he joined the Libya Dawn movement, which, backed by Islamists, had attacked and seized Tripoli in summer 2014. Fearing a coup by Haftar, the movement established its non-recognised administration and rejected the outcome of parliamentary elections that June. He enthusiastically defended the city attack and had close ties to militias in his home city of Misrata.

Now Swehli was living in the presidential suite of the Radisson Blu Al Mahary Hotel, where he had an office and dozens of people working for him. The interview was a farce. I came with my colleague Aidan and a cameraman, but an aide came down to tell us only one correspondent was permitted upstairs. I stayed with the cameraman, but after 20 minutes or so the aide returned and allowed me to join Aidan. I wanted to take the cameraman with me, but again the aide objected. After another 20 minutes or so our cameraman was also admitted, and we were all ushered through to the main room, where Swehli was waiting.

During the interview, in which he attacked Haftar and spoke about Libya's envisioned transition to democracy, Swehli had his own media team film us as well. He kept talking about the need for new elections, but made it clear he would not accept a result that saw Haftar's election. He kept asking when we would publish our story so he could issue a parallel statement about the interview. The interview contained little information of any news value. Swehli's main activity appeared to be meeting ambassadors and UN officials—all of whom visit him in the suite to try and persuade him to contribute to a peace settlement. The hotel lobby was packed with other officials who spent their days making phone calls and holding meetings without being able to do much actual work.

The disconnect between people like Swehli and their counterparts and rivals in other cities could be felt during a visit to Bani

Walid, a town nestled in rocky hills some 150 km southeast of Tripoli. I had visited Bani Walid in 2014, when people there talked cautiously of their support for Gaddafi. Now, having lost all faith in the new Libya, people were much more open—there was even a green flag in the city's main square. 'For us in Bani Walid it was much better before [under Gaddafi]. We had stability, salaries, security, health care,' said Mohamed Hussein, a 40-year-old public servant who was searching through the rubble of a hotel bombed by NATO looking for metal and corrugated iron to sell—his salary hadn't been paid for months. Even if it came through, he said, it was not enough to pay the bills inflated by the drop in value of the dinar. Such is the frustration that, at a meeting of leaders of the Warfalla tribe, some exclaimed they wanted Saif al-Islam, whose whereabouts are unclear, to run for president. Neither the UN Envoy Salamé, nor his recycled message, had ever visited them.

Back in the capital, journalists were experiencing hostility. In the first years after the revolution there was curiosity, but we were now met with suspicion and were even scapegoated by officials for the country's problems. A colleague of mine filed a story on the terrible conditions in detention centres, where migrants faced abuse, torture and starvation.[2] One official in the Gharyan facility south of Tripoli even admitted that the situation was dire: fewer boats were leaving due to intensified coastguard patrols, which led to overcrowded detention centres in the hinterland where desperate migrants from sub-Saharan countries were still arriving, unaware that the coast was now a dead end. But when the story and an accompanying TV report came out, the official and his colleagues accused us of distorting the reality and damaging Gharyan's reputation. The department's spokesman banned us from visiting any more detention facilities, demanding a written apology. I sat with several colleagues in the spokesman's office, pleading for access, but to no avail. 'You need to apologise for the article which smeared our reputation,' he said.

I went to his supervisor in the interior ministry—an open-minded officer who agreed that there was much abuse in detention centres and who called the spokesman to persuade him to change his mind. He even gave us a letter instructing the spokesman to give us access, which also proved unsuccessful. 'I'm not interested in any letter, I want an apology,' he insisted. It was a time when pictures of starving African migrants sleeping on top of one another in overcrowded hangars and cages were emerging, and CNN ran its report on a slave auction. Officials were on edge, but the episode showed again that the government in Tripoli was powerless. One public servant with a different agenda could easily defy an order with no threat of disciplinary action.

It wasn't just journalists being stonewalled: even diplomats and top foreign officials were struggling to carry out their duties. The French Foreign Minister, Jean-Yves Le Drian, flew to Libya in December 2017 to meet Serraj in Tripoli and then Haftar in Benghazi to discuss the latest UN talks and the conditions for migrants in detention centres. After meeting Serraj in his office he walked 100 m to one such facility, as planned and cleared by Serraj's government and the head of the department to fight illegal immigration, Hisham Bisher. But when he arrived, guards at the iron door of the decaying facility refused the delegation's admission. 'It's a detention centre,' said a tetchy man who said he was the facility's supervisor. 'Nobody is allowed in. Not the minister, and not journalists.' Le Drian's entourage had no choice but to leave, with the prime minister's authority not even stretching the short distance from his office to the centre.[3]

Shocking too was the surging poverty among Libyans, whose currency had dropped 200 per cent against the US dollar on the black market from 2014 to 2017, driving up inflation as Libya needs to import even basic food staples. Libyans had long managed to survive even after the country plunged into chaos in 2011 thanks to the generous welfare state, but this was now changing as low oil revenues made it difficult for the central bank to fund the system, delaying public salaries for up to six months for lack of liquidity. 'I haven't been paid for four months,' said Fatima, a 40-year-old woman from the southern city of Sabha—hit by anarchy and tribal fighting—selling small gold charms to pay for diabetes treatment in Tunisia for her sister standing next to her, who said: 'We're helpless.'

Just next to the gold market was the spot where the currency dealers were offering black market rates just behind the central bank headquarters. With a pistol tucked into the back pocket of his jeans, one of them was carrying a small plastic bag of dollars upstairs to a room in a courtyard above a restaurant. Minutes later, someone else came up with a larger bag of dinars. Ordinary people were losing out because the central bank kept the rate at 1.3 against the dollar, because officials feared there was no policy in place should the rate be adjusted closer to the black market rate of 9.6. But in reality the spread offered the door to massive corruption for a well-connected elite, because the bank allocated hard currency at the official rate for importers who used their credit letters to get cash to sell on the black market. The government temporarily stopped credit letters in October 2017 after one dodgy request to import tuna worth $120,000, more than the country's annual consumption, for 40 per cent of the released quantity.[4] That pushed the dinar further down, accelerating inflation and increasing hardship yet more. Many people even found themselves taking up the manual labour long shunned by Libyans. 'I got only three times salary since October,' said Salman Rashid, a public servant in the interior ministry visiting the market in the old city with his wife. 'I have started doing any work, apartment design and maintenance, just anything.'

Apart from the economic crisis, there was something sinister in the air in Tripoli and other cities where security had somehow improved. There were fewer major battles between militias, but the atmosphere had become more repressive, with the rise of Salafists—supporters of a puritanical interpretation of Islam—who have expanded across Libya, not just in the capital and western cities but also in the east, where Haftar has allied himself with Islamist brigades, who have been burning books in public and enforcing their 'morality rules'. Tripoli had never been much of a cultural or entertainment destination, but there were events like book fairs and workshops promoting women which had all but disappeared by 2017. The Rada Salafist militia raided a comic festival in Tripoli while I was there, and more and more Sufi shrines and mosques were attacked by Salafists who saw them, like comics, as un-Islamic. Libya has always been a conservative Muslim country, but the Salafists were turning mainstream—spreading intolerance and killing any hope for young people to gain access to modern entertainment or education.

'Supermilitias'

While the government was unable to provide reliable services, the militias—having successfully milked the state since 2011—thrived. Militias were now fully embedded in the state apparatus, and they had expanded their business interests by putting their men in ministries which could then appoint their comrades and supply them with weapons. Militiamen can make as much as 4,000 Libyan dinars, way above the average public servant salary (around 800 to 1,000).[5] Over the years, the militias diversified their interests, moving away from public salaries after the Tripoli-based central bank governor Sadiq al-Kabir made it more difficult to obtain a national identity card—a requirement to get on the public payroll.[6] Armed groups turned to other sources of income, using the territorial control of state bodies to blackmail officials.

For ordinary Libyans, militia control of ministries and banks made life more difficult. While citizens had to queue to receive cash (which was in short supply from the central bank), militias were able to help themselves whenever new stocks were delivered. They also decided who had access to cash, and even the forms needed to make domestic bank transfers. I met a 26-year-old female student who, while trying to send money home to her father in Benghazi, was blackmailed by a young militiamen who demanded to meet her late at night in a café—a no-go in such a conservative society. 'He wouldn't allow me to ask a bank employee to make a bank transfer to Benghazi unless I gave him my phone number,' she said. 'I gave him my number because I had no other choice, but I had to change it when he started pestering me late at night.'

The militias controlling Tripoli forced Serraj's Presidential Council and the central bank to hand out lucrative credit import letters to receive dollars at the official rate of 1.4, which they could then exchange on the black market rate for rates as high as 9.[7] Militias also kidnapped officials and businessmen to force the payment of ransoms and have them sign contracts or appoint their people to key positions. An armed group involved in fuel smuggling tried to force the head of the Brega Petroleum Marketing Company, a subsidiary of the National Oil Corporation (NOC), to resign after unsuccessfully lobbying the company to rescind the appointment. 'Armed men stormed the new chairman's office to threaten him and try to force him to resign. We saw how they also ran propaganda campaigns on social media,' the NOC said in September 2018.[8] Libya's sovereign wealth fund was forced to recruit staff from another militia group.[9]

By 2017, four 'supermilitias' consolidated power in Tripoli, officially working with Serraj's government but in reality blackmailing state institutions and banks to give them business. These were the Tripoli Revolutionaries' Brigade of Haitham al-Tajouri, which has switched loyalties several times since 2011, the Salafist forces of Rada, the Nawasi brigade and a group led by Abdelghani al-Kikli, yet another militia commander.

The supermilitias gradually sidelined other armed groups, especially those from Misrata who had backed Libya Dawn. Some militias stayed in Tripoli, clashing several times with the supermilitias before finally giving up.[10] 'By May 2017, central Tripoli, with its state institutions, banks, businesses, and the capital's only functioning airport, was divided between four large armed groups, clearly contrasting with the previous situation, in which a plethora of armed groups had directly competed for influence,' Libya researchers Wolfram Lacher and Alaa al-Idrissi wrote.[11]

The power consolidation had an unexpected consequence: it made Tripoli safer. There were clashes over the airport, but they fought fewer street battles (common when I lived in Tripoli from 2013–2015) and were focused instead on improving their businesses. Tajouri bought real estate in the UAE,[12] set up businesses and traded with credit letters for imports—all activities for which you need foreign partners, and thus, there were lulls in news reports of militia violence. The commander, who asked his followers to call him 'Haj Haitham' since doing the Muslim pilgrimage in Saudi Arabia in 2018, was driving around in his Mercedes S-Class, opening banks in the evening to the cheers of women who had been queuing for hours.[13]

The illusion of security was shattered when Tripoli militia leaders became millionaires, attracting the envy of other armed groups. A new Tripoli battle ensued when a group called the seventh brigade from Tarhouni, a town to the southeast of Tripoli, together with some Misratan groups, attacked the Tripoli cartel in August 2018, with clashes in a southern suburb around the old airport, scene of heavy fighting in 2014. The seventh brigade was little known to some Libya-watchers, who struggle to keep up with the number of armed groups emerging (and often very quickly disappearing) since 2011. They accused the four supermilitias of being '*Daesh*', or Islamic State (IS), for plundering state coffers.

The clashes showed how the parameters of politics had shifted since 2011. While the 2012 election was still partly about politics and the future direction of Libya, this battle was all about fighting over state funds, driven by a greed that transcended political convictions. Salamé managed to broker a shaky ceasefire after six weeks of clashes that left 100 civilians dead and many buildings in southern Tripoli damaged. Migrants in various detention centres were caught up in the fighting, forced to load ammunition onto trucks.[14] Others escaped after guards fled, but were re-arrested later.[15] Some 400 prison inmates also fled during the chaos, shattering the illusion of the safe parliamentary and presidential elections that had been scheduled for 10 December 2018.[16]

The ceasefire has largely held, but what followed was the usual tried and failed strategy: the UN launched a new 'security arrangement' for Tripoli, intended to bring a police force into operation to replace the militias. Ceremonies were held by the interior ministry, an entity controlled by militias, at key sites such as Tripoli Mitiga airport. These events, designed to 'hand over' control, were farcical: militiamen would disappear into one room and emerge minutes later, decked out in interior ministry uniforms.

I was unable to cover the Tripoli clashes as I was waiting for a visa for four months. When it finally came through in November, an eerie calm had returned to the capital. While the Serraj administration was still unable to provide basic services, the foreign media office swung into action to obstruct coverage. My colleague Aidan and I were joined by a minder, reinstating a rule from the Gaddafi era. The press office had become part of the foreign ministry; the minister, Mohamed Siyala, is a Gaddafi-era career diplomat, so this was a logical step from his point of view. We have known the minder, an employee from the media office, since 2011—he was a believer in a democratic Libya and was personally disappointed at having to work as a minder again, like in the old days. He let us do our work more or less without shadowing us, even apologising on trips outside Tripoli for having to report back every hour or so to his bosses.

What was worse were attempts by the media office to force us to pay imaginary taxes. They claimed this was a new law (and certainly it was one we had never heard of before)—officials obviously had got ideas from the militias about how to make money. To pressure us, officials withdrew accreditations for our local reporters for six months, forcing them underground with claims we had violated labour and other laws. I spent much of my time sorting out the paperwork, holding lengthy but unproductive meetings with officials—one of them always going out to report by phone to their boss as to whether I would give in to a long list of demands. I refused to budge, and was eventually promised the cards over dinner in Tripoli's best Lebanese restaurant, but when the director showed up he brought a female friend to the table and asked me to hire her as an office assistant, withholding the press cards again. I once again refused and got Salamé's office and Western embassies involved. Finally, I managed to reinstate the permits for our local team and fend off the tax claims. Unfortunately, much of the ten-day reporting trip was spent on such time-consuming meetings.

A police state in the east

In 2019 something unexpected happened—I got a visa to visit eastern Libya, which has its own immigration system. I and my successor as Libya correspondent had tried in vain to get a visa for Benghazi, home to the Haftar administration, ever since my last visit in 2015. Made up of former Gaddafi soldiers, security agents and other regime figures officials, the administration there is even less receptive to journalists than Tripoli. But with Western countries such as France, Italy and UK warming to Haftar, officials are more open to the idea of hosting a foreign reporter.

Coincidence and luck still played a big role in getting me there. Our Benghazi reporter Ayman al-Warfalli met a top LNA official at a social function and asked him whether we could submit questions to Haftar in writing (Haftar rarely gives sit-down interviews). We submitted some very general questions on the prospect of elections and a political settlement and turned the responses into a story, mainly to build a relationship and get a visa for me. The results weren't very interesting, save for the following quote: 'Which elections are you talking about?' Haftar asked, perhaps summing up his attitude towards a ballot. I braced myself for the usual complaints, but Haftar's officials were mainly concerned with whether we would address him by his 'official' title, Field Marshall. At first I declined, but they offered a visa if we did, so I added a line saying that his parliament had bestowed the title on him. That did the trick—though it still took five months to actually get the visa, which came in the form of a handwritten letter from Benghazi airport in which my name was spelt incorrectly, my nationality was changed to Dutch and my passport number was missing. Nevertheless, Haftar's officials assured me that this would be enough to make it to Benghazi.

Since my last visit, Haftar's administration had built up a parallel state—a real army, in the words of his advisers. I had assumed that there was more of a state than in Tripoli, but my first impressions were not good. Benghazi Benina appeared to be run by a ragtag band of officials—some in uniform, some not, some with badges, some not—who struggled to make sense of passports and visas. There were no computers, and my passport wandered from hand to hand. Our reporter Ayman, accompanied by a security officer, managed to get me through.

Benghazi was indeed much safer. There had been several suicide bombings in 2018 and at one point there were clashes between a Salafist brigade and other LNA units, but otherwise Benghazi was as safe as in the intermediate aftermath of the 2011 uprising—shops, restaurants and even theatres had reopened. The other contrast to Tripoli was the widespread destruction caused by Haftar's 2014–2017 city war. Entire districts had been flattened, but life for those who did not oppose Haftar openly was otherwise back to normal.

Eager to talk to civilians, I went with Ayman to the old city, a district which was one of the last strongholds for Haftar's opponents and which was almost entirely destroyed. It was here that the first protests against Gaddafi had erupted in February 2011, when relatives of prisoners killed in the Abu Salim massacre demanded answers. I wanted to talk to people who had backed the uprising about how they felt now. 'Muammar needed to go but democracy hasn't worked out in Libya,' said Miftah Atluba, sitting in the café he had reopened in 2011, but closed again three years later when fighting broke out. Now running his business once more, Atluba said 'We need a military ruler.' When I asked who that could be, he responded without hesitation: 'I can only see Khalifa Haftar as president. He has built the state.'

I heard this in many of my interviews in Benghazi. I was aware that some might be reluctant to talk openly to a reporter, but since I didn't have minder, speak Arabic and always assured people I wouldn't quote them by name, I have no doubt this was a sincere expression of support. Just as under Gaddafi, dissent is not tolerated under Haftar's rule, and thousands of his opponents and their families had fled west, like the female student Fatma (mentioned in Chapter 4) who I had met in Tripoli in 2018. The houses of those who left were seized by families loyal to Haftar's forces, while Human Rights Watch (HRW) has repeatedly documented extrajudicial executions, imprisonment, beatings and other forms of abuse of opponents in Benghazi.[17]

There is still some opposition inside Benghazi, with some residents accusing Haftar and his family of corruption on a similar scale to Gaddafi. Residents pointed out to me the central bank branch in the old city that had been robbed by an LNA elite unit commanded by Saddam Khalifa, Haftar's most prominent son.[18] But the overall mood in Benghazi was in favour of a strong state after years of chaos and violence. The debate was around whether or not people want Haftar to become president—many told me they didn't, but still supported the idea of having an army. Even civil society activists campaigning for a civilian state drew the line here: many of their colleagues had been assassinated in violence blamed on Islamist militants before the LNA was formed. 'In Benghazi, most people would not allow you to criticise the army because they've paid a price,' said Jamal Falah, an activist who wants to organise a national dialogue with the rest of the country.

Benghazi seemed to be enjoying a vibrant cultural life, too. I visited a theatre session which tackled state failure and corruption, portraying Libyans trying to get flights to Tunisia for medical treatment but finding that flights are booked out by officials who had bribed airline staff. While not criticising the LNA, the actors did dare to poke fun at Salafists. When one traveller, having finally arrived in comparatively liberal Tunis, is chided by a fellow countryman for drinking beer, he retorted to a laughing audience: 'In Tunisia, you don't need security approval to have a drink.'

But while cafés were packed and people were repairing their houses, activity in government offices was as unproductive as in Tripoli. In the east there is even less to do, as ministries have little or no budget. The east has carbon copies of Tripoli ministries and other state bodies, including the civil aviation authority and its own version of the NOC. The building carries the same logo at the entrance and boasts an extensive 'executive' car park packed with BMWs and sports-utility vehicles driven by senior officials, but otherwise the 500 or so staff have literally nothing to do. 'We are waiting for the authorisation to work. We are ready,' said a senior official,[19] sitting in front of a huge (but empty) desk. On another floor I bumped into a deputy prime minister who also had plenty of time to talk. 'We are ready to work,' he told me, over sweetened tea.[20]

It was a similar picture at the central bank, housed in a new building where Ayman and I spoke to governor Ali Salm al-Hibri for two hours. I wanted to leave, but he kept going, discussing theoretical economic models from US economist Milton Friedman and other academics whose work he thought could be useful in analysing Libya's economy. Of course, he too had very little to do, and several offices in the building were empty, with chairs still covered in plastic from the warehouse. I first met Hibri in 2013 when has still deputy governor of a united Libyan central bank. He and two other members of staff I met that day made the move east when the country broke up in 2014.

The inability of the eastern government to rebuild destroyed districts and provide basic services was fuelling public frustration, which only benefited Haftar and his military men. The message in the heads of many Libyans manipulated by pro-LNA media is that civilian officials get no work done and can't provide security—a sentiment which had helped Haftar to assemble his men in 2014. The fact that Tripoli sent no reconstruction budget exacerbated the overall feeling of neglect. 'I refurbished my shop, which had been heavily damaged, without any help from the government,' said Anis Tajouri, who had just reopened a one-room store selling wedding dresses in Benghazi's old market. He refused to endorse Haftar as a presidential candidate but, like others, he wanted a strong leader. 'The democracy we've had since 2011 hasn't worked out. We are a tribal society.'[21]

Diehard Haftar supporters called elections a waste of time unless the LNA was controlling Tripoli. They had little time for Salamé's roadmap and national reconciliation conference. In almost all interviews, opponents were labelled as members of the

Muslim Brotherhood, a designation widely used in the east for anyone from western Libya. 'The army has secured the east and, thank God, with the southern offensive now also the south,' said Fawzeia al-Furjani, head of a local business council run by women and who is from Haftar's tribe. 'How can you hold elections in the west when you have militias and the Muslim Brotherhood in control?'

So, is Haftar committed to elections, as Salamé and Western diplomats keep saying? His aides say so, but many have doubts. In interviews he has suggested that Libyans are not ready for elections or the idea of democracy. 'Democracy is a culture which builds itself, it's not a cup of instant coffee,' he said on one occasion.[22] He agreed to hold presidential and parliamentary elections on 10 December 2018 at a meeting brokered by French President Emmanuel Macron in Paris in May 2018. But there was no written agreement, and the next day LNA officials denied anything had been agreed at all. Besides, six weeks of clashes between Tripoli supermilitias were a reminder to Western diplomats that security was too fragile to hold a fair vote. The Tobruk-based rump parliament allied to Haftar failed to approve legislation in time because lawmakers, fearful they would lose their jobs after the election of a new assembly, dragged their feet.[23]

Haftar let his guard slip during two meetings with Western ambassadors at which his key advisers were not present, telling them a 'military solution' was best.[24] Western powers tried keep up their hopes of holding elections by bringing Serraj and Haftar together with other key players at another conference, this time in Palermo in November. I travelled there and spent much of the first day in a room with other reporters waiting for Haftar to arrive. The commander kept everybody waiting until late at night, when he finally arrived for a photo with Italian Prime Minister Giuseppe Conte—before skipping the official dinner.

To the horror of the Italians, Haftar's LNA issued a statement saying Haftar wouldn't be attending the conference, instead holding bilateral meetings in Palermo. The move was directed at his base, who were sceptical of the need to negotiate with opponents and hold a national conference to make a new attempt to prepare elections. LNA spokesman Mismari also tweeted in Italian for their hosts to understand that Haftar was not participating in the summit. A photo of him meeting Serraj, distributed by the Italian government, showed who really was in charge. Haftar embraced Conte with both arms, while Serraj, standing somewhat awkwardly to the side, put a hand on Conte's back to join the hug. Haftar departed early, skipping the normally obligatory official summit photograph, leaving participants wondering whether he was interested in the UN peace process at all. He did not address the press directly, leaving an Italian government official to convey waiting reporters something he had supposedly told Serraj: 'You don't change horses while crossing a river.' The Italians' interpretation was that Haftar would not seek to topple the Tripoli premier until elections took place. Diplomats took this as sign that Haftar was committed to elections and a political solution, but his next move would only serve to escalate tensions further.

EPILOGUE

PERPETUAL ENDGAME

As Reuters North Africa bureau chief I was responsible for coverage in Libya, Algeria, Tunisia and Morocco, so my focus switched when mass protests against veteran Algerian ruler Abdelaziz Bouteflika broke out in February 2019.[1] Our Tripoli reporter, Ahmed Elumami, alerted me when rumours about a move on Tripoli by Khalifa Haftar and his Libyan National Army (LNA) intensified in March. Sometimes the telltale signs can be subtle: he had seen some youths driving around the city late at night and playing loud pro-LNA songs on their car radios. I quickly put together a story, between near-constant output on Algeria's turmoil, just to flag to readers that something might happen. The headline sounded as dramatic as any other story from Libya, but I didn't believe an offensive would actually happen and later thought of the article as sensationalist.[2]

Haftar and his supporters had been talking for years about moving from the east to 'liberate' the capital from militias, framing this as a counter-terrorism operation by a real army. But few thought Haftar's forces would be able to stage such an assault, despite the massive military aid provided by Egypt and the UAE over the preceding few years. After all, they had needed more than three

219

years to take Benghazi, so Tripoli seemed a stretch for a force which was little more than a loose assembly of militias.

A military offensive simply didn't make sense: Haftar had, in recent years, gained international recognition, travelling several times to Italy and France, whose governments received him in quasi-official capacity. He had shifted from rogue general to a commander you had to work with, as his force controlled an alliance of tribes in the east. It was clear there would be no political solution that didn't include Haftar, so UN Envoy Ghassan Salamé and Western powers reached out to his camp after a French-led plan to hold elections in December 2018 collapsed.

On 3 April 2019, Haftar's forces published a statement about a deployment of troops to western Libya to fight militias, plus a video of a convoy of military trucks moving along a lonely coastal road.[3] It didn't specify the location, but it was clear the vehicles were headed west from Benghazi. I recognised it as the same wind-blown road I had driven when I had visited Ibrahim Jathran in his lair in 2013, after his forces had seized the eastern oil ports. The next day the LNA entered Gharyan, taking over the town and turning it into a forward base to stage an assault on the capital.

Talk of an offensive had been building since January, when Haftar began a surprise campaign to take the south after months of martial language from LNA figures and their supporters. Like the Benghazi and Tripoli campaigns, this was described as counter-terrorism—in this case to bring order to the long-neglected, lawless south, fight militants and secure the El Sharara and El Feel oilfields which produce some 400,000 barrels a day—a third of Libya's crude output at the time.

Haftar sent only a light force: some 40 vehicles[4] on 12 January, staying first at the Tamanhint air base outside the main city of Sebha, reinforcing its presence while avoiding all-out war. A further 40 vehicles followed, and troops finally entered Sebha—

taking the entire southwest within six weeks.[5] There was fighting with Tebu tribesmen over Murzuq town, but otherwise Haftar's forces co-opted tribal players to achieve their ends. The eastern parallel government was quick to fly in officials to claim ownership of Sebha, changing door signs at state bodies to read 'Interim Government', as we saw in Tripoli whenever a new government took charge. Officials also sent cash and petrol, much to the delight of locals who had long given up on state services.[6] The southern campaign was not as bloody as the battle over Benghazi, but Haftar's forces changed the social fabric of the region, leading to fighting between local groups that would put an end to the fragile stability announced by the fighters.

When the southern campaign was over, troops returned northeast. Some units went back to Benghazi, but others stopped roughly halfway at the oasis of Jufra, some 550 km away. LNA officials played down the move (saying they were only reinforcing an existing base) but in Tripoli alarm bells rang: the troops could head home or turn west towards the capital. More hints were dropped with letters posted on social media appearing to appoint officers to take charge of western regions. Even when I was in Benghazi in early February, officers told me that Special Forces Commander Wanis Bukhamada would be made commander of the Tripoli region. We tried to confirm the appointment, but LNA spokesman Ahmed Mismari claimed they were fake. Either way, it was clear there was a pattern.

Pressure tactics

Haftar's camp sought to pressure Tripoli Prime Minister Serraj, who met him in Abu Dhabi on 27 February to discuss a power-sharing deal as a first step to overcome divisions, with the ultimate goal of holding elections—a plan few Libyans believed would come to fruition anytime soon. The UAE brokered the meeting, showing itself once more as the real power in Libya, having armed Haftar's forces for years and even built an air base in the east. The UN envoy, the US charge d'affairs and other Western diplomats had to fly to Abu Dhabi to stay posted on what was going on. The UN Libya mission tweeted the next day that Haftar and Serraj had agreed to hold elections at some point, but it was clear there was no formal deal.[7] Both sides later accused each other of backtracking on promises made at the meeting. Haftar was not willing to share power and hand over command of the armed forces of a unified state to a civilian, a point he made to Western diplomats and ambassadors who met him in his base in Rajma as talk of his campaign intensified.

European ambassadors sat down with Haftar for three hours in March, telling him he would become an acclaimed national leader if he did not set his troops in motion towards Tripoli. Instead, the 76-year-old gave them a long lecture about how he started his 'Dignity' campaign in 2014 and wanted to continue his mission to rid Libya of 'terrorists'.[8] He had never changed his rhetoric, something diplomats and UN officials had failed to see when they reported for years to their governments that he was committed to the peace plan. 'I've wasted almost two years on Haftar,' said a European ambassador who met with him regularly. 'If the national conference doesn't happen, it was for nothing.'[9]

It didn't happen. UN Secretary General António Guterres flew to Tripoli to put the final touches to an event scheduled for two weeks' time on the same day the LNA announced it had dispatched troops west. I had been busy for weeks, anchoring our Algeria coverage from Tunis. I had applied for a Libya visa just in case the conference would take place. It would be a big story, but I suspected there wouldn't be a breakthrough. I was more interested in its venue, Ghadames, an oasis town 600 km southwest of Tripoli. Known as the 'pearl of the desert', it had once been a tourist attraction. I was keen to go.

My Libya visa application was approved just as the first of Haftar's troops were spotted in Gharyan. When I texted a UN official to find out what was going on, he responded: 'These are just psycho games.' The next day, UN Envoy Salamé sat stone-faced with folded arms next to Guterres in the heavily fortified UN compound. Guterres struggled to find words to make sense of the offensive. I too couldn't believe it was happening until I heard Haftar's voice urging his troops forward in an audio recording: 'To our army which is stationed at the outskirts of Tripoli: today we complete our march,' he said on the tape. Haftar saw himself on a mission to fight terrorism, but his real motive was unspoken: to fund his forces and the parallel administration, he needed to get access to the oil and gas revenues routed via the Tripoli-based central bank, which only paid some of the public servants in the east. Whether it was militias in western Libya fighting in September 2018 or Haftar in 2019 in Tripoli, Libya's conflict is not about ideology, but access to state funding.

Libya's energy wealth is a curse. It funds a welfare state which pays salaries for militia fighters and provides fuel, which also benefits armed groups—the LNA used kerosene made at the Zawiya refinery, west of Tripoli, or imported it from abroad. Their opponents also use subsidised fuel provided by the state oil firm. At the same time, Libya needed the help of the UN to send medical kits and top up the salaries of doctors and surgeons working in state hospitals on both sides of the Tripoli war to treat the wounded—fighters and civilians.[10]

Most Libya-watchers had been sceptical about the outcome of the Ghadames conference, and feared it would only rubber-stamp Haftar's leadership by making maximum concessions to him as the UN appeared desperate to find some sort of political agreement. It was impossible to say what would have happened had Haftar not launched his Tripoli campaign. But even if the conference had taken place, the UN planned to curtail the event for budgetary reasons. One hundred and fifty delegates had been invited,[11] and would be expected to agree on a political roadmap to hold parliamentary elections, a new transitional constitutional declaration and then later a presidential vote—all within two days. The Taif Accord, signed to end 15 years of civil war in Lebanon, took weeks to negotiate before it was ratified in October 1989.

Haftar and his top officers clearly expected a swift victory. His force's spokesman, Mismari, told reporters that Tripoli's women would welcome his troops. He gave daily updates with a map of Tripoli, using the same wooden stick he had used to show me the LNA positions in the south when I visited him with our local reporter Ayman in his villa in Benghazi. Haftar's forces charged up from Gharyan, meeting little resistance on the sparsely populated farmland plain to the southern Tripoli suburbs. Some fighters also tried entering Tripoli on the western coastal road and seized a highway bridge junction called Gate 27 before being chased away a few hours later. I had been there during the revolution, when anti-Gaddafi rebels entered Tripoli in August 2011. The LNA was helped by fighters in Tarhouna, a town southeast of Tripoli which had been home to a large tank unit under Gaddafi.

But this move was a misstep. Haftar's troops didn't make it past the southern suburbs, getting bogged down at Tripoli International Airport. Supporters had expected that some of the main Tripoli militias would join him, swapping loyalties like before. The Salafist forces looked sure to make up a contingent of the LNA.[12]

But Haftar had underestimated how unpopular he was, with many fearing he might impose military rule. Militias in Tripoli, Misrata and other towns—some of which had fought each other in September 2018 over control of Tripoli—now overcame their differences, working together to defend the capital in the biggest mobilisation since 2011. The Misrata militias now needed no encouragement to rush to Tripoli to fight off the LNA. After the initial shock the Tripoli defenders managed to keep the front line mostly unchanged for weeks, even pushing back the invaders.

To make matters worse, forces allied to Tripoli took some 200 LNA troops prisoner. Authorities organised a trip for reporters to showcase this group of mostly young men, some of them teenagers, the majority of them dressed in jeans and shirts. Only a few wore army uniforms. Around 50 sat in the courtyard of a prison, some holding their faces in their hands, while others ate from lunchboxes as masked policemen stood beside them. The prisoners had been forced to hand over their boots, which were piled up in a corner. They didn't look like they belonged to a real army, as the LNA had claimed: one said he was 16 and had been only recruited recently.[13] While the captured 'soldiers' finished their juice cartons, militia fighters allied to Tripoli showed the victory sign to reporters. It was a humiliation for Haftar.

The war for Tripoli

Wrapping up my Algeria work after President Bouteflika finally bowed to mass protests in April, I was eager to be back on the ground. I didn't try pick up my visa at the Libyan embassy in Tunis due to the usual obstructions put in place by consular staff. I asked that the approval letter be sent to the embassy in Cairo instead, but with Haftar having made his move on the capital, some staff there had changed sides overnight. I had already handed in my passport at the consulate and shown embassy staff the letter from Tripoli when an employee arrived claiming extra security approval was needed. It took me three days and many calls from my Tripoli colleagues to track down the consul, who finally issued me the visa. The same people who had earlier obstructed me ushered us in and served us coffee while the visa was issued. The embassy even waived the visa fee.

I headed to Tunis to meet with our security adviser who had flown in from the UK. Mitiga airport was still open for night flights (to minimise the risk of airstrikes). After half a day of waiting in Tunis, we were on our way. I was exhausted, having covered Algeria's protests for several weeks without a single off day, but I needed to stay focused for the next weeks to cover the war. Arriving in Tripoli I was greeted by the same foreign media officials who had obstructed me in November, shadowing my movements and forcing me to sit in endless meetings to discuss their complaints about our coverage. Now they claimed to be my friends as the Serraj government was eager to have journalists in town, hoping our presence would stop Haftar from turning entire districts to rubble, like in Benghazi. I thought I had an advantage over other journalists with my early visa application, but the media department had opened its doors overnight. I was under no illusion that work conditions would worsen again once the war was over.

Driving out of Mitiga airport on the coastal road to our office, I was reminded of my time in 2014 during the Libya Dawn attack. Groceries, fish restaurants and cafés were open and busy with customers even late at night, as Libyans had quickly adapted to yet another conflict. There was less traffic as those with families in the countryside had left, but otherwise it appeared to be business as usual. Most schools were still open, except for those used to house families displaced by the fighting. More than 30,000 people had been displaced in the first three weeks, a figure that would rise to 120,000 by August.[14] In central districts you hardly noticed the conflict, save for the sound of artillery booms and airstrikes, which were infrequent in the first weeks of the conflict. And it was business as usual for our office cat, King, who spent the afternoon sleeping in his favourite spot—a wooden garden table—oblivious to the artillery barrage.

But behind the facade, people were on edge. To gauge the mood, my Tripoli colleague Ahmed Elumami and I drove around the city to talk to residents living on the front line. We didn't have a minder this time—officials had dropped the rules as part of their new drive to make friends with reporters. Gunfire sounded much closer here than from our villa in the central district of Ben Ashur, and it didn't take long to get people to talk. 'We have heard gunfire since morning in here,' said a waiter, his voice almost a whisper, as he served customers while military vehicles rushed by. 'If the fighting gets any closer, I'll run away.' The owner of a grocery shop next door, Ameen Trabulsi, was rather fatalistic, planning to stay open, just as he has done during the previous—albeit smaller—armed clashes that have been a part of life in Tripoli since 2011. Business was good for him: displaced women and children living in the school were using his store to stock up. 'This is normal in Libya,' he said, before quickly adding: 'The situation now is calm but, who knows? it could worsen anytime.'[15]

And so people got on with their lives, but always staying in contact with friends or family living closer to the front line to see whether Haftar's forces came closer. Our team, made up of Ahmed, me, plus photographers and cameramen, went out in the morning to the front line, hospitals, shelters for the displaced, markets, schools and ministries to hunt for news. For lunch I usually went to my favourite Italian or Turkish restaurants or the Palestinian Falafel bistro I'd been to many times on previous visits, but now there were artillery booms in the background. 'How close was this?' I often texted my Pakistani friend Umar Khan, who had lived in Tripoli until 2015. We had often written to each other when I was based in Tripoli and had met again in Erbil in Iraq where we both happened to be on assignment, I for Reuters (covering the Mosul military campaign against IS militants) and he for the International Committee of the Red Cross (ICRC). We reconnected in 2018 when he relocated to Tunis to head ICRC's southern Libya operation. Now we were both on the ground to work on the war, me as a journalist, he as an aid worker.

At night, we were in constant contact as the battlefront picked up, with both sides using artillery. From the second week on, the LNA started to use drones, apparently supplied by the UAE. I didn't believe it until someone sent me audio of a typical drone humming sound he had recorded from his villa rooftop. The front line wasn't moving, but the war got nastier by the day. Shells and airstrikes hit residential districts even away from the front line. Seven people were killed when rockets hit the densely populated Abu Salim district, some 10 km from the front line. Retired public servant, Hadia al-Hariri, one of the survivors, was sleeping next to his wife when a shell struck the dining room of his two-story house, wounding his wife and their 3-year-old son. 'We've heard gunfire every night, but now I'm really afraid,' he said, showing me around the dining room as he was clearing debris from burned shelves and shattered windows. There was a large hole in the front wall. Serraj blamed Haftar's forces.

When not chasing news on the front line, I sat down with officials and supporters of the Tripoli defenders. Many were from Misrata and linked to the Libya Dawn government that ruled Tripoli from 2014 to 2016. Their commanders were now defending Tripoli, not attacking like in the summer of 2014, though the battle was raging in the same areas. They were keen to meet journalists to generate support for the fight against Haftar, but were less inclined to talk about 2014, when the Libya Dawn attack had heavily damaged the old airport, expelled the then internationally-recognised government and set up its parallel administration. Sitting down with a lawmaker in a café, I struggled to keep my cool when he claimed Serraj's government had delivered on public services and was committed to democracy. There was a power cut in the middle of the interview.

The front line changed several times a day, with the LNA charging (and taking selfies) before being chased out by the defenders' counter attack, who would then also take selfies, with both sides returning to their old positions by nightfall. In some areas the Tripoli forces pushed the attackers back and managed to take—with the help of residents from the town of Gharyan—the LNA's main forward base at the end of June. That was a shock to Haftar—there was still food burning in the ovens, supplies of ammunition and wounded fighters.[16] Haftar responded with an escalation of drone strikes, which diplomats believed were operated by UAE officers. The Tripoli forces had received drones and military vehicles from Turkey, which they put on display on official Libyan websites. Neither side made significant gains in the following months, despite the surge of the civilian death toll. Dozens were killed when the LNA hit a detention centre for African migrants in Tajoura in June. The centre was located next to a barracks—before the war the inmates had been forced to work there, loading ammunition and cleaning guns.[17]

Haftar still had the backing of Egypt and the UAE, while some Western countries also still saw him as a 'stabilising' force. It took the UN Security Council until 2020 to call for a ceasefire after the war started. Western countries and the EU kept issuing statements condemning the airstrikes and the civilian casualties, mostly without naming the aggressor. Even the UN mission rarely mentioned the LNA, which only encouraged Haftar to press the campaign further. France's duplicitousness helped Haftar from the start of the campaign: 'We were waiting for your victories,' French Foreign Minister Jean-Yves Le Drian told Haftar on 20 March, just as other Western diplomats and the UN were trying to avoid a showdown.[18] US President Trump helped Haftar by calling him in the second week of his campaign to discuss the 'ongoing counter-terrorism effort'. Trump 'recognised Field Marshal Haftar's significant role in fighting terrorism and securing Libya's oil resources, and the two discussed a shared vision for Libya's transition to a stable, democratic political system,' the White House said in a statement.[19] Perhaps these interactions could only be considered tacit endorsements; hands-off remarks from Western powers wary of wading too far into Libya's myriad struggles, but in any case, it begged the question: why would Haftar stop the war?

* * *

I stayed for a month and came back in June on a visa collected in London, home to the one Libyan embassy I know to be working totally professionally. When I arrived back in Tripoli, the war had long become part of everyday life. Fighting was much less intense, with both sides staging fewer ground operations, while the war had largely stopped making headlines. Power was off every day for 12 hours or more after an electricity plant was hit, which also hampered the water supply. Running water would be turned off for hours at a time, while people were queuing at a mosque with its own well just around the corner. 'Drinkable water is a daily issue for my family,' said Usama Mohamed Dokali, a cashier in a Tripoli café, who buys bottled water or gets it from a charity when money runs out. He was one of several people Ahmed Elumami and I interviewed for a report on Libya's water crisis, as a lack of maintenance and electricity had brought parts of the Great Man-Made River, which pumps water from the south to the cities on the coast, close to collapse.[20]

I unwittingly contributed to tensions between rival camps in the oil sector. I had heard from multiple sources that stocks of kerosene might be affected after monthly supplies to the central and eastern areas under Haftar's control had been boosted between April and July. The National Oil Corporation (NOC) wanted to make sure supplies were used for civilian purposes, diplomats and officials said. The minute the story[21] went live,

NOC Chairman Mustafa Sanalla was under attack in the east, with an NOC official and a diplomat imploring me to withdraw the story to defuse the situation. One of the NOC's foreign communications specialists sent me a text to complain that I had 'misrepresented' the company's position and put staff 'at risk'. But the story was accurate, and indeed it was one that the NOC had originally wanted to tell: the LNA was attacking Tripoli by air using fuel intended for civil aviation. With the backlash in full swing the company sought to distance itself from the claim by blaming my coverage—a tactic I was by now familiar with. The parallel NOC entity issued a statement criticising Sanalla for allegedly cutting off jet fuel supplies for a month. (Though I hadn't spoken to Sanalla, but to his spokesmen.) Then a senior lawmaker demanded Sanalla be referred to the eastern state prosecutor. More statements from eastern officials followed, and I even met a former eastern minister who complained about Sanalla's alleged cut of fuel supplies. He hadn't read my story, but its content and subsequent exaggerations had become common knowledge among easterners.

Ten days after the story broke, the eastern parallel government named a new board of the eastern branch of the Brega Petroleum Marketing Company, a unit of the NOC, to ensure fuel supplies.[22] Deputy Prime Minister Abdel-Salam al-Badri, who works out of the NOC parallel entity building, cited my story as the reason for the move (although I had included, at the urging of NOC Tripoli, a clarification that civilian jet fuel stocks were more than adequately filled). The starting point for my article had been indications from UN officials and oil industry sources that the east was setting up a firm to import fuel to offset restrictions from Tripoli. Now eastern officials used my article to go ahead with the new Brega board, risking the collapse of the NOC, which objected to the move. The NOC is one of the last links between both sides of the conflict, as it distributes oil revenues to the central bank, which pays much of the eastern public payroll. The NOC supplied fuel to the whole country until 2020, when the east began importing its own.

The war rumbled on with no end in sight, escalating into a foreign proxy war as both sides used drones supplied by the UAE and Turkey. Trucks from Jordan were also spotted alongside LNA forces.[23] By September residents reported airstrikes conducted by jets, not drones, with military experts pointing to the UAE and Egypt, who had both ordered strikes in Libya in the past. The outdated LNA jets, inherited from Gaddafi's arsenal of Russian-made planes, could not have been used to conduct such sophisticated and frequent airstrikes.[24] Hundreds of Russian mercenaries from a private army linked to the Kremlin were also spotted fighting alongside Haftar's forces from September, as Moscow filled a Western policy void as it did in Syria, where its military intenvention helped President Assad to survive.[25] They brought with them modern Russian weapons, manned artillery and even pilots flying Sukhoi-22 jets.[26] It remains to be seen whether the Russians will be successful in helping Haftar's forces to break the stalemate on the Tripoli front line.

Germany called for a conference to bring the UAE, Egypt and Turkey to the table with Western powers, but it was doomed from the start. Haftar's foreign backers have invested too much in him to drop him overnight, and with weapons flowing into the country, both sides can sustain their war for the foreseeable future. Haftar seems unable to enter Tripoli by force, but the capital's defenders can't push his forces back east. If Serraj agreed on a ceasefire, as proposed by France, then he would have to concede territory to the LNA, from where the force could start a new campaign.

Russian mercenaries had helped Haftar's forces make enough gains on the Tripoli front to prompt Serraj's officials to seek urgent assistance from Turkey. President Recep Tayyip Erdoğan sent military personnel (advisers and up to 2,000 fighters, mainly ethnic Turkmen) from Syria's civil war. They arrived by plane via Istanbul.[27] Outsourcing the fighting this way minimised the risk of casualties among regular soldiers—which could become a political problem back home—and would give Erdoğan cover if things went wrong. Turkey supplied Bayraktar drones (named after Erdoğan's son-in-law, who heads the firm that produces them) but began to cut back its military support in October 2019. This savvy move made officials in Tripoli desperate enough to sign a maritime deal with Ankara, giving Turkey exclusive exploration rights in the Eastern Mediterranean—much to the dismay of Israel, Egypt, Greece and Cyprus. Only after the agreement was signed did Turkey agree to a military deal with Tripoli. The Turkish move restored the old front line positions but added another layer of foreign involvement in Libya, with Moscow and Ankara now becoming major players in addition to the UAE, Egypt and Jordan—all of whom were vying to fill the Western policy void. Russia's President Putin agreed to call for a ceasefire and mercenaries from the Russian Wagner firm suddenly withdrew from the Tripoli front line.[28]

Fighting abated in January 2020, but this was due less to a genuine desire to make peace and more to the sophisticated air defences Turkey had given Tripoli, which deterred strikes by UAE-supplied drones.[29] Serraj signed a proposal for a permanent ceasefire at a Turkish-Russian summit, but Haftar proved elusive once again, leaving Moscow unannounced without putting his name on the document.

That boded badly for the Berlin conference on 19 January. Reporters covering the event were seated far away from the chancellery, watching Erdoğan, Putin, Egypt's Sisi, France's Emmanuel Macron, US Secretary of State Mike Pompeo and other Western and Arab officials arrive in their limousines on a TV screen. Serraj and Haftar were also invited to separate last-minute meetings with German Chancellor Angela Merkel, Macron and others. Officials ensured there were bathrooms for the rivals to use, arrangements made so that neither they nor their delegations would bump into each other.[30] Even UAE Crown Prince Mohamed bin Zayed al-Nahyan, the main backer of Haftar and de facto ruler of the Gulf Emirates, showed up to meet Merkel. For the summit proper he sent his foreign minister, highlighting his country's duplicity: publicly claiming to support diplomatic efforts while shipping in new, advanced weapons along with ammunition and fighters.[31] The summit resulted in an arms embargo and an agreement to enforce a ceasefire on the ground. But with no sanctions in place for violators, the pledge was rendered, as the UN Deputy Special Representative to Libya put it a few weeks later, 'a joke'.[32]

Haftar was, as ever, not interested in compromise. His forces had closed all the eastern oil ports and the El Sharara oilfield, cutting 1 million barrels of exports in just two days while his foreign backers in Berlin pretended to push for a political solution. The commander's behaviour had become increasingly erratic, much like Gaddafi's: to try and avoid an early departure like the one in Moscow, German officials treated him like a state guest, putting him in a luxury hotel in central Berlin. He still didn't agree to anything and returned to the hotel after his meeting with Merkel, refusing to come back in the afternoon for a briefing on the summit's outcome.[33] A picture from a meeting with German Foreign Minister Heiko Maas, who had travelled to Haftar's lair outside Benghazi to invite him to Berlin, demonstrated the general's attitude: he sat relaxed in his chair under his force's emblem and next to the Libyan flag while Maas and one of his aides leaned in, trying to get his attention.

I met a tired-looking UN Special Envoy Ghassan Salamé the day before the summit. Salamé had been conducting shuttle diplomacy in a bid to end the conflict. He offered only a vague hope that Haftar and his backers might agree to make peace. Arranging a colleague's interview with the envoy proved to be as complicated as dealing with Libyan militias. The UN mission spokesman, an expatriate, was still angry about a story I had posted on the first week of Haftar's war, which quoted a surprised UN official dismissing the arrival of the first LNA troops as 'psycho games'.[34] As punishment, the mission spokesman, who had tried to get me to reveal the name of the official, insisted that I not be present for the interview on threat of cancellation. However, I managed to join eventually; Salamé was unaware of the spat and welcoming as always. A few days after the summit, Salamé resigned from his role as special envoy, announcing on Twitter that he had "sought for two and a half years to unite Libyans" but that his health "no longer allows [him] to take this much stress."[35] The UN spokesman joins a list of Libyan officials and militiamen who have stopped talking to me because of my stories, which often generate intense reactions in Libya's charged-up atmosphere. Gunmen shout at those who speak to the media and some diplomats favour self-censorship to avoid fueling further tensions.

And so the battle goes on, with Turkey, the UAE, Jordan and Egypt sending even more weapons and fighters into a country that was already brimming with hardware and foreign militants. The war risks becoming a permanent reality in Libya, as does the erosion of living standards—the state is less and less able to provide basic services such as electricity, water and salary payments (for a lack of banknotes). By 2018, the UN was providing water pipelines for schools and paying for basic childhood vaccinations, as it does in many poor sub-Saharan countries.[36] What makes it so difficult to end Libya's conflict is that too many people benefit from the status quo.

The Tripoli war provided plenty of opportunities for militias allied to Serraj's government to enrich themselves, as the embattled premier directed ever more resources to the military effort.[37] In the east, Haftar and his supporters have expanded their parallel administration. In November 2018, the Tobruk-based rump parliament, still loyal to Haftar, set up a military investment authority based on Egypt's model, where the military controls much of the economy. This has allowed Haftar's forces and their backers to expand their most lucrative activities: exporting scrap metal, gaining access to land and introducing waivers for taxes and duties to raise extra revenue.[38] The investment authority is essentially a patronage network for Haftar and his forces, distributing wealth to help them stay in power: many LNA officers and their supporters now make money in 'predatory economies'.[39] These actors are unlikely to give up their interests easily—another barrier to any potential integration of the LNA into the national army and the unification of institutions in the east and west.

The same goes for the civilian parallel administration. The eastern-based Prime Minister Abdullah al-Thinni, with whom I dealt with as reporter when we both were living in Tripoli in 2014, was still in office five years later, despite stating in April 2014 that he would resign after an attack on his home.[40] He kept his title when he fled east in 2014 after the Libya Dawn militias took over Tripoli, but lost it when Serraj was set up in Tripoli as part of the UN-brokered deal rejected by the eastern camp. Despite having no real budget, Thinni simply carried on—issuing orders on official letterheads without exercising power or addressing pressing matters such as the electricity supply or the need for new schools. He is now the longest-serving premier since the revolution, but is still not taken seriously by Haftar's supporters. His position merely allows Haftar to claim the east is run by a civilian government.

His Tripoli 'counterpart' Serraj leads the longest-serving internationally recognised government in office, though he was never elected, since UN and Western diplomats put him on a boat in March 2016 in southern Tunisia to take power in Tripoli. Libya hasn't had national elections since 2014 and seems unlikely to hold elections anytime soon.

NOTES

INTRODUCTION

1. Based on publications from the Tripoli-based central bank and interviews conducted with central bank officials in 2013 and 2014. Sovereign wealth fund assets were placed under UN sanctions in 2011 to prevent the Gaddafi regime from selling the funds.
2. 'GDP per capita (current US$)—Morocco, Libya, Tunisia, Algeria, Egypt, Arab Rep.' World Bank, https://data.worldbank.org/indicator/NY.GDP.PCAP.CD?end=2015&locations=MA-LY-TN-DZ-EG&start=2008
3. There are no official figures for how many exiled Libyans returned home after Gaddafi's overthrow, but Britain is home to one of the largest Libyan exile communities.
4. On one day in June 1996, security forces killed up to 1,200 prisoners at the Abu Salim prison in Tripoli. 'Libya: June 1996 Killings at Abu Salim Prison', Human Rights Watch, https://www.hrw.org/news/2006/06/27/libya-june-1996-killings-abu-salim-prison
5. This was 21 Aug. 2011. I and my then Tripoli-based colleague Missy Ryan filed this report: 'Libyan Rebels reach Tripoli, no sign of resistance', The Jerusalem Post, https://www.jpost.com/Middle-East/Libyan-rebels-reach-Tripoli-no-sign-of-resistance
6. Saudi officials had complained about small protests that erupted in the oil-rich east, home to the Shi'ite Muslim minority accusing the Sunni kingdom of discrimination; and in Riyadh, as officials got nervous about

the Arab spring toppling rulers in Tunisia and Egypt. Reuters published two stories about my expulsion, endorsing my coverage: 'Saudi Arabia withdraws Reuters reporter's permit', Reuters, https://www.reuters.com/article/us-saudi-media-reuters/saudi-arabia-withdraws-reuters-reporters-permit-idUSTRE72E5WD20110315; 'Witness—searching for reforms in King Abdullah's Saudi Arabia', https://www.reuters.com/article/oukwd-uk-saudi-idAFTRE72N39E20110324

7. After leaving Tripoli in 2014, I came back regularly for visits lasting up to five weeks each. Whenever I was out of the country for longer than eight weeks I felt I was losing my grip on the complicated Libyan story and its myriad players. I could have stayed in Cairo, but I believe you need to have to be on the ground, mixing with Libyans, to be able to report properly.

8. The Sunni Muslim extremist group is variously known as Islamic State of Iraq and the Levant, Islamic State of Iraq and al-Sham and by its Arabic acronym, *Daesh*. I use the most common abbreviation, IS.

9. He was later replaced by someone more hostile. Luckily for me, my paperwork had already been finalised.

10. Based on interviews with Tunis-based diplomats. The consul is a former commander in the militia of Haitham al-Tajouri, a key figure in Tripoli, as we will see in Chapter 2. See also: 'Capital of militias: Tripoli's armed groups capture the Libyan state', Small Arms Survey, http://www.smallarmssurvey.org/fileadmin/docs/T-Briefing-Papers/SAS-SANA-BP-Tripoli-armed-groups.pdf

11. I know of seven foreign journalists denied a visa from the Tunis consulate, despite having obtained approval from the foreign media office. Even Tunis-based diplomats sometimes struggle to obtain the correct paperwork.

12. 'Militia shells Tripoli airport, UN pulls staff out of Libya', Reuters, https://www.reuters.com/article/us-libya-violence/militia-shells-tripoli-airport-u-n-pulls-staff-out-of-libya-idUSKBN0FK05B20140715,

13. Interview with Tunisian official in Oct. 2017.

14. Tunisia reopened its consulate in April 2018, but the foreign ministry declined to officially confirm the move, for fear of attracting the atten-

tion of militias who might be looking for people to kidnap. We confirmed the story via a diplomatic source: 'Tunisia reopens consulate in Libyan capital Tripoli', Reuters, https://www.reuters.com/article/us-libya-security-tunisia/tunisia-reopens-consulate-in-libyan-capital-tripoli-idUSKBN1HS0BI

1. AN ACCIDENTAL STATE

1. Evans, Martin, *Algeria: France's Undeclared War*, Oxford, UK: Oxford University Press, 2012, p. 33.
2. To read more about Tunisia's modern history, see Masri, Safwan, *Tunisia: An Arab Anomaly*, New York, US: Columbia University Press, 2017.
3. Indeed, this somewhat haphazard assembly of autonomous regions was a key feature of postcolonial boundary drawing, as seen across Africa and of course the Subcontinent. Modern-day Libya's composite parts became whole by virtue, as much as anything else, of their proximity. The title of this chapter is also intended as homage to Dirk Vandewalle's indispensable *A History of Modern Libya* (referenced extensively in this potted history), which includes the term in the title of its chapter about the reign of King Idris.
4. Interview in Sept. 2019.
5. Interview with Harchaoui, who said the closest to an attempt to build an army was when the British, with the help of the Sanoussi movement, formed a Libyan armed force to fight the Italians in the 1940s.
6. Vandewalle, Dirk, *A History of Modern Libya*, Cambridge, UK: Cambridge University Press, 2012, pp. 30–31; Baldinetti, Anna, *The Origins of the Libyan Nation: Colonial Legacy, Exile and the Emergence of a new Nation State*, London, UK: Routledge, 2010, p. 48.
7. El Ghomeny, M. Riad, *Land, Food and Rural Development in North Africa*, London, UK: Routledge, 1993, p. 71.
8. The closure lasted until 1975.
9. Gaddafi closed the foreign military bases a year after his coup. See Wright, John, *A History of Libya*, New York, US: Columbia University Press, 2010, p. 200.
10. Ahmida, Ali Abdullatif, *The Making of Modern Libya: State Formation,*

Colonization, and Resistance, New York, US: State University of New York Press, 2009, p. 85.

11. Hayford, Elizabeth R., *The Politics of the Kingdom of Libya in Historical Perspective*, dissertation at Tufts University, 1970, p. 220.

12. Wright, op. cit., p. 169.

13. Pargeter, Alison, *Libya: The Rise and Fall of Gaddafi*, Connecticut, US: Yale University Press, 2012, p. 37.

14. The name 'Libya' hails from the ancient Greeks, who left their footprints in the Cyrene settlement. 'Libya' was used by the Greeks to refer to much of North Africa.

15. Vandewalle, op. cit., p. 61.

16. Hayford, op. cit., p. 191.

17. Wright, op. cit., pp. 177–179.

18. Wright, op. cit., p. 179.

19. Vandewalle, op. cit., p. 147.

20. Vandewalle, op. cit., p. 26; Ahmida, op. cit., p. 117.

21. Reporting trip to Tobruk in Sept. 2014.

22. Vandervalle, op. cit., p. 53.

23. Gurney, Judith, *Libya: The Political Economy of Oil*, Oxford, UK: Oxford University Press, 1996, p. 195.

24. For a copy of the five-year plan, see Hayford, op. cit., p. 444.

25. Interview with Harchaoui.

26. Gurney, op. cit., p. 200.

27. See Vandewalle, Dirk, 'Libya's Revolution in Perspective 1969–2000' in *Libya Since 1969: Gadhafi's Revolution Revisited*, New York, US: Palgrave Macmillan, 2008, p. 13.

28. Wright, op. cit., p. 189.

29. Vandewalle, Dirk, *A History of Modern Libya*, Cambridge, UK: Cambridge University Press, 2012, p. 69.

30. Hayford, op. cit., p. 243.

31. Testimony from such incidents can be found here: 'The last days of Tripoli', Six Day War, http://www.sixdaywar.co.uk/jews_in_arab_countries_doris.htm

32. Pargeter, op. cit., p. 46.

33. Wright, op. cit., pp. 191–192.

34. Pargeter, op. cit., p. 47.

35. Pargeter, op. cit., p. 69.

36. For more on the committees and Gaddafi's security apparatus, see Jawad, op. cit., pp. 1–6.

37. All codified in Gaddafi's Green Book, which you can find at: http://openanthropology.org/libya/gaddafi-green-book.pdf

38. Pargeter, op. cit., pp. 79–80.

39. In Dec. 2019 the biggest online retailer in Nigeria, Jumia, listed Gaddafi's My Vision, co-authored with Edmond Jouve (London, UK: John Blake Publishing, 2005) in its 'bestselling books' category. 'He is a prophet and a revolutionary', the advertisement reads: https://www.jumia.com.ng/jumia-books-my-vision-by-muammar-gaddafi-with-edmond-jouve.-his-revolute-42231469.html

40. Wright, op. cit., p. 206.

41. In 1986, the title was amended to the 'Great Socialist People's Libyan Arab Jamahiriya' following Operation El Dorado Canyon, a bombing of Libya by the US in retaliation for Libya's alleged sponsorship of a terrorist attack on a nightclub in West Berlin, which killed three and injured more than 200 the same year.

42. An excellent book exploring life and persecution under Gaddafi is the debut novel by Libyan-American writer Hisham Matar. Matar, Hisham, *In the Country of Old Men*, New York, US: Viking Press, 2006.

43. Al-Senoussi married a sister of Gaddafi's second wife, Farkash.

44. Vandewalle, op. cit., p. 190.

45. Lacher, Wolfram, 'Families, tribes and cities in the Libyan revolution', *Middle East Policy Council*, 18, 4, pp. 140–154.

46. Wright, op. cit., p. 209.

47. Vandevalle, op. cit., p. 106–107.

48. Vandewalle, op. cit., p. 167; various Reuters stories: www.reuters.com/search/news?blob=lockerbie

49. He was the eldest son from Gaddafi's second wife, Safiya.

50. Pargeter, op. cit., p. 201.

51. Pargeter, op. cit., p. 192; Vandewalle, op. cit., p. 192.

52. In Tripoli's Gargaresh district, Italian and Spanish restaurants and cafés opened and global sports retailers such as Nike arrived. Western hotel

group Intercontinental unveiled plans to establish itself in the country, but many projects stood unfinished when the 2011 revolution began, with planners abandoning construction sites due to the country's chaos.

53. Vandewalle, op. cit., p. 212.

54. Pargeter, op. cit., p. 206.

55. 'Gaddafi aides present car crash baby as NATO victim', Reuters, http://af.reuters.com/article/libyaNews/idAFLDE7540M220110606

2. WELCOME TO MILITIALAND

1. 'Trapped in a Tripoli hotel, journalists were the enemy', Reuters, http://af.reuters.com/article/libyaNews/idAFLDE77N0W520110824

2. I recommend reading her account: Jawad, Rana, *Tripoli Witness: The Remarkable First-hand Account of Life Through the Insurgency*, London, UK: Gilgamesh, 2011.

3. 'Libya: Col Gaddafi damns the 'rats' as he clings to power', The Telegraph, https://www.telegraph.co.uk/news/worldnews/africaandindianocean/libya/8341567/Libya-Col-Gaddafi-damns-the-rats-as-he-clings-to-power.html

4. McQuinn, Brian, 'History's warriors—The Emergency of Revolutionary Battalions in Misrata', *The Libyan Revolution and its Aftermath*, edited by Peter Cole and Brian McQuinn, London, UK: Hurst & Company, 2015, pp. 251–252.

5. 'Armed militias hold Libya hostage', Reuters, https://www.reuters.com/article/us-libya-militias insight/armed-militias-hold-libya-hostage-idUSBREA2T05H20140330

6. I interviewed Wehrey in July 2015. See also his excellent book, *The Burning Shores: Inside the Battle for the new Libya*, New York, US: Farrar, Straus and Giroux, 2018.

7. Interview in Tobruk, Feb. 2015.

8. A hotel guard told me this in Aug. 2011.

9. The US said the group was behind the attack on a US diplomatic compound in Benghazi in Sept. 2012 that killed Ambassador Chris Stevens and three other Americans. Ansar al-Sharia was just one of several groups which took control of the eastern city, carving out fiefdoms and taking

over the tasks of the absent state. For more on the group's role at a hospital, see 'Militants or no, Islamist fighters praised at Benghazi hospital', Reuters, https://www.reuters.com/article/us-protests-benghazi-hospital-idUSBRE88L0AL20120922

10. Interviews with Libyan officials, militiamen and diplomats, 2013–2015. See also the June 2019 Chatham House report, 'Conflict Economies in the Middle East and North Africa', p. 15: https://www.chatham-house.org/sites/default/files/publications/research/2019-06-21-Conflict-Economies-MENA_0.pdf

11. 'Libya halts cash for ex-fighters over corruption', Reuters, https://www.reuters.com/article/libya-corruption/libya-halts-cash-for-ex-fighters-over-corruption-idINDEE83901Y20120410

12. Around $3,080, based on the official exchange rate.

13. 'Finding their place—Libya's Islamists during and after the revolution', in *The Libyan Revolution and its Aftermath*, edited by Peter Cole and Brian McQuinn, London, UK: Hurst & Company, 2015, p. 179.

14. This perhaps helps to explain the ferocity of the battle for control of Benghazi that started in May 2014.

15. 'Libyan police unit admits kidnapping ex-spy chief's daughter', The Guardian, https://www.theguardian.com/world/2013/sep/05/libyan-police-kidnap-senussi-daughter

16. 'Like Captain Haitham Tajouri, all #Libya-ns should join together to build their country's future.', tweet from Deborah Jones (@safiradeborah) on 11 Dec. 2013: https://twitter.com/safiradeborah/status/410804654553849856

17. Interview with AFP in 2013.

18. As we will see in Chapter 9.

19. Megerisi provided me with this analysis of the militias in his valuable comments on a draft of this book.

20. See several studies from the 'Costs of War' project by the Watson Institute for International and Public Affairs at Brown University, https://watson.brown.edu/costsofwar/papers/human

21. Various interviews with officials, political players and diplomats.

22. Various interviews with officials and diplomats during my time in Tripoli. Pinning down the number of Libyan soldiers was one of my main research themes.

23. Visit to Tripoli in May 2015.

24. Interview in Tripoli in Oct. 2013.

25. Various interviews in Libya, 2013–2015.

26. Interview in May 2015.

27. Interview in Ghat in May 2014.

28. Various exchanges with the Tripoli-based central bank between 2013 and 2015.

29. 'Libyan force was lesson in limits of U.S. power', Washington Post, https://www.washingtonpost.com/world/national-security/a-security-force-for-libya-becomes-a-lesson-in-failure/2015/08/05/70a3ba90–1b76-11e5-bd7f-4611a60dd8e5_story.html

30. 'UK to end training of Libyan troops early after sex attacks', Reuters, http://uk.reuters.com/article/uk-britain-defence-libya-idUKKBN0IO1E220141104

31. France acknowledged the presence of some soldiers only when three were killed in July 2016 in a helicopter crash during what was described an 'intelligence gathering' mission. Diplomats also said French special forces had advised Haftar on his campaign to seize Benghazi. 'France says three soldiers died in accident on Libya intelligence mission', Reuters, https://www.reuters.com/article/us-libya-security-france-idUSKCN1000R3

32. Interview with Pakistan's military attaché in Tripoli in May 2015. Pakistan was one of the few countries to keep its embassy open after the takeover by Libya Dawn, but diplomats avoided dealings with officials in public; staff dealt mainly with its large community in consular affairs.

33. The military support has been described in detail in UN reports from the panel of experts monitoring the arms embargo imposed on Libya in 2011. See: https://www.un.org/securitycouncil/sanctions/1970/panel-experts/reports

34. The panel regularly issues such a report to verify compliance with a UN arms embargo, asset freeze and travel ban. 'Final report of the Panel of Experts established pursuant to resolution 1973 (2011)', UN Security Council, https://www.undocs.org/S/2015/128, p. 43.

35. 'Jordanian ambassador seized in Libya, kidnappers demand prisoner

release', Reuters, https://www.reuters.com/article/us-libya-jordan-kidnapping/jordanian-ambassador-seized-in-libya-kidnappers-demand-prisoner-release-idUSBREA3E0CO20140415

36. Interview in Nov. 2013.
37. Various interviews with officials and diplomats in Tripoli in 2013 and 2014.

3. THE OIL PORT REBEL

1. His opponents, meanwhile, dismiss this narrative, claiming he had been a petty criminal in the Gaddafi years, jailed for trading in stolen cars. This version of events is repeated even by those within the eastern federalist movement he claimed to support.
2. 'One family against Gaddafi' Al Jazeera, https://www.aljazeera.com/indepth/features/2011/03/2011318121134680476.html
3. Gaddafi hired African mercenaries during the 2011 uprising, meaning already widespread racism against black Libyans worsened after the revolution.
4. Estimate by a central bank official, made in interview in June 2014. 'Lost oil revenues have cost Libya $30 billion: central bank', Reuters, https://www.reuters.com/article/us-libya-cenbank/lost-oil-revenues-have-cost-libya-30-billion-central-bank-idUSKBN0EH0WU20140606
5. A copy of the report, which Reuters obtained in 2011, was incorporated into the following article: 'Special Report: the Gaddafi oil papers', Reuters, https://www.reuters.com/article/us-libya-oil-corruption-idUS-TRE7BM0JF20111223
6. Visit to Hariga port in Sept. 2014.
7. The port is also known as Es Sidra. I use the spelling used by Reuters and other news outlets.
8. Obtaining reliable economic data is a major challenge in Libya. The figure here is based on the estimate made by a central bank official in an interview in June 2015. The economy minister gave me slightly lower figures in Nov. 2013, putting losses at $6 billion since August. 'Libya has lost $6 billion from oil protests: minister', Reuters, https://www.reuters.com/article/us-libya-oil/libya-has-lost-6-billion-from-oil-protests-minister-idUSBRE9AD0RX20131114

9. Jathran asked us not to call him a militia commander in our coverage, but to quote him with his 'official' title, Director of the Politburo of the Federalist Cyrenaica Movement.

10. The letter was circulated to foreign oil traders in early Jan. 2014. Reuters and other media obtained a copy.

11. The same prosecutor would later side with the Islamist-backed Libya Dawn administration set up in 2014.

12. The Tripoli government published the brief agreement on its website to prevent Jathran from later backing out or denying what had been agreed upon.

13. More on this in Chapter 4.

14. I use the official rate.

15. In office from 2014 to 2015.

16. Libya researcher Jalel Harchaoui dated the period of cooperation as from May 2014 to Sept. 2015. Interview in Oct. 2019.

17. 'Final report of the Panel of Experts on Libya established pursuant to resolution 1973 (2011)', UN Security Council, http://www.statewatch. org/news/2017/jun/un-libya-final-report-res-1973–11-migrant-abuses. pdf, p. 63.

18. Haftar's forces claimed the existence of Chadian mercenaries, a fact confirmed by Western diplomats. Sudanese fighters fought for Jathran as well as the Libyan army in the oil port clashes, according to a UN report. 'Final report of the Panel of Experts on the Sudan established pursuant to resolution 1591 (2005)', UN Security Council, https:// reliefweb.int/sites/reliefweb.int/files/resources/Final%20report%20 of%20the%20Panel%20of%20Experts%20on%20the%20Sudan%20 established-10jan2019.pdf, p. 26

19. In a statement dated 14 June 2019, the NOC confirmed a loss of 240,000 barrels a day. An official later told Reuters that export losses had risen to 400,000 barrels a day.

20. NOC statement from 18 June 2019. 'Catastrophic damage at Ras Lanuf terminal', National Oil Corporation, https://noc.ly/index.php/en/new-4/3748-catastrophic-damage-at-ras-lanuf-terminal

21. 'الجضران: نعلن بدء العمليات العسكرية في منطقة الهلال النفطي' ('Jathran: We announce the start of the military operation in the Oil Crescent'), Libya

Al-Ahrar, https://www.youtube.com/watch?v=ClKciRUhQnA&feature=share

22. Quote taken from Millett's then Twitter account, @PeterMillet1, which was suspended at the time of going to press. He now tweets from @PeterMillett1

23. Interview with Emad Badi in Jan. 2019.

4. LIBYA DIVIDED

1. The Tunisian state carrier, Tunisair, continued flying to eastern Libya until Aug. when it suspended flights for security reasons. Turkish Airlines kept flying from Misrata to Istanbul until Jan. 2015, when threats from Haftar's fighters forced it to abandon Libya. A small charter airline flew from Mitiga until 2019.

2. UNHCR statement from 10 Oct. 2014.

3. 'Elite' might not be the right term, at least in comparison with units in other countries. The Saiqa has around 3,500 men and mainly uses Soviet-era tanks and weapons, its commander told me in Feb. 2019.

4. Interviews with Islamists, 2013 and 2014.

5. Interviews with residents.

6. The suspect's brother claimed this in an interview with Reuters' Benghazi reporter, Ayman al-Warfalli. We published a story, 'Benghazi suspect fighting anti-Islamist general before US raid', Reuters, http://www.reuters.com/article/us-libya-security-usa-khatallah-idUSK-BN0EV1II,20140620, on 20 June 2014. Bukhamada made it clear several times (although privately) that his forces were too weak to make such arrests.

7. Interview with Libya researcher Jalel Harchaoui, who has studied Haftar's life and rise, in Mar. 2019.

8. 'In the Desert, Chad exhibits spoils of war', The New York Times, http://www.nytimes.com/1987/04/13/world/in-the-desert-chad-exhibits-spoils-of-war.html

9. 'The unravelling', The New Yorker, www.newyorker.com/magazine/2015/02/23/unravelling

10. Interview with Fawzeia al-Furjani, a business leader from Haftar's tribe, in Feb. 2019.

11. The New Yorker, op. cit.

12. 'Gunmen loyal to ex-general storm Libyan parliament, demand suspension', Reuters, https://www.reuters.com/article/us-libya-violence/gunmen-loyal-to-ex-general-storm-libyan-parliament-demand-suspension-idUSBREA4G04A20140518

13. He later used the name of Libyan Arab Armed Forces (LAAF), which is the now standard title on the force's official letterhead. The word 'Arab' is a source of concern for non-Arab minorities such as the Amazigh, who were supressed under Gaddafi. LNA remains the most widely cited name in the media. In the February 2014 coup video Haftar used 'Libyan National Army' again. When I visited the eastern city of Bayda in 2015 I saw documents stamped with the same moniker. He uses the same name in a manifesto calling for the overthrow of Gaddafi in 1995, which Libya researcher Jalel Harchaoui shared with me. Haftar's supporters have also used the title 'Libyan Armed Forces' *or al-jaish* ('army').

14. See, for example, Annex 10 in 'Letter dated 5 September 2018 from the Panel of Experts on Libya established pursuant to resolution 1973 (2011)', UN Security Council, http://www.securitycouncilreport.org/atf/cf/%7B65BFCF9B-6D27-4E9C-8CD3-CF6E4FF96FF9%7D/s_CF6E4FF96FF9%7D/s_2018_812.pdf, p. 79. The annex contains a copy of an LNA document which confirmed that Sudanese opposition forces had been integrated.

15. Interviews with several former Haftar aides and officials.

16. 'Libyan troops block PM visit, may signal rift with government', Reuters, https://www.reuters.com/article/us-libya-security-visit/libyan-troops-try-to-block-pm-visit-may-signal-rift-with-government-idUSKBN0L62B920150202

17. Interview in May 2015.

18. 'Final report of the Panel of Experts established pursuant to resolution 1973 (2011)', UN Security Council, https://www.undocs.org/S/2015/128, p. 36.

19. Haftar told me in a phone interview in May 2015 that the campaign would last 'at least three months'. 'Renegade former general says PM must go, vote must wait,', Reuters, https://www.reuters.com/article/us-libya-general/renegade-former-libyan-general-says-pm-must-go-vote-must-wait-idUSBREA4P0C720140526

20. 'Letter dated 5 September 2018 from the Panel of Experts on Libya established pursuant to resolution 1973 (2011)', UN Security Council, http://www.securitycouncilreport.org/atf/cf/%7B65BFCF9B-6D27–4E9C-8CD3-CF6E4FF96FF9%7D/s_2018_812.pdf

21. UN Security Council, op. cit.

22. UN Security Council, op. cit.

23. I will keep using the most common name and term: LNA or Haftar's forces.

24. 'Libyan troops try block PM visit, may signal rift with government', Reuters, http://www.reuters.com/article/us-libya-security-visit-idUSK BN0L62B920150202

25. Interview with LNA officers.

26. The HoR stayed on beyond the planned 15 months, despite only a minority of the originally elected lawmakers attending sessions and the house turning into a pro-Haftar institution, saying parliament needed to remain until future elections. This narrative was accepted by foreign powers and the UN, who wanted to keep up the illusion of having an assembly with which to negotiate a future political solution.

27. Figure cited by the High National Elections Commission, https://hnec.ly/?page_id=7454; see also 'Poor turnout in Libyan parliament vote as prominent lawyer killed', Reuters, https://www.reuters.com/article/us-libya-election/poor-turnout-in-libyan-parliament-vote-as-prominent-lawyer-killed-idUSKBN0F000720140626

28. The assembly had initially been intended for Benghazi, but officials eventually conceded that these plans were unrealistic due to security, hence the second choice of Tobruk where a Libyan businessman based in the UAE paid for accommodation in the first months. The Benghazi plans were a purely political decision with no practical meaning—even without Haftar's campaign, a move there would still have been hampered by security concerns.

29. Various interviews, 2014.

30. 'Libya—Spiraling militia attacks may be war crimes', Human Rights Watch, https://www.hrw.org/news/2014/09/08/libya-spiraling-militia-attacks-may-be-war-crimes; 'Libya—Rule of the gun' Amnesty USA, http://www.amnestyusa.org/research/reports/libya-rule-of-the-gun-abductions-torture-and-other-militia-abuses-in-western-libya

31. It turned out that this was the same official being yelled at by a militiamen on speakerphone over what the thug saw as a paltry fee for me visiting front line troops, in Chapter 3.

32. Interview in Tripoli in Nov. 2015.

33. This is the story I filed: 'Exclusive—Libya's rival oil minister wants to attend OPEC meeting', Reuters, www.reuters.com/article/us-libya-security-oil-exclusive-idUSKCN0JA0RV20141126

34. We wrote this story: 'Rival Libyan PM meets Turkish envoy in fist known meeting with foreign visit', Reuters, www.reuters.com/article/us-libya-security-turkey-idUSKCN0IA2I520141021

35. I filed this story after the news conference: 'UN to widen Libya peace talks by including rival parliament', Reuters, www.reuters.com/article/us-libya-security-talks-idUSKBN0JN00P20141209

36. I included some quotes from the interview in a broader piece on the situation in eastern Libya, published on 22 Feb. 2015: 'Embattled Libyan government loses grip as general expands power', Reuters, www.reuters.com/article/uk-libya-security-idUKKBN0LQ0D720150222

37. 'Libya starts dipping into wheat reserves to overcome flour shortages', Reuters, www.reuters.com/article/libya-security-wheat-idUSL6N0VE34D20150204

38. 'Libya plans smart cards to cut fuel subsidies that boost smuggling', Reuters, www.reuters.com/article/libya-subsidies-idUSL6N0N94UP20140417. It is very difficult to get official data, and where figures do exist, they are often wrong. There is no reliable official figure for fuel subsidies, but in 2013 the International Energy Agency estimated the subsidies cost Libya $3 billion in 2011. 'Libya aims to end fuel subsidies in three years', Reuters, http://www.reuters.com/article/us-libya-oil-idUSBRE93T0N120130430

39. See Chapter 9.

5. TRIBE VS. REGION VS. TOWN VS. FAMILY

1. 'There is no political language in Libya. There is no language for democracy or any level of political sophistication,' Mary Fitzgerald, a Libya researcher, told Reuters for this story: 'Libya's first post-Gaddafi vote

to test Islamists', Reuters, https://uk.reuters.com/article/uk-libya-election-islamists/libyas-first-post-gaddafi-vote-to-test-islamists-idUKBRE8640DC20120705

2. Interview in Sept. 2014 in Tobruk.

3. Anderson, Lisa, *The State and Social Transformation in Tunisia and Libya: 1830–1980*, New Jersey, US: Princeton University Press, 1986, pp. 41–42.

4. Anderson, op. cit., p. 49.

5. Lacher, Wolfram, 'Families, tribes and cities in the Libyan revolution', *Middle East Policy Council*, 18, 4, pp. 140–154.

6. Warfalla members tried to oust Gaddafi in 1993 in a failed coup, having split with one camp comprising 42 officers from Bani Walid. Cole, Peter, 'Loyalism in a time of revolution', *The Libyan Revolution and its Aftermath*, edited by Peter Cole and Brian McQuinn, London, UK: Hurst & Company, 2015, p. 179.

7. Interview in 2015 with a researcher who was present during a phone call between Misrata forces and Karami.

8. Perhaps the best example of such an alliance is the one between the Wahabi Salafi sect and the House of Saud.

9. 'A quick guide to Libya's main players', European Council on Foreign Relations, https://www.ecfr.eu/mena/mapping_libya_conflict

10. The Warfalla tribe were key to Gaddafi's security apparatus. During visits in 2014 and 2017, most residents I met were pro-Gaddafi. There were even green flags hoisted in the central square in Nov. 2017.

11. Anderson, op. cit., pp. 197–198.

12. It's not difficult to beat Tripoli International—a cubicle construction from the 1970s, it was heavily damaged in 2014 and subsequently taken out of service. Still, Misrata airport is hardly more comfortable, with passengers sitting in a container-like terminal building next to a military air base.

13. A year before he had refused to show me the port, citing my lack of a security permit I had never heard of, while boasting about the success of Misrata as a trading hub and the country's biggest port.

14. 'Libya spends $7 billion from reserves to cover loss of oil revenues', Reuters, www.reuters.com/article/libya-oil-budget-idUKL5N0JI3GV 20131203

15. I continued to use the reserve figure in later stories, careful to make clear that I had taped the interview. That wouldn't have protected me against angry militiamen, but I felt I had to make a point.

16. 'Libya steps up fuel imports as strikes hobble refinery', Reuters, www. reuters.com/article/libya-oil-refinery-idUKBQE7DN0FH20131219

17. 'Overview of violations of international human rights and humanitarian law during the ongoing violence in Libya', UN HCHR, http:// www.ohchr.org/Documents/Countries/LY/OverviewViolationsLibya_UNSMIL_OHCHR_Sept04_en.pdf

18. It should also be noted that Zintani forces committed similar acts. 'Libya: Spiralling militia attacks may be war crimes', Human Rights Watch, https://www.hrw.org/news/2014/09/08/libya-spiraling-militia-attacks-may-be-war-crimes

19. An eyewitness told me this.

20. Name changed to protect the subject.

21. Interview with Tarek Orafi, head of the elected Benghazi council in Apr. 2018. The story I published was: 'Benghazi's displaced: a litmus test for Libya', Reuters, https://www.reuters.com/article/us-libya-security-displaced-insight/benghazis-displaced-a-litmus-test-for-libya-idUSKCN1II0FZ

22. Haftar's supporters blame his radical Islamist opponents, who posted a video of the attack online. The LNA also bombed residential districts using older planes that lacked precision weapons.

23. The offensive is discussed in detail in the Epilogue.

6. FUELLING CONFLICT

1. Interview in Musaid in Sept. 2014.

2. Estimates by diplomats, analysts and economists in 2019.

3. Interview in Aug. 2015.

4. Interview with Husni Bey in 2015.

5. Since 2016, Libya has had only so-called 'financial arrangements' to reflect the split and lack of formal vote as the House of Representatives is based in eastern Libya and linked to a parallel administration there. Lawmakers do not work with the GNA, so the IMF, World Bank and

the US mediated between the GNA, the Tripoli central bank and a senior lawmaker, usually the head of the finance committee at the Tobruk-based parliament, to work out a budget serving the whole of Libya by paying public salaries and fuel subsides without a formal vote.

6. 2014 report, Libya Audit Bureau, http://audit.gov.ly/pdf/LABR_2014.pdf, p. 32.

7. Libya Audit Bureau, op. cit.

8. Central bank statement, 5 Jan. 2019.

9. 'Gaddafi 2011 inspecting identities of some poor Libyans (with English subtitles)', salim000001, https://www.youtube.com/watch?v=2hgPyK6s3Bs

10. Interview in Aug. 2015.

11. Data from the US Energy Information Administration website, https://www.eia.gov/beta/international/analysis.php?iso=LBY

12. Amazigh activists shut down the Mellitah gas port in 2013, from where the Greenstream pipeline starts, to demand increased minority rights. But gas exports have been much less disrupted than oil exports; militias tend to target gas facilities less because gas is needed for local electricity generation.

13. For more on Libyan oil policy, see Vandewalle, Dirk, *A History of Modern Libya*, Cambridge, UK: Cambridge University Press, 2012, pp. 53–55.

14. 'Gunmen kill 12 Libyans, foreigners at oilfield raid,' Reuters, https://www.reuters.com/article/us-libya-security/gunmen-kill-12-libyans-foreigners-at-oilfield-raid-idUSKBN0L80LF20150204

15. It was a shock to many Libyans (including militias) when gunmen loyal to IS attacked the NOC headquarters in Sept. 2018. When I visited Tripoli in June 2019 the damage had still not been fixed.

16. Sanalla in Reuters interview in Oct. 2018.

17. The Tripoli government finally allocated 1.5 billion dinars (almost $1.1 billion) to NOC to invest in oil and gas fields. 'Tripoli government gives Libya's NOC $1 billion in funding', Reuters, https://www.reuters.com/article/us-libya-oil/tripoli-government-gives-libyas-noc-1-billion-in-funding-idUSKCN1WK0J6

18. Central bank statement, Jan. 2019.

19. Response from NOC to questions submitted by Reuters for a story I did on fuel smuggling to Tunisia. 'Pasta and petrol: smuggling crackdown stirs dissent in Tunisia's south', Reuters, https://www.reuters.com/article/us-tunisia-libya/pasta-and-petrol-smuggling-crackdown-stirs-dissent-in-tunisias-south-idUSKCN1N30KL

20. NOC statement, Sept. 2018.

21. 'Libya Rich in Oil, Leaking fuel', Chatham House, https://chatham-house.shorthandstories.com/libya-rich-in-oil-leaking-fuel/index.html

22. The central bank governor announced this during a debate on al-Ahrar TV on 30 Dec. 2018, but it was confirmed to me by Deputy Prime Minister Ahmed Maiteeq in an interview in Nov. 2018.

23. Interview in Tripoli in Feb. 2015. The PSF was for several years in charge of organising flour production. But after the Tripoli government liberalised the market and lifted food subsidies it reduced the fund's role in emergency interventions should private importers fail to provide sufficient flour, the Tripoli-based Economy Minister Ali Abdulaziz Issawi told me in Apr. 2019.

24. Data from the British flour miller industry body, Nabim, http://www.nabim.org.uk/flour-and-bread-consumption

25. Interview with businessmen in Tripoli in June 2019.

26. Interview in Tripoli in Feb. 2015.

27. See the June 2019 Chatham House report, 'Conflict Economies in the Middle East and North Africa', p. 15: https://www.chathamhouse.org/sites/default/files/publications/research/2019-06-21-Conflict-Economies-MENA_0.pdf

28. I use the official rate of 1.4 dinars to the dollar.

29. Public data is very scarce and unreliable in Libya, another legacy of the secretive Gaddafi era. The accounting of expenditures became more complicated in 2014, when Libya effectively spilt into a western and eastern region with separate parliaments. The Tripoli-based central bank said in Dec. 2014 that Libya had spent 21.1 billion dinars on public salaries and 12.7 billion dinars on subsidies from January to November of that year. I used data from the Tripoli-based Libyan Audit Bureau report for 2014: www.audit.gov.ly/pdf/LABR_2014.pdf

30. Libyan Audit Bureau, op. cit., p. 43.

31. Estimate by NOC Chairman Mustafa Sanallah in a Reuters interview in Jan. 2016. 'Libya lost $68 bln in oil revenue since 2013-NOC', Reuters, af.reuters.com/article/libyaNews/idAFL8N1593H6

32. Interview in Tripoli in Mar. 2014.

33. Libyan Audit Bureau, op. cit., p. 169.

34. Libya does not publish reliable inflation data on a regular basis, but the evidence was all around: most notably in the rise of food prices in supermarkets.

35. For details on the eastern parallel financial system see 'Of tanks and banks: stopping a dangerous escalation in Libya,' International Crisis Group, https://www.crisisgroup.org/middle-east-north-africa/north-africa/libya/201-tanks-and-banks-stopping-dangerous-escalation-libya

36. Diplomats describe the rising debt as a time bomb. 'The east has sold bonds they don't plan to settle. How do you value them in a future deal, at face value or less?' one Western diplomat told me in Feb. 2019.

37. 'Debts pile up as rival Libyan governments struggle for power', Reuters, www.reuters.com/article/us-libya-economy-insight/debts-pile-up-as-rival-libyan-governments-struggle-for-power-idUSKCN1QN1VL

38. Interview in Tripoli in Dec. 2013.

39. I wrote this story based on the conference: 'Libya says aims to run economy, banking system along Islamic lines', Reuters, https://www.reuters.com/article/us-libya-islamic-banks/libya-says-aims-to-run-economy-banking-system-on-islamic-lines-idUSBREA050PX20140106

40. Speech by NTC Chairman Mustafa Abdul Jalil on 22 Oct. 2011.

41. In its article, 'Leaked Emirate emails could threaten peace talks in Libya', https://www.nytimes.com/2015/11/13/world/middleeast/leaked-emirati-emails-could-threaten-peace-talks-in-libya.html, The New York Times quoted Ahmed al-Qasimi, a senior UAE diplomat, in a leaked email as saying: 'The matter of fact is that the UAE violated the UN Security Solution [imposing an arms embargo] and continues to do so.'

42. The eastern Prime Minister Abdullah al-Thinni said this in an interview with Saudi-owned al-Arabiya television.

43. More on this in Chapter 9.

44. For example, the group issued a statement in Aug. 2015 saying that it had tested a mortar gun it had developed.

7. THE STRUGGLE TO SECURE LIBYA'S BORDERS

1. 'The sex trafficking trail from Nigeria to Europe', CNN, https://edition. cnn.com/2017/12/04/africa/nigeria-benin-city-sex-trafficking/index. html

2. 'No escape from hell', Human Rights Watch, https://www.hrw.org/ report/2019/01/21/no-escape-hell/eu-policies-contribute-abuse-migrants-libya

3. 'EU gets one million migrants in 2015, smugglers seen making $1 billion', Reuters, www.reuters.com/article/us-europe-migrants/eu-gets-one-million-migrants-in-2015-smugglers-seen-making-1-billion-idUSKBN0U50WI20151222

4. During a visit to Tunis, then European Commission President Jean-Claude Juncker said the issue was no longer on the agenda: 'Juncker says North Africa migrant 'camps' not on EU agenda', https://www. reuters.com/article/us-europe-migrants-africa/juncker-says-north-africa-migrant-camps-not-on-eu-agenda-idUSKCN1N01TU

5. 'European Council: Malta declaration by the members of the European Council on the external aspects of migration: addressing the central Mediterranean Route, 2017', European Council, https://www.consil-ium.europa.eu/en/press/press-releases/2017/02/03/malta-declaration. EUBAM had a budget of 17 million euros approved for the period from Aug. 2016 to Aug. 2017. 'Eubam Libya mission extended', European Council, https://www.consilium.europa.eu/en/press/press-releases/2016/08/04/eubam-libya-mission-extended/

6. Human Rights Watch report, Jan. 2019: https://www.hrw.org/ report/2019/01/21/no-escape-hell/eu-policies-contribute-abuse-migrants-libya

7. 'Gaddafi: Europe will turn black unless EU pays Libya 4 billion [GBP] a year,' The Telegraph, https://www.telegraph.co.uk/news/worldnews/ africaandindianocean/libya/7973649/Gaddafi-Europe-will-turn-black-unless-EU-pays-Libya-4bn-a-year.html; 'Gaddafi causes storm in Italy

with Islam comments', Reuters, reuters.com/article/idINIndia-51171
220100830

8. Interview in Tripoli in May 2015.

9. For more, see 'Armed group seeks legitimacy with Tripoli migrant deal,
   source says', Reuters; https://www.reuters.com/article/us-europe-
   migrants-libya/armed-group-seeks-legitimacy-with-tripoli-migrant-
   deal-source-says-idUSKCN1BW0HA

10. I filed the following story with my colleague Aidan Lewis, who trav-
    elled with me: 'Migrant flows slow to trickle in Libyan former smug-
    gling hub', Reuters, reuters.com/article/libyaNews/idAFL8N1XX5R3

11. Interview with Italian diplomat in Tripoli in Nov. 2018.

12. Libyan security forces used tear gas to force 65 migrants off a cargo
    ship docked at Misrata port in Nov. 2018: 'Libyan coastguards force
    stranded migrants off container ship', Reuters, reuters.com/article/us-
    europe-migrants-libya-idUSKCN1NP21A

13. The human trafficking business has been covered in various UN and
    Human Rights Watch reports. See http://www.securitycouncilreport.
    org/atf/cf/%7B65BFCF9B-6D27–4E9C-8CD3-CF6E4FF96FF9%
    7D/s_2018_812.pdf for example.

14. 'Europe's plan endangers foreigners in Libya,' Human Rights Watch,
    https://www.hrw.org/news/2016/07/06/eu/nato-europes-plan-endan-
    gers-foreigners-libya

15. A total of 473 migrants were brought back to Libya within four days
    in Jan. 2019, according to the UN and the Libyan coastguard.

16. Interview with coastguard official in Dec. 2018.

17. Interview with coastguard officials in Misrata in May 2015.

18. Interview in Misrata in May 2015.

19. Interview at Mellitah port in Nov. 2013.

20. Interview in Misrata in May 2015.

21. See, for example, the report by UNSMIL issued on Dec. 2018 which
    noted a 'complicity of some State actors, including local officials, mem-
    bers of armed groups formally integrated into State institutions, and
    representatives of the Ministry of Interior and Ministry of Defence, in
    the smuggling or trafficking of migrants and refugees.' 'Migrants and
    refugees crossing Libya subjected to "unimaginable horrors"—UN',

UNSMIL, https://unsmil.unmissions.org/migrants-and-refugees-crossing-libya-subjected-%E2%80%9Cunimaginable-horrors%E2%80%9D-%E2%80%93-un

22. For more details on EUBAM see: www.europa.eu/csdp/missions-and-operations/eubam-libya/index_en.htm

23. Estimates from diplomats.

24. Interview in Nov. 2013.

25. Interviews in Nov. 2013.

26. Interviews in several prisons in western Libya in May 2015.

27. See reports from Human Rights Watch and Amnesty International: www.hrw.org/middle-east/n-africa/libya; www.amnesty.org/en/countries/middle-east-and-north-africa/libya

28. Interview in Gharboulli in May 2015.

29. Interior Minister Matteo Salvini demanded this in July 2018. 'Italy wants end to Libyan embargo to help it tackle migrants', Reuters, reuters.com/article/uk-europe-migrants-italy-libya/italy-wants-end-to-libyan-embargo-to-help-it-tackle-migrants-idUKKBN1JV2GL

30. Interview with Libya's defence minister and interviews with other officials and diplomats in Tripoli, 2013–2014.

31. Interviews with diplomats and security contractors in Libya in 2013 and 2014.

32. Interviews in May and Sept. 2018 in Tunis.

33. Interview with EUBAM official.

34. More information is included in the Epilogue.

35. Interviews in Ghat and Tripoli in 2015.

36. Interview in Ghat in May 2015.

37. Interview in Tripoli in May 2015.

38. 'Letter dated 5 September 2018 from the Panel of Experts on Libya established pursuant to resolution 1973 (2011)', UN Security Council, http://www.securitycouncilreport.org/atf/cf/%7B65BFCF9B-6D27-4E9C-8CD3-CF6E4FF96FF9%7D/s_2018_812.pdf

39. Interview in May 2015. To my knowledge, no trial case has been opened since then.

40. Interview with the Tripoli-based Foreign Minister Ghirani in May 2015. 'Insight—unable to halt Europe-bound migrants, Tripoli

demands help', Reuters, https://www.reuters.com/article/uk-europe-migrants-libya-insight/insight-unable-to-halt-europe-bound-migrants-tripoli-demands-help-idUKKBN0O907J20150524

8. THE ARRIVAL OF ISLAMIC STATE

1. Many were released in 2010 after a reconciliation dialogue between the LIFG (and other Islamist groups) and the regime. Fitzgerald, Mary, 'Finding Their Place: Libya's Islamists During and After the Revolution, in Cole, Peter and McQuinn, Brian (eds.), *The Libyan Revolution and its Aftermath*, London, UK: Hurst & Company, 2015, pp. 180–197.
2. Around 556 Libyan fighters were thought to be in Syria at the time, according to estimates by the International Centre for the Study of Radicalisation. 'Up to 11,000 foreign fighters; steep rise among Western Europeans', Washington Institute, https://www.washingtoninstitute.org/policy-analysis/view/up-to-11000-foreign-fighters-in-syria-steep-rise-among-western-europeans
3. 'The origins and evolution of ISIS in Libya', Atlantic Council, https://www.atlanticcouncil.org/images/publications/The_Origins_and_Evolution_of_ISIS_in_Libya_web_0705.pdf
4. Government briefing attended by Reuters and other outlets in Nov. 2017.
5. 'The Islamic State's first colony in Libya', Washington Institute, https://www.washingtoninstitute.org/policy-analysis/view/the-islamic-states-first-colony-in-libya
6. 'Dozens of Libyans in eastern town pledge allegiance to Islamic State', Reuters, reuters.com/article/us-mideast-crisis-libya/dozens-of-libyans-in-eastern-town-pledge-allegiance-to-islamic-state-leader-idUSKBN0I-L2YR20141101
7. You can find the video at archive.org/details/w.tarablus.resala.to.mowahdeen.original.quality
8. Interview in Tobruk in Sept. 2014.
9. Reuters hired a British security adviser to escort me when travelling around or visiting offices. That was great for my wellbeing, but it was often difficult to explain his presence at checkpoints—former elite soldiers and police officers struggle to pass as camera assistants.

10. He said this in a news conference after his release.
11. They published a video about their arrival.
12. His company, Team Crucible, named him in a statement as David Barry.
13. Buraq needed foreign subcontractors to get landing permissions in the EU.
14. The café visit was in May 2015.
15. 'Islamic State militants claim attacks on Iranian ambassador's residence in Libya', Reuters, https://www.reuters.com/article/us-libya-security-iran/islamic-state-militants-claim-attacks-on-iranian-ambassadors-residence-in-libya-idUSKBN0LQ0DX20150222
16. Tunisians were among the foreigners.
17. 'Islamic State claims suicide attack in Libya that kills 42', Reuters, https://www.reuters.com/article/uk-libya-security/islamic-state-militants-claim-suicide-attacks-in-libya-that-kill-42-idUKKBN0LO0ST20150220
18. 'Libya: long term arbitrary detentions', Human Rights Watch, https://www.hrw.org/news/2015/12/02/libya-long-term-arbitrary-detentions
19. Interview with Swiss ambassador in June 2014. His residence was a welcome getaway for me and my wife from our villa and presented a rare opportunity to get a drink in a dry country.
20. Interview in Sirte in May 2015.
21. 'Islamic State executes rival fighters after revolt in central Libyan city: residents', Reuters, https://www.reuters.com/article/us-libya-security/islamic-state-executes-rival-fighters-after-revolt-in-central-libya-residents-idUSKCN0QL0EH20150816; 'Islamic State fights to emulate Iraq, Syria success', Reuters, https://www.reuters.com/article/us-libya-security-insight/islamic-state-in-libya-fights-to-emulate-iraq-syria-success-idUSKCN0T20J520151113
22. Interviews in Ben Jawad in Feb. 2015.
23. I visited Sirte in May 2015.
24. Interview in Misrata in May 2015.
25. 'Seven shot dead at protest against Islamic State in Libya', Reuters, https://www.reuters.com/article/us-libya-security-protests/seven-shot-dead-at-protest-against-islamic-state-in-libya-residents-idUSKBN0OS1OK20150612

26. Phone interview from Ayman al-Warfalli.

27. Interview in Tripoli in June 2015.

28. Interview in Sirte in May 2015.

29. 'A place of distinctive despair', Carnegie Middle East Center, https://carnegie-mec.org/diwan/76997

30. Carnegie Middle East Center, op. cit.

31. Carnegie Middle East Center, op. cit.

32. There was no final death toll given for the attack, but the Tobruk-based parliament issued a statement announcing the deaths. 'Islamic State claims responsibility for attack on central Libyan town', Reuters, https://www.reuters.com/article/us-libya-security/suspected-islamic-state-fighters-attack-central-libyan-town-idUSKCN1N3

9. A COUNTRY BEYOND REPAIR?

1. Statement issued by the GNA on 17 Dec. 2017.

2. 'Disastrous conditions for migrants displaced by Libya clashes, official says', Reuters, reuters.com/article/us-europe-migrants-libya/disastrous-conditions-for-migrants-displaced-by-libya-clashes-official-says-idUSK-BN1CH33D

3. 'Contrasting realities in Libya for French minister's visit', Reuters, https://www.reuters.com/article/us-libya-security/contrasting-realities-in-libya-for-french-ministers-visit-idUSKBN1EG1PU

4. Interview with businessmen and diplomats in Nov. 2017.

5. Interviews with Libyan officials and militiamen.

6. Interview with eastern central bank governor Ali Salim al-Hibri in Benghazi on 4 Feb. 2019. The eastern parallel administration, as we have seen in Chapter 6, has been forced to sell bonds outside the official banking system because adding new staff to the public payroll has become increasingly difficult without identity cards. This was then confirmed to me by various other Libyan sources.

7. The black market rate dropped to 4.1 dinars to a dollar in Mar. 2019, down from as much as 9 in Nov. This fall comes after the central bank and Serraj's government agreed on a quasi-devaluation of the official rate of 3.9 in Sept. by slapping a fee on private hard currency transactions.

8. Written responses from NOC to questions from Reuters in Sept. 2018.

9. 'Letter dated 5 September 2018 from the Panel of Experts on Libya established pursuant to resolution 1973 (2011)' UN Security Council, https://www.securitycouncilreport.org/atf/cf/%7B65BFCF9B-6D27–4E9C-8CD3-CF6E4FF96FF9%7D/s_2018_812.pdf

10. 'Capital of militias: Tripoli's armed groups capture the Libyan state', Small Arms Survey, http://www.smallarmssurvey.org/fileadmin/docs/T-Briefing-Papers/SAS-SANA-BP-Tripoli-armed-groups.pdf, page 9.

11. Small Arms Survey, op. cit., p. 9.

12. Interviews with diplomats in 2018.

13. Interviews with Tripoli residents and witnesses.

14. Interview with UN officials.

15. Interviews with interior ministry officials in Nov. 2018.

16. 'Some 400 prisoners escape prison in Tripoli chaos', Reuters, https://www.reuters.com/article/us-libya-security/some-400-prisoners-escape-prison-in-tripoli-chaos-idUSKCN1LI0SU

17. See, for example, the Human Rights Watch reports: 'Libya: War crimes as Benghazi residents flee', https://www.hrw.org/news/2017/03/22/libya-war-crimes-benghazi-residents-flee; 'Libya: Mass extra judicial execution', https://www.hrw.org/news/2017/11/29/libya-mass-extra-judicial-execution; 'Libya: videos capture summary executions', https://www.hrw.org/news/2017/08/16/libya-videos-capture-summary-executions. In another incident in July 2019, an armed group seized lawmaker Siham Sergewa and her husband in Benghazi, hours after she had criticized Haftar's Tripoli war.

18. Officials have offered conflicting explanations: officials linked to the LNA said the money had been moved to an unspecified location for security reasons, while the governor of the eastern central bank branch, Ali Salim al-Hibri, said the banknotes had been damaged by sewage. 'The statements were contradictory and incomplete,' said a UN report, concluding: 'Multiple credible sources indicated that most of the funds had been shared among LNA top commanders following their transfer from the Bank's branch in Benghazi.' 'Letter dated 5 September 2018 from the Panel of Experts on Libya established pursuant to resolution 1973 (2011)', UN Security Council, https://www.securitycoun-

cilreport.org/atf/cf/%7B65BFCF9B-6D27-4E9C-8CD3-CF6E4FF96FF9%7D/s_2018_812.pdf, pp. 10–11.

19. He asked me to withhold his name for reasons of personal security.
20. Interview in Feb. 2019.
21. Interview in Feb. 2019.
22. Interview with Jeune Afrique, Jan. 2018.
23. UN envoy Salamé accused Tobruk-based lawmakers of deliberately obstructing the legislation in a briefing to the UN Security Council in Nov. 2018. The assembly passed it later that month, but by then the 10 Dec. date had already become unrealistic.
24. Interviews with diplomats in Dec. 2018 and Feb. 2019.

EPILOGUE: PERPETUAL ENDGAME

1. I anchored and wrote up the stories of our overworked local team reporting from the streets. This is one example: 'Tens of thousands of Algerian students extend protests against Bouteflika', Reuters, https://www.reuters.com/article/us-algeria-protests/thousands-of-algerian-students-extend-protests-against-bouteflikas-re-election-plan-idUSKCN1QF-1SP. I was also on duty when Bouteflika quit after another dramatic day. 'Algerian leader Bouteflika ends 20-year rule after mass protests', Reuters, https://www.reuters.com/article/us-algeria-protests/algerian-leader-bouteflika-quits-after-mass-protests-idUSKCN1RE1CH
2. 'Libyans fear showdown as eastern commander eyes capital', Reuters, reuters.com/article/us-libya-security/libyans-fear-showdown-as-eastern-commander-eyes-capital-idUSKBN1QQ069
3. '#Libya. April 3rd, 2019: #LNA announces it has "moved several military units to the Western Region", thus #Tripolitania. https://www.facebook.com/1719515878289208/posts/2314753065432150/ ...', tweet from Alessandro Pagano (@PaganoDritto) on 3 Apr. 2019: https://twitter.com/paganodritto/status/1113441202395865088
4. According to a confidential report from a humanitarian agency active in southern Libya and corroborated by interviews with local sources.
5. Interviews with local and humanitarian sources.
6. 'Debts pile up as Libyan governments struggle for power', Reuters,

reuters.com/article/us-libya-economy-insight/debts-pile-up-as-rival-libyan-governments-struggle-for-power-idUSKCN1QN1VL

7. Interviews with Western diplomats.

8. Interview with Western diplomats in Mar. 2019.

9. Interview in Apr. 2019. I used the quote in my article: 'How Libya's Haftar blindsided world powers with advance on Tripoli', Reuters, https://www.reuters.com/article/us-libya-security-haftar-insight/how-libyas-haftar-blindsided-world-powers-with-advance-on-tripoli-idUSKCN1RM0PJ, which I filed when the war started.

10. Interview with World Health Organization (WHO) official in Tunis, June 2019.

11. A source involved in organising the event showed me the list of invitees in May 2019.

12. For more on Salafis, see 'Addressing the Rise of Libya's Madkhali-Salafis', International Crisis Group, https://www.crisisgroup.org/middle-east-north-africa/north-africa/libya/addressing-rise-libyas-madkhali-salafis

13. 'Libya forces battle for Tripoli despite UN truce calls', Egypt Independent, https://egyptindependent.com/libya-forces-battle-for-tripoli-despite-un-truce-calls/

14. Estimate by WHO on 22 Apr. 2019.

15. 'Life goes on in Tripoli—but residents wonder for how long', Reuters, reuters.com/article/us-libya-security-life/life-goes-on-in-tripoli-but-residents-wonder-for-how-long-idUSKCN1RO1S3

16. 'Haftar vows to attack Turkish assets in Libya', France24, https://www.france24.com/en/20190629-haftar-vows-attacks-turkish-assets-libya

17. Interviews with human rights activists.

18. 'How Libya's Haftar blindsided world powers with advance on Tripoli', Reuters, reuters.com/article/uk-libya-security-haftar-insight/how-libyas-haftar-blindsided-world-powers-with-advance-on-tripoli-idUKKCN1RM0PL

19. 'White House says Trump spoke to Libyan commander Haftar on Monday', Reuters, https://www.reuters.com/article/us-libya-security-trump/white-house-says-trump-spoke-to-libyan-commander-haftar-on-monday-idUSKCN1RV0WW

20. We wrote this story: 'In battle for Libya's oil, water becomes a casualty', Reuters, reuters.com/article/us-libya-security-water-insight/in-battle-for-libyas-oil-water-becomes-a-casualty-idUSKCN1TX0KQ

21. 'Exclusive: Libyan state oil firm cuts back fuel supplies to east amid battle over capital', Reuters, reuters.com/article/us-libya-cuts-back-fuel-supplies-to-east-amid-battle-over-capital-idUSKCN1VR1E9

22. 'Libyan state oil firm rejects eastern parallel board for oil firm', Reuters, reuters.com/article/libyaNews/idAFL5N26A3KZ

23. LNA sources confirmed the existence of Jordanian trucks (as reported on social media) to Reuters.

24. Just to give a few examples, Egypt flew airstrikes against suspected militant positions in Derna, then controlled by IS, in Feb. 2015 in retaliation of the beheading of 21 Egyptian Copts on a Libyan beach. President Sisi also ordered airstrikes on Libya after IS claimed responsibility for a massacre of dozens in Minya, a city in Upper Egypt, in May 2017. The UAE conducted airstrikes against Libya Dawn militias in Tripoli in Aug. US officials told Reuters.

25. The Russians are believed to be private military contractors linked to the Wagner group which has been active in Syria and Ukraine, among other countries: 'Putin-linked mercenaries are fighting on Libya's front lines', Bloomberg, https://www.bloomberg.com/news/articles/2019-09-25/-putin-s-chef-deploys-mercenaries-to-libya-in-latest-adventure; 'Frontline clashes ebb and flow as Libya's war hits impasse', Reuters, https://www.reuters.com/article/us-libya-security/frontline-clashes-ebb-and-flow-as-libyas-war-hits-impasse-idUSKBN1XA1OX

26. 'U.S. warns against Russia's growing role in Libya war', Bloomberg, https://www.bloomberg.com/news/articles/2019-11-15/u-s-warns-against-growing-russian-role-in-libya-s-war; 'Arrival of Russian mercenaries adds deadlier firepower, modern tactics to Libya's civil war', Washington Post, https://www.washingtonpost.com/gdpr-consent/?destination=%2fworld%2farrival-of-russian-mercenaries-adds-deadlier-firepower-modern-tactics-to-libyas-civil-war%2f2019%2f11%2f05%2ff330820c-fa03-11e9-9534-e0dbcc9f5683_story.html%3f

27. UN Special Envoy Ghassan Salamé told me in January 2020 that between 1,000 and 2,000 fighters from Syria, allied to Turkey, had

arrived. They were from northern Syria and had fought for rebel groups in Syria's civil war. According to diplomats, these fighters see Libya as a way to make money.

28. They were still present in Libya as of February 2020, but were deployed to hinterland LNA positions such as the Al Jufra airbase in central Libya.

29. It was open secret among diplomats and UN officials that Egypt and the UAE conducted airstrikes on behalf of the LNA.

30. As told to me by a German government official.

31. UNSMIL said in a statement on 25 January, six days after the Berlin summit: 'Over the last ten days, numerous cargo and other flights have been observed landing at Libyan airports in the western and eastern parts of the country providing the parties with advanced weapons, armoured vehicles, advisers and fighters.' It did not specify the country of origin for any of the planes, identifying them only as from 'member states, including several who participated in the Berlin conference'. 'UNSMIL statement on continued violations of arms embargo in Libya', https://unsmil.unmissions.org/unsmil-statement-continued-violations-arms-embargo-libya

32. 'U.N. says Libya arms embargo a "joke", demands accountability', Reuters, https://uk.reuters.com/article/uk-germany-security-libya/libya-arms-embargo-a-joke-says-u-n-official-idUKKBN20A0AB

33. As told to me by diplomatic sources. See also: 'International powers call for cease-fire in Libya's long civil war', The New York Times, nytimes.com/2020/01/19/world/africa/libya-peace-talks-berlin-summit.html

34. 'How Libya's Haftar blindsided world powers with advance on Tripoli', Reuters, reuters.com/article/us-libya-security-haftar-insight/how-libyas-haftar-blindsided-world-powers-with-advance-on-tripoli-idUSKCN1RM0PJ

35. 'United Nations Libya envoy resigns citing stress', Reuters, reuters.com/article/uk-libya-security-un/united-nations-libya-envoy-resigns-citing-stress-idUKKBN20P2JV

36. Interview with Abdel-Rahman Ghandour, Libya Special Representative for UNICEF in June 2019 in Tunis.

37. Serraj's government allocated by decree 2 billion dinars for the war effort. Officials first confirmed and then sought to deny the figure. Serraj told me in an interview in June 2019 that funds meant for schools and hospitals would instead be used to defend Tripoli.

38. The central bank in Tripoli does not fund the LNA. The nine-page law can be found in this Chatham House report: 'Will economic instability undermine Khalifa Haftar's offensive in Libya?', https://www.chathamhouse.org/expert/comment/will-economic-instability-undermine-khalifa-haftar-s-offensive-libya

39. For more on the expanding LNA business activities, see 'Predatory economies in Eastern Libya, the dominant role of the Libyan National Army', Nokia Research, https://globalinitiative.net/eastern-libya-lna/

40. In 2015 he promised again to resign, but simply stayed on. This was our story: 'Libyan PM Thinni says on TV he will resign but spokesman says he stays', reuters.com/article/libya-politics/update-2-libyan-prime-minister-thinni-says-he-will-resign-tv-idUSL5N10M4Q 220150812

FURTHER READING

Ahmida, Ali Abdullatif, *The Making of Modern Libya: State Formation, Colonization, and Resistance*, New York, US: State University of New York Press, 2009.

Anderson, Lisa, *The State and Social Transformation in Tunisia and Libya: 1830–1980*, New Jersey, US: Princeton University Press, 1986.

Baldinetti, Anna, *The Origins of the Libyan Nation: Colonial Legacy, Exile and the Emergence of a new Nation State*, London, UK: Routledge, 2010.

Carnegie Endowment for International Peace, 'A place of distinctive despair', https://carnegie-mec.org/diwan/76997

———— 'Libya's coming forever war: why backing one militia against another is not the solution', https://carnegieendowment.org/2019/05/15/libya-s-coming-forever-war-why-backing-one-militia-against-another-is-not-solution-pub-79143

Chatham House, 'Libya's war economy: predation, profiteering and state weakness', https://www.chathamhouse.org/publication/libyas-war-economy-predation-profiteering-and-state-weakness

———— 'Libya: rich in oil, leaking fuel', https://chathamhouse.shorthand-stories.com/libya-rich-in-oil-leaking-fuel/index.html

———— 'Will economic instability undermine Khalifa Haftar's offensive in Libya?', https://www.chathamhouse.org/expert/comment/will-economic-instability-undermine-khalifa-haftar-s-offensive-libya

Clingendaal, 'Libya's looming contest for the Central Bank', https://www.clingendael.org/publication/libyas-looming-contest-central-bank

FURTHER READING

———— 'Libya: When Haftar obliterates years of diplomacy', https://www.clingendael.org/publication/libya-when-haftar-obliterates-years-diplomacy

Cole, Peter and McQuinn, Brian (eds.), *The Libyan Revolution and its Aftermath*, London, UK: Hurst & Company, 2015.

Crawford, Alex, *Colonel Gaddafi's Hat: The Real Story of the Libyan Uprising*, London, UK: HarperCollins, 2012.

El Ghomeny, M. Riad, *Land, Food and Rural Development in North Africa*, London, UK: Routledge, 1993.

European Council on Foreign Relations, 'Order from chaos: stabilising Libya the local way', https://www.ecfr.eu/publications/summary/order_from_chaos_stabilising_libya_the_local_way

———— 'Libya's global civil war', https://www.ecfr.eu/publications/summary/libyas_global_civil_war1

Evans, Martin, *Algeria: France's Undeclared War*, Oxford, UK: Oxford University Press, 2012.

Fitzgerald, Mary, *Finding their Place: Libya's Islamists During and After the Revolution*, London, UK: Hurst.

———— 'Jihadism and its relationship with youth culture and ideology: the Case of Ansar al-Sharia in Libya', in: Narbone, Luigi, Favier, Agnès and Collombier, Virginie (eds.), *Inside Wars, Local Dynamics of Conflicts in Syria and Libya*, Florence, Italy: European University Institute, 2016.

———— 'What happened to political Islam in Libya', in: Mezran, Karim and Varvelli, Arturo (eds.), *The Arc of Crisis in the MENA Region Fragmentation, Decentralization, and Islamist Opposition*, Milan, Italy and Washington, US: ISPI and Atlantic Council, 2018.

Fitzgerald, Mary and Megerisi, Tarek, *Libya: Whose Land Is It? Property Rights and Transition*, London, UK: Legatum Institute, 2015.

Gaddafi, Muammar (with Edmond Jouve), *My Vision*, London, UK: John Blake Publishing, 2005.

Gurney, Judith, *Libya: The Political Economy of Oil*, Oxford, UK: Oxford University Press, 1996.

Hayford, Elizabeth R., *The Politics of the Kingdom of Libya in Historical Perspective*, dissertation at Tufts University, 1970.

FURTHER READING

Hilsum, Lindsey, *Sandstorm: Libya in the Time of Revolution*, London, UK: Penguin Press, 2012.

Human Rights Watch, 'The endless wait: long-term arbitrary detentions and torture in Western Libya', https://www.hrw.org/report/2015/12/02/endless-wait/long-term-arbitrary-detentions-and-torture-western-libya

———— 'Death of a dictator: bloody vengeance in Sirte', https://www.hrw.org/report/2012/10/16/death-dictator/bloody-vengeance-sirte

———— 'No escape from hell: EU policies contribute to abuse of migrants in Libya', https://www.hrw.org/report/2019/01/21/no-escape-hell/eu-policies-contribute-abuse-migrants-libya

International Crisis Group, 'Addressing the rise of Libya's Madkhali-Salafis', https://www.crisisgroup.org/middle-east-north-africa/north-africa/libya/addressing-rise-libyas-madkhali-salafis

———— 'Of tanks and banks: stopping a dangerous escalation in Libya', https://www.crisisgroup.org/middle-east-north-africa/north-africa/libya/201-tanks-and-banks-stopping-dangerous-escalation-libya

Jawad, Rana, *Tripoli Witness: The Remarkable First-hand Account of Life Through the Insurgency*, London: UK, Gilgamesh, 2011.

Lacher, Wolfram, 'Libya's local elites and the politics of alliance building', *Mediterranean Politics* 21, 1 (2016), pp. 64–85.

———— *Who is Fighting Whom in Tripoli? How the 2019 Civil War is Transforming Libya's Military Landscape*, Geneva, Switzerland: Small Arms Survey, 2019.

Lacher, Wolfram and al-Idrissi, Alaa, *Capital of Militias, Tripoli's Armed Groups Capture the Libyan State*, Geneva, Switzerland: Small Arms Survey, 2018.

Lacher, Wolfram and Cole, Peter, *Politics by Other Means: Conflicting Interests in Libya's Security Sector*, Geneva, Switzerland: Small Arms Survey, 2014.

Masri, Safwan, *Tunisia: An Arab Anomaly*, New York, US: Columbia University Press, 2017.

Matar, Hisham, *In the Country of Old Men*, New York, US: Viking Press, 2006.

FURTHER READING

———— *The Return: Fathers, Sons and the Land in Between*, New York, US: Viking Press, 2016.

Middle East Institute, 'Libya's Hifter and the false narrative of authoritarian stability', https://www.mei.edu/publications/libyas-hifter-and-false-narrative-authoritarian-stability

Pack, Jason (ed.), *The 2011 Libyan Uprisings and the Struggle for the Post-Qadhafi Future*, London, UK: Palgrave Macmillan, 2013.

Pargeter, Alison, *Libya: The Rise and Fall of Gaddafi*, Connecticut, US: Yale University Press, 2012.

Simons, Geoff, *Libya: The Struggle for Survival*, 2nd edition, London, UK: Palgrave Macmillan, 1996.

———— *Libya and the West: From Independence to Lockerbie*, London, UK: Bloomsbury, 2003.

St. John, Ronald Bruce, *Libya: From Colony to Independence*, London, UK: Oneworld Publications, 2008.

———— *Libya: From Colony to Revolution*, London, UK: Oneworld Publications, 2012.

Vandewalle, Dirk (ed.), *Libya Since 1969: Gadhafi's Revolution Revisited*, New York: Palgrave Macmillan, 2008.

———— *A History of Modern Libya*, Cambridge, UK: Cambridge University Press, 2012.

Wehrey, Frederic, *The Burning Shores: Inside the Battle for the new Libya*, New York, US: Farrar, Straus and Giroux, 2018.

Wright, John, *A History of Libya*, New York, US: Columbia University Press, 2010.

Zuckoff, Mitchell, *13 Hours: The Inside Account of What Really Happened in Benghazi*, New York, US: Hachette Book Group, 2014.

INDEX

INDEX

INDEX

INDEX

INDEX

INDEX

INDEX

INDEX

INDEX

INDEX

INDEX

285

INDEX

INDEX

INDEX

INDEX

INDEX

INDEX

INDEX

INDEX